Filming the Nation

Italian neo-realism has inspired film audiences and fascinated critics and film scholars for decades. This book offers an original analysis of the movement and its defining films from the perspective of the cultural unconscious.

Combining a Jungian reading with traditional theorizations of film and national identity, *Filming the Nation* reinterprets familiar images of well-known masterpieces by Roberto Rossellini, Vittorio de Sica and Luchino Visconti and introduces some of their less renowned yet equally significant films.

Providing an illuminating analysis of film images across a particularly traumatic and complex historical period, *Filming the Nation* revisits the concept of national identity and its 'construction' from a perspective that combines cultural, psychoanalytic and post-Jungian theories. As such this book will be essential reading for all students and scholars of film and psychoanalysis.

Donatella Spinelli Coleman teaches Film and is Honorary Research Fellow at the Cinema and Television History (CATH) Research Centre at De Montfort University, Leicester.

Filming the Nation

Jung, Film, neo-realism and Italian national identity

Donatella Spinelli Coleman

Routledge
Taylor & Francis Group
LONDON AND NEW YORK

First published 2011
by Routledge
27 Church Road, Hove, East Sussex BN3 2FA

Simultaneously published in the USA and Canada
by Routledge
270 Madison Avenue, New York, NY 10016

Routledge is an imprint of the Taylor & Francis Group, an Informa business

© 2011 Donatella Spinelli Coleman

Typeset in Times New Roman by
RefineCatch Limited, Bungay, Suffolk
Printed and bound in Great Britain by
TJ International Ltd, Padstow, Cornwall
Paperback cover design by Andrew Ward

All rights reserved. No part of this book may be reprinted or reproduced or utilized in any form or by any electronic, mechanical, or other means, now known or hereafter invented, including photocopying and recording, or in any information storage or retrieval system, without permission in writing from the publishers.

This publication has been produced with paper manufactured to strict environmental standards and with pulp derived from sustainable forests.

All reasonable attempts have been made to contact copyright holders, but in some cases this was not possible. Any omissions brought to the attention of Routledge will be remedied in future editions.

British Library Cataloguing in Publication Data
A catalogue record for this book is available from the British Library

Library of Congress Cataloging-in-Publication Data
Spinelli Coleman, Donatella, 1963–
  Filming the nation : Jung, film, neo-realism and Italian national identity / Donatella Spinelli Coleman.
    p. cm.
  ISBN 978-0-415-55513-5 (hardback)
  ISBN 978-0-415-55514-2 (paperback)
  1. Motion pictures – Italy. 2. Italy in motion pictures. 3. Motion pictures – Psychological aspects. 4. Culture in motion pictures. I. Title.
  PN1993.5.I88S65 2011
  791.43'65845—dc22
                                                    2010031307

ISBN: 978-0-415-55513-5 (hbk)
ISBN: 978-0-415-55514-2 (pbk)

To Alessandro, Francesco and Sara Lily and in fond memory of my grandmother

Contents

Acknowledgments ix

Introduction 1

Primo tempo 9

1 The uninvited guest: film, psychoanalysis and the Jungian absence 11
2 Archetype and complex: the paradox of dynamic structures 31
3 Jung, film and nation: image as witness of a process of becoming 48

Intervallo 67

4 Italian neo-realism and the unmitigated darkness of historical truth 69

Secondo tempo 95

5 1942–1945: War and archetypes – an orphan nation with a legacy of murder 97
6 1947–1949: clearing the debt to the maternal between war and reconstruction 141
7 1949–1952: Redeemers, tricksters and the wisdom of the unconscious 167

Conclusion 204

Bibliography 216
Index 225

Acknowledgments

I would like to thank my editor, Sarah Gibson, for her support, her reassurance and her reliable answers, invaluable during the final phase of the development of this book.

Very special thanks must go to Renzo Rossellini for his generosity and openness and for his commitment to the continued appreciation of Roberto Rossellini's work which made it possible for me to illustrate the book with the striking images of his father's timelessly beautiful films.

I am grateful to Laura Summerton from the Bridgeman Library for her knowledgeable support and prompt, fruitful responses.

Michael Walker from South Nottingham College generously gave of his time and expertise in capturing from the films the images that appear in this book.

At a particularly critical point during the research for this book (then a doctoral thesis) I had a dream that seemed, at the time, particularly significant and became the inspiration to continue with the work. I relate it here as my gratefulness to those who helped me fulfil the potential of this project originates from it. In the dream, I was talking to a woman and as I expressed to her my doubts about the value of my project's hypothesis she showed me how the words *knowledge* and *patience* could be written as in a crossword, intersecting on the letter 'e'. She insisted that I base my work on that understanding. Acquiring both patience and knowledge has certainly helped me navigate the horizonless seas of interdisciplinary research, but I also came to understand how not only mine but the patience and knowledge of those supporting me made this research possible.

I would like to thank my Director of Studies, Viv Chadder, whose knowledge and clarity of mind has consistently provided the positive challenge and the pressure to test my assumptions against a thorough and systematic approach to theory.

A really special thank you goes to my Supervisor, Professor Richard Johnson. He is an example of that open, clear, supportive, energetic and caring spirit which is at the heart of the very best of academia. His reliable, always constructive feedback has tactfully contained my sometimes directionless exuberance and his questionings often opened doors to new areas of knowledge and understanding. It has been a privilege to benefit from his experience and great wisdom.

I am also thankful for the encouragement of Dr Jacinda Read, Professor Robert Murphy and Dr Parvati Raghuram at the very beginning of this study and to Professor Tim O'Sullivan for his unfaltering belief in my research skills and for his support throughout the full span of my academic studies.

Those who have demonstrated their support by patiently waiting for my return from a long and demanding journey deserve equal gratefulness to those who have provided academic direction. First of all I would like to thank my children who have demonstrated incredible resilience, independence and maturity throughout the times of my many 'disappearances'. My family in Italy who have patiently accepted my compulsive film viewing at every recent visit deserve my gratitude, and so do my friends Angela, Elisabetta, Cecilia and Geraldine who, from different geographical and emotional locations, sustain me with the priceless gifting of their unconditional and uniquely beautiful friendships.

And finally I'm profoundly grateful to my husband, Ian, for standing by me with the tender, endless patience that testifies, again, to his great capacity for love.

Introduction

'Cinema is something like the royal road to the cultural unconscious' (Lebeau 2001: 6). With this simple and appropriate statement Vicky Lebeau places cinema at the intersection between psychoanalysis and culture. The sentence's structure and the powerful metaphor are, in fact, directly borrowed from the widely acknowledged reference Freud himself made to the interpretation of dreams as 'the *via regia* to a knowledge of the unconscious element in our psychic life' (Freud 1900: 441). Lebeau's play with words and with the concept they deliver suggests a possible widening of the field of enquiry which has fostered, for at least three decades, the successful development of a theory of film informed by a constructive dialogue with psychoanalysis.

The Jungian theoretical construct, in its so-called 'post-Jungian' rephrasing, acknowledges the functional presence of the cultural unconscious as an intermediate layer between the collective and the personal. The introduction of this concept, coupled with its renowned emphasis on the centrality of the image, firmly places the Jungian approach in a position to competently respond to the encouragement, implicit in Lebeau's words, to reassess the cultural specificity of the relationship between cinema and the unconscious. The renewed academic interest in the fruitful intersection between film studies and analytical psychology is finally testing the validity of this response and it has opened fascinating new avenues of research. Inspired and supported by this re-evaluation, this book explores the potentials of the Jungian contribution to an understanding of cinematic images as descriptive of a movement which, akin to the process of psychological growth endured individually, drives a culture towards change.

The association of cinematic images with those produced as dreams has proven irresistible to both psychoanalysis and film theory. As early as the late 1940s psychoanalysis was in fact using the 'analogical-conceptual elaboration' of '*dream screen*' (Heath 1999. 32). Film theory also sealed, with Daudry (1974–5) and Metz (1977), the postulate of a cinematic situation reproductive of a dream process as one of the points of incessant attraction and of contested departures for theoretical developments.

The analogy between cinematic and oniric images was not destined to remain the only point of intersection between theories of the unconscious and the study of film. In the past three decades other fundamental concepts of psychoanalysis have alternated with each other on the centre stage of psychoanalytic film criticism and the debate, essentially hosted by the journal *Screen*, has seen the shift of interest from the original elaboration of the idea of fetishism to the appreciation of the concept of fantasy, from the application of the notion of suture to complex redefinitions of the boundaries of the real and of the meaning of the concept of symptom (Mulvey 1975; Heath 1976; Silverman 1988; Zizek 1992; De Lauretis 1995).

The centrality of a psychoanalytical approach and its relevance to the solidity of theoretical constructs developed as a framework for the study of cinema, have not been discouraged by what seems a fundamental difference between the relationship to the image of film and psychoanalysis. As Stephen Heath synthetically describes:

> Extending the domain of the visible into dreams, reveries, fantasies and so on, psychoanalysis at the same time crosses the image, disturbs that domain and its domination; what counts is not what is there to be seen but the insistence through it of unconscious desire, which indeed is decisively operative in what is seen.
>
> (1999: 30)

Film, on the other hand, is structured around the support of the image; its aim is that of sustaining 'vision, to entertain – to bind in – the spectator with images' (Heath 1999: 31). Rather than an irredeemable divergence, this very difference has provided an interface, making of the psychoanalytical necessity to interrupt 'the vision of images' and to challenge 'the sufficiency of the representation they make' (Heath 1999: 31) the ideal methodological framework for the exposure of the political and ideological discourses underpinning cinema's construction of the spectator-subject.

The positive contribution of a film criticism intended as an instrument of social analysis and oriented towards an idea of cinema as a 'symptom' of the culture which produces it cannot be underestimated. Indeed, bearing witness to its importance is the extraordinary contribution of feminist film criticism to the understanding of women's position within a system of representation structured on patriarchal values. However, neither the use of psychoanalysis as a model for the description of the relationship between subject/spectator and the cinematic apparatus nor of film as the place where psychoanalytic theory can be verified make the most of the viability of that 'royal road to the cultural unconscious' that cinema is also supposed to represent.

If indeed the reductionist Freudian approach 'illuminates . . . the motivations driving a leading protagonist' (Izod 2001: 4) and successfully describes and ideologically inscribes the process of subject positioning in relation to the cinematic image, it finds its resolutions backwards, in the repressed material it recovers from childhood's amnesia or in the retracing of elementary psychic processes (Izod 2001: 25). Moreover, the powerful attraction and emotional effect that certain images elicit cannot satisfactorily be explained, contained and redirected by a theory intent on discovering hidden corpses – contents repressed from infancy – behind the deceiving curtain of repetitive alibis – cinematic techniques, character development, narrative styles, modes of closure, etc.

This work originates from a frustration with a theory of cinema that, in its devotion to a Freudian 'distrust' of the image, endlessly searches for the non-image, for the abstraction hidden behind the distraction of the visible. Indeed, this theoretical approach manages to postpone, with the aid of hyperbolic rewritings of the history of psychoanalysis, that intuitively fruitful meeting with the cultural unconscious if not for the one these rewritings implicitly presuppose. This frustration found resonance in a comparatively small cluster of academic voices supportive of the re-evaluation of the Jungian contribution to the understanding of film.

Considering Jungian analytical psychology's focus on the image in its theorizing of the unconscious, it is surprising to find how negligible its intersections with film have been in the years which have seen the escalating association of psychoanalysis with the study of cinema. It is only with the beginning of the new millennium that the rare trickle of dedicated Jungian publications has increased to a dignified flow, raising hopes for the development of a constructive dialogue with existing, more solidly accepted modes of film analysis. A number of these publications (Hauke and Alister 2001; Hockley 2001; Izod 2001) have provided the propelling inspiration for this research and a suitable springboard for a more in-depth exploration of the still under-realized potential of this perspective.

The Jungian approach to the unconscious is teleological; it presupposes the existence of purpose in the unconscious's relationship of dialogue with consciousness. To the Freudian belief in the tendency of the unconscious to obscure meaning and store repressed desires and traumas Jung opposed a view which proposes that, as well as holding the memory of the scars of conflict, the unconscious offers suggestions for resolution and active compensation, displaying a natural tendency towards healing. Rather than a search oriented backwards towards the unveiling of the truncated trajectories which left in the unconscious the sediments of suppressed and unsatisfied desires, Jungian analysis is 'oriented forward towards the future'. It is sustained by the belief that 'the products of the unconscious compensate for the contents of the conscious and counterbalance them' (Izod 2001. 25) in the striving towards the ultimate goal described by Jung as *individuation*: 'the tendency for an organism to continue to become itself, to fulfil its unique potential to become wholly itself' (Hauke and Alister 2001: 245).

This projection towards the future is then naturally inscribed within a developmental perspective supported by the seminal proposition of the existence of a collective unconscious, repository of 'inherited modes of psychic functioning', the archetypes, which when activated 'govern patterns of behaviour' (Izod 2006: 25). Archetypes can be described as 'centres of energy' that remain forms without content until their activation, made necessary by the psyche's tendency towards realization, attracts them to consciousness where they become manifest as individually and culturally specific images and affects.

Although undoubtedly implicit, the developmental aspect of Jung's theory of the unconscious is only fragmentarily present across his extensive writings. Its potential has, however, been successfully realized through the work of Erich Neumann who, in his comparative studies of mythology throughout history, draws the parallel between the development of individual consciousness and that of society as a whole. If a degree of determinism is inherent in the tentative sequencing of the archetypal material, Neumann manages somewhat to avoid rigid definitions and the description of definitive chronologically organized stages of development by adopting the inductive, comparative method, characteristic of the Jungian approach, and by insisting on the dynamic nature of the psyche and on its interdependency with an environment (natural and cultural, internal and external) that effects, as well as bearing the effects of, its functioning.

Jung had himself encouraged a systematic approach to dreams which would encompass an attention to material descriptive, across a span of time, of the movement towards individuation. When discussing the function of dreams he explained:

> With deeper insight and experience, these apparently separate acts of compensation arrange themselves into a kind of plan. They seem to hang together and in the deepest sense to be subordinated to a common goal, so that a long dream-series no longer appears as a senseless string of incoherent and isolated happenings, but resembles the successive steps in a planned and orderly process of development. I have called this unconscious process spontaneously expressing itself in the symbolism of a long dream-series the individuation process.
>
> (*C.W.*, Vol. 8: para. 550)

By investing mythology with the function of describing collectively the same process that dreams describe individually, Neumann's research has the characteristic of pointing to the relevance of images that mediate the universality of the archetype with the specificity of the culture which hosts its emergence. This characteristic makes his work particularly relevant to a study of film understood as a cultural product that, through the sensitivity of the individual artist, mediates between the collective unconscious and the collective consciousness which it addresses and describes.

This book develops the hypothesis of the traceability, through the isolation of cinematic images of archetypal value, of a process akin to that of individuation in a group sharing a unique cultural history. The necessity to select a culturally specific, historically coherent and sufficiently representative body of films for the analysis has led to the choice of the work of three Italian directors who are universally recognized as the fathers of Italian neo-realism: Roberto Rossellini, Vittorio De Sica and Luchino Visconti. The directors' declared willingness to produce cinematic work characterized by adherence to reality and depicting the true conditions of post-war Italy provides a precious insight into a cultural attitude, forged by political forces and certainly grounded on a cultural unconscious profoundly conditioned by religion. Moreover, neo-realism's renowned claim to objectivity entails an eagerness to release control over the narrative and to trust in the dramatic and emotive power of reality. The implied yielding to the relative ability of reality to structure its own narration produced characteristic tales that seem to catch fractions of a movement which often does not find resolution within the films' diegesis. Images of archetypal value surprisingly emerge throughout the texts, punctuating a journey which certainly transcends the conscious intentions of the minimalist narrative.

The films considered were produced between 1942 and 1952, a decade which saw the fall of a regime, a war fought on two sides, the abolition of the monarchy, the birth of a republic, the beginning of recovery and of the building of an economic stability unmatched by political consensus. The journeys that the films describe individually become, when the films are considered in relationship with each other and against the specific historical context of their production, the clear episodes of a narrative of loss and of the rebirth of a sense of national unity.

Both the process leading to the emergence of a collective, if unstable, sense of identity as 'nation' and that of active negotiation of boundaries implicit in the development of ego-consciousness as described by Jungian developmental psychology share the archetypal reference to the Self.[1] Considered 'an archetypal image of man's fullest potential and the unity of the personality as a whole', the Self demands throughout life 'to be recognized, integrated, realized', a demand which not only remains forever 'in process' because of the vast totality of the Self in relation to the limitations of human consciousness, but which also requires an ability on the part of the ego to maintain flexibility while setting individual and conscious boundaries (Samuels, Shorter and Plaut 1986: 135). Similarly, the ideal of nation as an abstract unifying notion requires in order to be 'recognized, integrated, realized' that the group longing for its realization strive to maintain flexibility while setting conscious boundaries.

Suggesting the possibility of drawing a parallel between the process leading to the construction of a national identity and that descriptive of the birth of ego-consciousness, the images emerging across the selected films will be read as both a re-elaboration of past events and as 'signposts' to an ongoing process of psychological evolution. Taking into consideration the possibilities this book explores, Freud's original suggestion can perhaps be asked to bear another rephrasing: Cinema is the popular road *from* the cultural unconscious *towards* the future.

This book is organized in two parts: Part I (Primo Tempo), comprising three chapters, is mainly concerned with theoretical issues. Part II (Secondo Tempo) directly engages, across three chapters, in the detailed Jungian reading of the selected films. Between the two parts is a chapter which stands between the two as a hybrid (Intervallo): it introduces Part II as well as summing up the methodological

---

1 Capitalized throughout the book when referring to the archetype of the Self.

issues fragmentarily addressed across Part I. The presence of a 'chapter in between' has inspired a renaming of the parts which make the book's structure according to a now obsolete organization of cinema viewing where the two parts are broken/joined by an interval. Honouring the texts that have inspired this project I have opted for the Italian translation as Primo Tempo, Intervallo, Secondo Tempo.

Chapter 1 explores the possible reasons for the relative absence of the Jungian contribution from the academic debate on cinema. Briefly retracing the development of the prolific dialogue between psychoanalysis and theories of film, this chapter also presents a parallel history of the rare appearance of Jungian publications across the same period. Despite having suffered the most disheartening and frustrating indifference, those same publications have become part of a recent wave of engaging material that is finally soliciting responses and attracting academic interest. A detailed review of some of the most relevant texts based on a Jungian perspective reveals, however, a reluctance to consider films outside of their possible healing function within the analytic experience. The contributions of Hockley (2001), Izod (2001, 2006) and Hauke and Alister (2001) represent, however, a definitive move away from that limiting approach and because of their relevance and direct involvement with existing academic discourses become a springboard for further development.

Chapter 2 provides a manageable synthesis of the central concepts of Jung's theory of the unconscious. A history of the development of archetypal theory demonstrates how the original idea of archetypes as primordial images has been significantly developed by Jung himself to include a distinction between the archetypal representation (images and ideas) and the archetype-as-such. The latter is considered to be the paradoxically irrepresentable form which finds in representation a visible approximation of its meaning. A revisiting of this concept informed by a scientific perspective offers a clear, updated and functional definition of archetype and it introduces Jung's Complex[2] theory. Directly deriving from the latter, Jung's discussion of the origin of artistic inspiration is presented parallel to Freud's thoughts on daydreaming and phantasy. The analysis of the relationship between archetype, complex, artist and culture leads to the exploration of the connections between the work of art and the context of its production further developed in Chapter 3.

Beginning with a discussion on the Jungian definition of symbol and of its emergence and function in art, Chapter 3 introduces the post-Jungian debate on the importance of a newly specified, intermediate layer between the individual and the collective unconscious: the cultural unconscious. A parallel is drawn between the function of mythological images as markers of the evolving of the consciousness of a culture and as means of support of specific cultural orders, and new narrative forms which, still relying on symbolic material, have inherited such

---

2 The capital letter will be used to distinguish the use of the word Complex as a noun descriptive of an element of Jung's theory from its use as adjective.

functions. The ego development traced throughout mythology is tentatively compared to the process of nation building described by the culturally specific images of symbolic value in art. The specific function of film within this perspective is analysed vis-à-vis revisiting the concept of nation within the Jungian theoretical framework. Italy is finally introduced as a nation with a particularly troubled history that ran parallel to the history of the development of its national cinema. The salient moments of a movement towards the achievement of national unity left traces recognizable in the specific cinematic images of a period, images which will be thoroughly analysed and discussed in the following chapters.

The choice of neo-realism as a textual reference demands, because of the films' social and political commitment and their immediately relevant themes, a clear overview of the historical context that harboured their production. World War II and the immediate post-war years form the backdrop, visually as well as politically, to the selected texts. The traumatic effects of the events characteristic of this period would perhaps provide sufficient reference when searching for the historical motivations behind the hypothesized longing for a sense of nationhood. Italy, however, did not become a nation with the proclamation of the Republic in 1946 but it had been one for almost 80 years. Indeed, both the history that led to the war and that leading to the establishment of the fascist dictatorship spanning across the two decades preceding the conflict had significant consequences and certainly affected the unfolding of events as well as influencing cultural and political attitudes. Chapter 4 provides an overview of the history of Italy from unification in 1861 to the beginning of World War II. A parallel history of national cinema is also outlined together with a review of the attitudes towards women, family, masculinity and gender relations that, fostered by the fascist regime, continue to influence Italian post-war society. The chapter finally introduces neo-realism, its fluid definitions and the directors responsible for the production of quietly beautiful documents of a reality that, in its psychological significance, has a universality which makes them movingly intimate.

Presenting the analyses of the films produced during the five years of the war, Chapter 5 is divided in two parts (1942–1943 and 1943–1945), reflecting the division which characterized the unfolding of the war on Italian soil. Rossellini's *Un Pilota Ritorna* (1942), Visconti's *Ossessione* (1943) and De Sica's *I Bambini ci Guardano* (1943) stand somewhat at the point of passage, both chronologically and stylistically, between the cinema of the regime and one that, responding to rapidly precipitating events, begins to show a desire for a more direct involvement with reality. The themes presented by the films, the children's presence, the representation of motherhood and the absence of fathers in the narratives are discussed in relation to both their social and symbolic significance. The second part of the chapter, covering the historical period which saw the emergence of an active Resistance as a token of Italy's plight to regain its dignity as nation, reviews De Sica's *La Porta del Cielo* (1944) and Rossellini's *Roma Città Aperta* (1945). The decidedly Catholic iconography and underlying motifs are considered as indicators of the powerful influence of a Church that represents, at this particular time, the only seemingly solid point of reference and, most importantly, the only guarantor of unity. It is, however, through the archetypal value attributable to such images that apparently hopeless endings become the necessary steps leading to the possibility of rebirth represented by the end of the war.

The films analysed in Chapter 6 were produced at a time when the potential for political reform, economic rebirth and positive international relations should have certainly projected a positive image of the country's future on to the celluloid strip. Rossellini's *Germania Anno Zero* (1948), Visconti's *La Terra Trema* (1948) and De Sica's *Ladri di Biciclette* (1949), with their narratives of suicide, failure and irretrievable loss, seem to refute the positive reading of this particular time in the history of Italy. Indeed, a close analysis of the events that led to the 1948 elections and the unexpected victory of the Christian Democrats reveals a situation in politics which is actually matched by the frustratingly disheartening journeys of the films' protagonists who lose their moral rectitude, their dignity and their enthusiasm for change. The archetypal reading, however, retraces their movements as a safe psychological option and as a compensatory choice protecting with temporary dissolution what would otherwise be antagonized as 'other' (shadow).

The three films presented in Chapter 7, although stylistically at the edge of a definition of neo-realism, remain honest witnesses to the changes that are taking the country towards economic stability. *Europa '51* (Rossellini, 1952), *Bellissima* (Visconti, 1951) and *Miracolo a Milano* (De Sica, 1951), as well as delivering the directors' conscious criticism of the corrupting effect of American colonization of Italian culture, offer with their symbolically rich narratives the opportunity for a revealing psychological analysis. The three films present remarkably similar narrative closures, suggestive of and mostly critically recognized as surrenders to the corrupting power of patriarchal capitalism. The in-depth analysis of the archetypal content reveals, however, a positive trajectory compensating for the hopelessness of the otherwise disempowering retreats. The images punctuate, in fact, a journey towards individuation. Undeterred by the defeat that had taken the country to face profound division rather than enjoy the psychological progress that integration would entail, the wisdom of the unconscious suggests a temporary solution. This chapter offers a thorough exploration of this possible reading.

The Conclusion offers a review of the salient arguments developed throughout the book and revisits the question of the place occupied by Jungian research within film theory. The analyses developed across the last three chapters are also brought together to reconstruct a narrative which, parallel to that described by history, becomes the history of the development of a national identity understood archetypally.

Primo tempo

Chapter 1

The uninvited guest
Film, psychoanalysis and the Jungian absence

Introduction

The relatively recent history of film theory as an academic discipline runs parallel to the history of the development of its ambivalent relationship with psychoanalysis. Despite the ambivalence, or maybe because of it, the dialogue between the two has been and continues to be outstandingly prolific and intense, producing academically rigorous and challengingly complex publications that have certainly contributed to raising the discipline's prestige.

For reasons this chapter will explore, Jungian analytical psychology has remained excluded until recently from this dialogue, in spite of its declared emphasis on the image as positive witness to the unfolding of unconscious processes. Beginning less than a decade ago, a more consistent flow of contributions supporting a so-called post-Jungian perspective on cinema has only marginally readdressed the imbalance, notwithstanding the relevance and originality of the approach. Indeed, in 1999 Janet Bergstrom, when introducing a collection of essays discussing the parallel histories of film and psychoanalysis, briefly but sharply reclaimed the exclusive suitability of the Freudian perspective to the study of film. In a footnote she mentions a collection of Jungian papers on cinema summarily describing Jung's work as 'rather far afield of the study of psychoanalysis and cinema as we know it' (Bergstrom 1999: 23). As well as discretely dismissing possibilities for further dialogue, Bergstrom clearly suggests an understanding, shared with her reader ('we'), of the presupposed margins of psychoanalytic film theory, margins which when faced with the daunting task of defining them seem, on the other hand, rather arduous to delineate. This chapter, endeavouring to situate the approach to film proposed by Jungian analytical psychology within the academic discourse, retraces the symptomatic infrequency of Jungian-based interventions alongside a synthetic revisiting of the development of the most widely acknowledged contributions to date. The intention, rather than the unnecessarily over-ambitious one of providing a complete and satisfactory overview of the vast and varied history of psychoanalytic film theory, is that of offering a context to the sporadic appearances of publications centred on a Jungian theoretical construct.

The understanding of cinema as 'a signifying practice of ideology' (Creed 2000: 77) and the desire to expose its function of reinforcing women's passivity within a patriarchal order were amongst the issues animating the theoretical discussions on film in the early 1970s. The contributions of Jean-Louis Baudry (1974–5), Christian Metz (1974) and Laura Mulvey (1975) will be closely considered as each provided innovative and influential critiques around which the academic debate became particularly animated. It is against such a debate that Don Fredericksen's essay (1979), the first coherent attempt at bringing a Jungian perspective to the study of film, made its appearance, introducing the 'symbolic approach' as an alternative to the perceived limitations of the 'semiotic attitude' (Fredericksen 1979: 170).

The lack of critical response to the article can only partially be justified by its inadequacy to question the 'supremacy of materialist theories in academic studies of film since the late 1960s' (Izod 1992: 1). A detailed analysis will isolate the article's possible points of divergence from contemporary theoretical issues while discussing them alongside the acknowledgement of the value of Fredericksen's pioneering insights.

Fredericksen only briefly mentions Lacan in his critique of Metz's 'imaginary signifier' (Fredericksen 2001: 25), yet Lacanian variations of Freudian psychoanalysis provide the central theoretical reference to most poststructuralist film literature. The recently renewed interest of Jungian analysis in film studies is coincidentally contemporary to a revision, essentially accomplished by Copjec (1989, 1994) and Zizek (2001), of the perceived misuse of Lacan's central concept of the gaze in film theory. A brief analysis of Copjec's contribution in particular reveals one of the fundamental differences between the approach her work epitomizes and that which is based on the Jungian theoretical framework. Consistent with the difference between a Freudian and a Jungian perspective, the fundamental divergence between the approaches to film remains, unsurprisingly, to be found in their purpose.

This chapter reviews the most relevant Jungian literature that, beginning in 2001, has finally brought Jungian film theory to the foreground. The review not only confirms the extent of such divergence, but also highlights the potential inherent in the new directions proposed by some of the works considered. Luke Hockley (2001), Christopher Hauke (Hauke and Alister 2001) and John Izod (2001a, 2006) in particular, engage in a dialogue that, rather than selecting a specifically Jungian interlocutor, is finally open to the challenging scrutiny of film studies academics. Consistent with the opening towards new directions suggested by these authors, this work pursues an analysis intended as complementary rather than in conflict with a psychoanalytically informed theoretical framework.

Film theory and psychoanalysis: a history of the Jungian absence

From the late 1960s, striving to legitimize film as an object of academic study, film theorists began to favour approaches which suggested the possibility of modes of analysis independent from other disciplines (Doane 1990: 4). This struggle towards theoretical autonomy coincided with a period of social and political upheaval both in western Europe and in the USA, conditioning the shift from a criticism centred on issues of realism, authorship and film form to an analysis of the role of cinema as an instrument of ideology. Psychoanalysis and semiotics, with their shared focus on the analysis of the process of signification in the human psyche and in systems of language respectively, seemed to provide film theory with that sought for autonomy, while offering an adequate framework for a politically informed analysis of film. Consistent with an understanding of social reality influenced by Marxist and feminist perspectives, film theory became centred on a scrutiny of the relationship between screen and spectator aimed at revealing the role of cinema as participating in the construction of a subject in line with the interests of specific social systems.

It was indeed with the intent of exposing cinema as partaking in the promotion of a dominant ideology that both Jean-Louis Baudry (1970, 1975) and Christian Metz (1975) analysed, in the early 1970s, the relationship between subject and image, screen and spectator, screen and dream. In 'Ideological Effects of the Basic Cinematographic Apparatus' (1970) Baudry introduced the theories of Jacques Lacan as a framework to an understanding of the processes at work within the relationship between screen and spectator. Baudry maintained that such a relationship could be considered as reminiscent of the Lacanian mirror stage. In his theory of subjectivity Lacan describes the mirror stage as the moment when the misrecognition of a sufficiency that belongs to the image reflected outside of himself or herself leads the infant to the identification with a fictional self, imagined as complete. Baudry saw in the reproduction of this situation in cinema the working of an ideology that aims at 'creating a fantasmatisation of the subject' by functioning as 'a sort of a psychic apparatus of substitution corresponding to the model defined by the dominant ideology' (Baudry 1970: 46). As Barbara Creed succinctly rephrases it, for Baudry 'the cinematic institution is complicit with ideology ... whose aim is to instil in the subject a misrecognition of itself as transcendental' (Creed 2000: 78).

In his subsequent analysis of the 'apparatus' of cinema as the ideologically biased mechanism supportive of the relationship between spectator and film, Baudry (1975) suggested that the cinematic experience, characteristically enjoyed in conditions of darkness, passive immobility and distancing from daily preoccupations, stimulates a regression similar to that afforded by the dream state. These conditions concur to produce an 'impression of reality', an impression that, he specified, 'is different from the usual impression which we receive from reality, but which has precisely this characteristic of being more than real which we have detected in dream' (Baudry 1975/1999: 772).

Metz (1975) shared, in part, Baudry's theoretical standpoint and made the connection between the 'impression of reality' afforded by the cinematic experience and the regression to a mode of satisfaction characteristic of the primary process involving, in Freud's own words, the 'hallucinatory revival of the perceptual images' (1900: 383). The power of cinema is, then, acknowledged as its ability to respond to the unconscious desire or need for a regressive return to an infantile narcissism which allows for the satisfaction of desire through the entering in relationship with a reality where 'the separation between one's body and the exterior world, between ego and non ego, is not clearly defined' (Stam 2000: 163). Cinema provides the means for the perception, in the achieved regressive state, of an image that, in accordance with the responses typical of the primary process, is one with the object and yet, being a recorded projection, testifies to the absence of the object it represents. Metz introduced the notion of the 'imaginary signifier' when he argued that cinema, in making present what is absent, offers a unity which is only imaginary and forces the spectator to deal with the lack as part of the viewing process.

In line with Baudry, Metz argued that this process is analogous to that described by Lacan's mirror phase, understood as a reworking of Freud's description of the Oedipal trajectory. The child's (a male child) identification with the image in the mirror is accompanied by the awareness of the difference from his mother. The castration anxiety deriving from the realization of her lack requires the repression of the desire for her which marks the entry into the Symbolic (defined by law, language and loss). Letting go of the mother is the prerequisite to the acquisition of a social identity but it also implies the beginning of the desire, of the search for the lost object. The options open to the boy (again the sexing is specified) are either disavowal or fetishism, processes that are also reproduced in the cinematic situation, both in narrative solutions and in the actual relationship between screen and spectator. Apparatus theory suggests that cinema actually compensates for what the viewing subject lacks by offering 'an imaginary unity to smooth over the fragmentation at the heart of subjectivity' (Creed 2000: 80). Although extremely influential, apparatus theory has been repeatedly contested for failing to take into account the 'economic, social, or political determinations of cinema' (Penley 2000: 459), for the inaccurate application of Lacanian concepts and, most strongly, for constructing an analysis of the cinematic situation which presupposes a male gendered spectator.

With her article 'Visual Pleasure and Narrative Cinema' (1975), Laura Mulvey set out to review the position of the female spectator and provided the cornerstones for an extremely prolific feminist film criticism. She suggested that the dual trapping of woman into possibilities of identification either with passive femininity or with the denial of it and with the objectifying gaze of the male spectator could only be resisted through an analysis of pleasure intent on destroying it. Criticized for assuming the impossibility of positive identification outside the one with a male character, Laura Mulvey has subsequently revised her statement and yet in that seminal article she had clearly anticipated that her analysis would be limited by its very psychoanalytic nature. The near impossible challenge of fighting an 'unconscious structured like a language ... while still caught within the language of the patriarchy' was to be faced, according to Mulvey, by examining 'patriarchy with the tools it provides, of which psychoanalysis is not the only but an important one' (1975: 7). Mulvey described the Freudian concept of scopophilia as a perverted looking aimed at 'taking other people as objects, subjecting them to a controlling and curious gaze' (1975: 8) and proposed again the analogy between the cinematic situation and the process of identification as described in Lacan's mirror phase. When considering the relevance of these concepts to the cinematic situation Mulvey concluded that 'cinema seems to have evolved a particular illusion of reality' where the tensions between instinctual drives (where pleasure is obtained through objectification of the other through looking) and self-preservation (where identification with the image leads to recognition/fascination and/or rejection) are reconciled.

According to Mulvey, however, classical narrative cinema has played on these mechanisms of objectification and identification in order to support the ideology of patriarchy. In fact not only is woman presented visually as the sexual object of the male gaze, as a signifier of male desire, but the narrative structure will work in favour of an active male hero, whose power in controlling the action is made to coincide with 'the active power of the erotic look, both giving a satisfying sense of omnipotence' (1975: 12). The threat of castration that the female image supposedly evokes produces an anxiety, which, breaking the illusion of a seamless diegesis, would create a distancing leading to awareness. The surfacing of this anxiety needs to be contained either through 'fetishistic scopophilia', which by fetishizing the female body disavows difference, or through voyeurism which in its association with sadism punishes it. Film then becomes a patriarchally constructed signifying practice contributing to the maintaining of women's passivity while endeavouring to offer visual pleasures to a viewer who will necessarily be male.

The breaking down of the cinematic codes that concur in the creation of an 'illusion cut to the measure of desire' becomes, according to Mulvey, a necessary feminist action which, in freeing 'the look of the camera into its materiality in time and space', will in turn free 'the look of the audience into dialectics, passionate detachment' (1975: 17–18).

The limitations of such an approach to film are to be found in the way the analysis revolves continuously around the relation of the female spectator to the screen and in an analysis of a look and pleasure conditioned by gender. However, from a feminist point of view these limitations would have to be considered strengths. Mulvey's work has indeed brought feminism into a dialogue with film theory that advances the understanding of the position of women in culture. In suggesting that this position is 'ascribed' by a patriarchal unconscious she entered a distinctively political discourse which finds its validation in the mapping of theories of subjectivity on to classical, mainstream narrative cinema.

The theoretical interventions considered so far all imply a revisiting of the Lacanian idea of the mirror stage as apt analogy for the relationship between screen and spectator. This revisiting is, however, a revisiting with a difference as the image reflected by the cinema screen is not a mirror image of the spectator, so that the subsequent and, according to these theorists, inevitable identification which ensues is not with the image on screen but with the act of perception itself.

This moment, which Joan Copjec translates as 'identification with the gaze' (1989: 442), is the prerequisite for a subsequent recognition of the images on screen. Copjec highlights how, for Metz, identification with the gaze is the step that allows the subject to see itself as the one 'supplying the image with sense'. If the gaze is 'the signified of the image' then the subject 'comes into being by identifying with the images signified' (1989: 442). It is in this claim to the construction, by the cinematic apparatus, of a subject who places himself in a position of centrality in relation to representations that Copjec sees the distancing of film theory from a truly Lacanian perspective. With a brief and rather condensed reference to Lacan's Seminar XI she revisits his definition of the gaze.

Rather than a gaze as possessed by or identifiable with the subject, Copjec redefines it, quoting Lacan, as 'that which "determines" the I in the visible; it is "the instrument through which ... [the] I [is] *photo-graphed*"[1] (Lacan 1977: 106)'. While film theory has positioned the subject as coinciding with 'the geometrical point from which perspective is grasped', Lacan describes the construction of another non-punctiform position (Lacan 1977: 96). Lacan's description takes into account the way in which that 'misrecognition', which Metz related to the lack of reflection of the subject's own image, is produced in the intersection between the triangle described by the gaze and that produced by the interference of the signifier, a signifier which, because of its reference to other signifiers rather than to a signified, would maintain the subject trapped within the imaginary, as the subject cannot imagine anything outside of it. Representations, Copjec continues, are considered by Lacan as a 'trap for the gaze' as they 'induce us to imagine a gaze outside – and observing – the field of representation' (Copjec 1989: 450).

According to Copjec's understanding of Lacan, it is by generating a 'beyond', by suggesting the question of what remains invisible and by marking the absence of a signified, that representation produces the response of desire. This desire is for a representation of what the subject 'wants to see', and it is this desire which 'institutes the subject in the visible field' and constructs a lack commensurate with desire itself (Copjec 1989: 450). So the separation between the subject's unconscious and its conscious 'semblance' is described here as a traumatic and rather desperate breaking up, performed against (and because of) the perceived deception which is considered to be an effect of representation. The ensuing desire, as intended in the previous paragraph, is supposed to 'impede [the subject's] progress' and, according to Copjec, 'must be reconstructed if the subject is to be changed' (1989: 452).

While Copjec seems successfully to redirect psychoanalytic film theory towards a clearer understanding of central Lacanian concepts, her final suggestion, to be taken supposedly as a conclusion, of the need for a deconstruction of desire and a changing of the subject leaves the reader wanting more, hanging from an unfulfilled promise of a solution which is not provided.

---

1 Italics in the original.

Is it possible then to avoid this circumnavigating of 'the absence that anchors the subject and impedes its progress' (Copjec 1989: 452)? Or are we not trapped by the very definition of a truth that can never be grasped by language, by a cause of being to be found in the impossibility of seeing the object of a desire which is beyond representation? And if the change that Copjec would aspire to is to be performed through the analytical relationship (we can only infer this from the note which refers to the concept of 'the pass' in Lacan, 'Study Notes', Vol. 3, Jacques Alain-Miller), what then is the role of cinema if not to accept its own deceptive nature?

These questions are left unanswered. The theoretical attitude is towards an uncovering of ideologically motivated intentions to be accomplished through the analysis of the relationship between spectator and screen. This analysis is to be performed with the aid of an understanding of psychoanalysis and of its methods, and with a critical approach based on claims of accuracy and of pertinence of interpretation of the original conceptual framework provided by the Freudian and Lacanian literature. The 'resistance' or 'change' is then claimed as a conclusion which is justified by the thorough analysis but does not point, with equally thorough attention, to the discussion of a programme of action.

In 'Remembering Women: Psychical and Historical Constructions in Film Theory' (1990) Mary Ann Doane reflects on the possible reasons for the apparent impasse that psychoanalytic film theory seems to have come to. Her paper describes how psychoanalytic film theory, in proposing a 'static, inflexible theorization of an apparatus which is always in place, always functioning', has failed to consider the fact that psychoanalysis, because of its origin in the relational and temporal space of the analytic encounter, 'would seem to propose the articulation of theory and history rather than their polarization' (1990: 57). First published in 1987, Doane's paper is chronologically distant from both the first tentative Jungian approaches to film and the revisions of the applicability of Lacanian concepts exemplified by Copjec's contribution. Nevertheless her 'diagnosis' of the reason which has brought psychoanalytic film theory to a point of 'apparent exhaustion' (1990: 49) would probably still make sense today and, as it implicitly points to an alternative approach centred on a relationship of dialogue with history, invites an exploration of the potential of the Jungian paradigm.

Jungian analytical psychology's anchoring in history is, in fact, effected in its methodology as well as in its purpose. The comparative method involves both the horizontal interaction of the object of analysis with other cultures and its vertical relationship with past representations (in mythology, folklore, visual arts, literature). The intention is that of isolating a meaning which is both descriptive (past) compensatory (present) and suggestive (future), an intention that sustains the Jungian appreciation of a three-dimensional relationship of art with time which will be explored in chapter three. An understanding of the teleological perspective characteristic of the Jungian construct as well as making it a potentially suitable alternative, also, paradoxically, partially justifies its temporary exclusion from early academic discourses. Jungian film theorists seem to accept such exclusion as inevitable.

Indeed, Luke Hockley (2001) suggests that for the purpose of a criticism focused on a reading of film as an instance of the repressive, all-pervading power of patriarchy 'a Jungian perspective would not have been as well suited to use in deconstructing images as psychoanalysis' (Hockley 2001: 4). Before him Don Fredericksen in his article 'Jung/Sing/Symbol/Film' first published in 1979 by the *Quarterly Review of Film Studies* had also distanced his position from that of other interpretative models by proposing a Jungian 'symbolic' approach in opposition to poststructuralist perspectives (Fredericksen 2001: 17). However, a close analysis of Fredericksen's essay reveals that rather than in opposition to contemporary theoretical approaches his position did not actually engage with the interpretative models that he set out to reject. It is in fact an approach with a different purpose: that of defining 'symbolic art' and to prove its compensatory, healing function. More specifically Fredericksen argues that 'by intruding themselves upon the ego's awareness, neurotic symptoms and symbolic art draw attention to the fact that a change of conscious standpoint is necessary. They thus perform a positive and healing function' (2001: 35). The 'change' hailed by Fredericksen as necessary does not echo the ideological intention of Mulvey's resistance nor Copjec's suggestion of a reworking of desire free from the dependency on representation. Although pioneering, his paper introduced Jungian analytical psychology as the tool for a parallel, non-dialectic alternative to a Freudian/Lacanian approach to the understanding of film.

John Izod in his Jungian study of Nicolas Roeg's films (1992) also presents Jungian analytical psychology as an alternative to which film theorists must have remained indifferent because of the 'supremacy of materialist theories in academic studies of film since the late 1960s' (Izod 1992: 1). Maybe in order to explain more substantially the reasons for such indifference Izod adds: 'Jung's theoretical work on the mind's activities constructs an altogether fuller picture of the interior life of the human being than that given by the currently dominant model.' Unlike his fellow Freudian and Lacanian film theorists, Izod finds this model 'particularly attractive in that it corresponds with the individual's ever-present, ever-fluctuating sense of an active inner being' (Izod 1992: 1).

Indeed 'materialist theories' might not see themselves as benefiting from a 'fuller picture of the interior life of the human being' and the idea of 'the individual's ever-present . . . sense of an active inner being' does not seem compatible with that of a split subject. It is more than just a question of incompatibility of language; the difference is in perspective and in purpose. Ricoeur (1970) in *Freud and Philosophy: An Essay in Interpretation* described Freud, together with Marx and Nietzsche, as a 'master' of what he called the hermeneutic of suspicion (p. 32) as in psychoanalysis the search for meaning happens behind the text which is believed to deceptively mask reality. This same distrust for the image is characteristic of a film theory that, derived from a Freudian standpoint, is set to uncover what has been misplaced or disguised by the image or concealed behind it. A Jungian perspective sees the image as the potential catalyst of the transformations which serve the purpose of individuation, the inner process directed towards psychic development. This teleological approach, being central to Jung's theory of the unconscious, can only remain central to Jungian theories of film and it is bound to be welcomed with scepticism by those who see in the relationship with the image the manifestation of a desire to see what is beyond, suggestive of an 'absence that anchors the subject and impedes its progress' (Copjec 1989: 452).

Nevertheless the flow of Jungian participation has certainly seen an increase after the contemporary publications in 2001 of three texts which have finally brought Jungian film theory to the foreground of academic discourses. A more comprehensive analysis of these texts will point to the place that a Jungian perspective has chosen to occupy and clarify the perceived gap this work intends to fill.

Jung and film and how symbols will never be the same

Don Fredericksen's paper, first published in 1979, is also presented as the opening contribution in Hauke and Alister's (2001) *Jung and Film: Post-Jungian Takes on the Moving Image*. As well as representing, in its first edition, the beginning of a competent interaction of Jungian analysis with film theory, Fredericksen's essay is asked to provide, within the more recent text, a suitable theoretical framework and as such it demands closer analysis. The essay was actually presented as a paper at the Society for Cinema Studies Conference in 1978. Fredericksen presented the paper under the title 'Does Jung's distinction between Sign and symbol set a limit upon film semiotics and point to the need for a broader notion of film meaning?'. It later become 'Jung/Sign/Symbol/Film' and edited and restructured it is now part of the edited collection. The paper's intention was and remains that of demonstrating the value of what Jung has described as a 'symbolic' attitude as an alternative to what Fredericksen calls the semiotic attitude in film studies.

First the notion of the 'impression and/or illusion of reality' as it is conceived of in film theory is briefly discussed and criticized as it would not satisfactorily explain the numinous and uncanny qualities of a 'living symbol experienced as such, whether in film or in dreams and fantasies'. The power and the effect of the symbol define, according to Fredericksen, its 'unassailable *reality*'[2] (1979: 174).

Understood as part of a Jungian vocabulary the 'numinous and uncanny' qualities should be seen as the consequence of the experience of a symbol. They are considered elements, and possibly the most characteristic, of its effect and a proof of the symbols' power. The birth of the symbol into *reality*[3] is, however, a rushed phenomenological delivery, and it is rendered more unstable by Fredericksen's comment on Metz's understanding of the symbolic image as one that 'overtakes' its motivational origin. Metz suggested that the cross, although chosen as a reminder of the fact that Christ died on one, has also come to represent Christianity

---

2 Italics in the original.
3 Italics mine. Reality is not intended here as the Lacanian *real* and this remains a necessarily ambiguous term.

with all its complexity, thus 'overtaking' its simpler original motivation. Fredericksen describes Metz's as a 'strikingly mundane' notion of the symbolic. If the image of the cross stands for that known entity which Christianity supposedly is, then it should be considered a sign, not a symbol. The cross, Fredericksen continues, is used as a symbol of Christianity because Christianity is itself the manifestation of the tendency towards psychic wholeness embodied by Christ but symbolized by crosses before Christianity and across cultures.

Once described as a psychic reality, this tendency towards wholeness has become 'known', it has been 'dressed' in order to become describable. It has lost its symbolic nature or, as Jung points out in the passage which Fredericksen himself quotes: 'once its meaning has been born out of it, once that expression is found that formulates the thing sought, expected, or divined even better than the hitherto accepted symbol, then the symbol is *dead*' (*C.W.*, Vol. 6: para. 816). Jung acknowledged the personal and cultural importance of a meaning derived from what is 'relatively unknown' but at the same time he also admitted to the fragility of the symbol which does indeed come to possess only an historical significance once it dies to bear meaning. Understanding manipulates the nature of the symbol in order to leave behind something with an historical significance (in the history of a culture as much as in that of an individual), probably a sign. Jung's description is indeed clear and extensive:

> Whether a thing is a symbol or not depends chiefly upon the attitude of the observing consciousness . . . there are undoubtedly products whose symbolic character does not depend merely on the attitude of the observing consciousness, but manifests itself spontaneously in the symbolic effect they would have on the observer. Such products are so constituted that they would lack any kind of meaning were not a symbolic one conceded to them.
> (*C.W.*, Vol. 6: para. 818)

The 'effect' defines the symbolic and a temporary absence of meaning calls for the concession of one, a concession whose purpose is the true difference between a Jungian and a Freudian approach. Fredericksen introduces Jung's own distinction between the two attitudes exemplified by the difference between symptoms and symbols: if symptoms are 'merely derived from something', no more than consequences, symbols are 'processes which bear within them a hidden meaning, processes which . . . seek to become something' (Fredericksen 2001: 169). The difference is in the purpose: the function of the symbol is that of a marker, it appears as a manifestation of the psyche's natural urge for individuation, for self fulfilment. The symbols' 'becoming' is a translation into a rich meaning that outlives it as the symbolic process finds its temporary fulfilment in consciousness. Fredericksen acknowledges this transformation when he distinguishes between 'cultural symbols', recurrently appearing within a culture and elaborated to the point of being reducible to signs, and 'natural' symbols, which appear in dreams and cultural products beyond the confines of a culture or of an historical period.

Fredericksen, still attempting to define the symbolic approach against the limitations of the Lacanian/Freudian perspective, introduces at this point a discussion centred on the Lacanian definition of meaning. In a concise analysis based on Richard Wolheim's *The Cabinet of Dr. Lacan* (1979) Fredericksen criticises the acceptance in Lacan of the possibility of meaning as based on, and 'arising from the known or knowable' (Fredericksen 1979: 177). Lacan actually clearly admitted that 'there is no such thing as knowledge in the pure state, for the strict community of ego and other in desiring the object initiates something completely different, namely recognition' (Lacan 1988: 51). He also insisted on the impossibility of grasping meaning when he described it as 'an order, that is to say, a sudden emergence. A meaning is an order which suddenly emerges. A life insists on entering into it, but it expresses something which is perhaps completely beyond this life' (Lacan 1988: 232).

Persistent in his search for differences, Fredericksen argues that the Jungian symbol, being connected to pre-linguistic 'indeed pre-human, layers of the unconscious' (1979: 177), cannot find equivalent in the Lacanian unconscious which is defined against the infant's entering the Symbolic through language. It seems as if the Jungian symbol is made here to be identical with instinct (part of the 'pre-human' layers of the unconscious), and, and this is more confusing, has come to bear the characteristics Jung had ascribed to the archetype-per-se, understood as the psyche's inherent potential for psychic development (the distinction between the archetype and the archetype-per-se will be discussed in detail in the next chapter). The arrival of the symbol into consciousness necessarily marks its separation from the unconscious. We may therefore infer the existence of its origin in the unconscious but cannot say that the symbol itself exists before language. Before language, symbols are unnecessary; it is language that gives the unconscious the never quite adequate shape it does not need before it, the shape of symbols. The felt irreducibility of a symbol to its fullness of meaning in consciousness, its numinosity, its felt power, testify to the impossibility of its representation and to it being a visual approximation of something irreducibly invisible, the archetype.

The symbol, as Fredericksen puts it, is the manifestation of the tie existing between deep layers of the unconscious and consciousness. It is a glimpse which resists semiotic imprisonment in rational categories. And, because of its ability to transcend personal associations, because of the power of its fascination and energy, the symbol is considered a manifestation of an unconscious that itself is beyond the personal: the collective unconscious. Dreams, fantasies, fairy tales, myths, legends and works of art offer the canvas for the manifestation of symbols, providing access to that unconscious, calling for meaning and recognition in consciousness. The search for symbolic imagery in films must then be at the heart of a Jungian film analysis. When the semiotic readings reach a standstill and when after all has been said there still remains more, we might be, according to Fredericksen, in the presence of a symbol. The way to a deeper understanding, to a 'symbolic' reading of the film is then through the process Jung called amplification. Amplification within the therapeutic context has the aim of clarifying the content of symbolic images that appear in dream by drawing mythical, cultural and historical parallels. These will bring the dream image within the context of the collective; it will provide a perspective from which a resolution or an understanding of the psychoanalytic situation that the image describes can be accomplished. The understanding, still within the therapeutic confines, will lead to a synthesis of opposing psychological principles which, together with an awareness of unconscious processes and a learnt ability to respond to their manifestations, represents the aim of a Jungian analysis. In describing the function of amplification Jung specifies that 'this procedure widens and enriches the initial symbol. . . . Certain lines of psychological development then stand out that are at once individual and collective' (*C.W.*, Vol. 7: para. 299). This description reinforces the suggestion of the importance of the symbols as markers of a process and of their reading within a context.

Fredericksen expands the possibilities offered by amplification to the understanding of cinema and, deriving his suggestion from Jung's reference to the function of the symbol within the therapeutic situation, he extends that function to what he calls symbolic cinema. The presence of images of symbolic value is invested then with a compensatory purpose; its existence should point, in Fredericksen's words, to the need to 'listen to that inner space which is at once uniquely individual and transpersonal (archetypal)' (2001: 51). While 'listening to that inner space' is a suggestion spoken in a language inaudible to the academic ear trained to respond to the vertiginous and sharp Lacanian logic, the idea of the possibility of tracing a psychological development at once individual and collective through the analysis of film seems to call, at least, for a specific methodological approach sustained and validated by a Jungian understanding of the symbolic value of images. Such an approach not only informs this work but justifies the selection of a specific cultural and historical context as its field of analysis.

Jung and film into the new millennium: old limitations and new potentials

If the first three decades of the history of film study as an academic discipline only saw rare instances of Jungian participation, the beginning of the new millennium marked a decidedly clearer commitment of the Jungian perspective to the study of film. In 2001 three books were published: Luke Hockley's *Cinematic Projections: The Analytical Psychology of C.C. Jung*, John Izod's *Myth, Mind and the Screen: Understanding the Heroes of Our Time* and the collection of essays edited by Christopher Hauke and Ian Alister *Jung and Film: Post-Jungian Takes on the Moving Image*. These books were to represent an incentive and an inspiration for a more consistent flow of publications that certainly supported the final recognition of the positive value of the Jungian approach to the analysis of the cinematic image.

In order to understand more clearly the reasons for academia's long-lasting indifference towards Jung it is important to realize how those issues which have attracted much suspicion from the academic community have often inadequately being addressed. These are issues related to Jung's personal life, his perceived views on racism and politics, and his dubious closeness to some of the women in his analytical care. The suspicions have turned into caustic accusations with the publication of Richard Noll's *The Jung Cult: Origins of a Charismatic Movement* (1994) and *The Aryan Christ: The Secret Life of Carl Jung* (1997). The negative impact of the unforgiving views epitomized by these two books is probably lessened by the approximation and lack of evidence which characterizes them, paralleled by a recent re-evaluation of the Jungian contribution to literary theory. A consideration of Jung's own attitude and life choices in the light of the context of his upbringing and cultural surroundings should ease the weight of judgement and allow for a critical and more selective reading of his work.

In an article first published in 1992 Andrew Samuels specifically addresses these issues and discusses Jung's perceived anti-semitism. His conclusion is a balanced perspective which, while acknowledging the problem also limits the extent of its negative effect to the benefit of the positive application of Jung's pioneering theoretical statements. Samuels maintains:

> If one were to abandon Jung's method, then one might be able to revalue what he was trying to do. For, make no mistake about it, alongside the many problems with Jung's ideas about nation, race and religion, there are also the seeds of a marvellously useful approach to difference. Even if Jung's method and ideology are suspect, his intuition of the importance of exploring difference remains intact. We can preserve a connection to Jung's intuition of the importance of difference but unhindered by excessive dependence on complementarity
>
> (Samuels 1992:3)

Luke Hockley in *Cinematic Projections* (2001) also considers the characteristics of the Jungian attitude and of a theoretical standpoint which might have negatively affected its academic reception. Besides admitting to the unsuitability of the Jungian position, founded on a developmental and teleological view of the psyche, to match the politically motivated film analyses of the early 1970s, Hockley, in his introduction, suggests other reasons for the limited presence of Jungian contributions to the study of film. As well as acknowledging the problems associated with Jung's personal life Hockley points to the lack of clarity in Jung's own writing which reflects the continuous development of his own understanding of the psyche. Moreover, when reading *The Collected Works* one finds definitions that seem unstable and it is often difficult to pinpoint a concept. If Freud's writings are focused and to the point, Jung often takes the reader along to experience the thought processes leading to a theorization. Lacan puts it rather sharply when he declares that 'Freud isn't Jung. He doesn't spend his time finding all the echoes. When Freud puts something in his text, it is always extremely important' (Lacan 1988: 131).

Having set a context for the Jungian lack of participation in the theoretical discourse on film, Hockley is then keen to emphasize how the Jungian teleological and developmental model of the psyche suggests an analysis of images, whether emerging from dreams or from other forms of expression, profoundly different from the one supported by a Freudian perspective. Rather than 'the royal road to the unconscious', dreams would be 'the royal road *from* the unconscious, *to* the future' and as the psyche, in Jung's own words, 'consists essentially of images' Hockley derives the idea that, on the bases of this theoretical assumption, cinema can be seen to provide us with our own *'psychological* portrait' (Hockley 2001: 2–5). Although Hockley's suggestion that 'perhaps just the act of watching a film *might* have a therapeutic effect' (Hockley 2001: 6) seems to introduce a clinically oriented analysis, the exploration of meaning he attempts leads decisively beyond the discussion of the remedial function of film. Most relevant to the unfolding of this research is Hockley's reference to Monaco's and Wright's vision of films as 'culturally shared dreams' (Hockley 2001: 40) and his conclusion that, having understood the psychological meaning of the 'individuation process' as a core concept of analytical psychology, it should become clear how 'individuation is something that happens not just to individuals but also to cultures . . . According to this model, cultures individuate, they become aware of the diversity and opposition within them, and they come to accept their shared, collective unconscious qualities' (Hockley 2001: 43).

Developing on this affirmation Hockley, in his discussion of the dynamic and formal aspects of the archetypal, draws a direct parallel between individual situations that are believed to activate and allow for the emergence of archetypal images, and the psychological conditions of a culture which motivate the abundance, in the cultural products of a time, of images with a common, specific archetypal core. The conventional Jungian analytic procedure is 'inductive' in method as it moves from the images presented by individuals or cultures to the psychological condition that they describe. In line with Hockley's reminder that it is not the content (image) but the 'archetypal patterns . . . that influence the development of individuals and cultures' (Hockley 2001: 64–65), it seems important to add that the inductive method needs the essential support and wider perspective of a comparative approach. And it is this collaboration that forms the methodological backbone of this work.

Hockley's work is motivated by a desire to provide a practical model that will allow for the isolation of the mythological themes and archetypal images and clarify the way they describe the process of individuation within a film. Such a model, together with Hockley's schematic diagram of the 'Phases of Individuation' (Hockley 2001: 118), is of great value as it eases the way towards a Jungian understanding of film text. And yet it feels as if the potential of a view that sees the symbolic imagery emerging from a film as the psychological representation of the culture from which it derives cannot fully be realized unless such representations are returned to their originating context. Hockley does actually point to an understanding that, in widening the angle of the analysis, becomes inclusive of a perspective where symbols are deeply rooted into the originating cultures. In the detailed analysis of *Trancers* (Band, 1984) he notes how 'the hero archetype is not separate or divorced from the culture . . . *Trancers* can be interpreted as a mythological representation of the American descent into the underworld, in which the hero's individuation mirrors the individuation of American culture' (Hockley 2001: 127) and according to Hockley, in representing the cultural quest for individuation, the hero's own journey, as portrayed in this particular film, will also aid this process.

Hockley's presentation of the work of Jung and of post-Jungian developments represents a clear advance towards the integration of analytical psychology within academia. Hockley's definition of the difference between sign and symbol rather than a play against semiotic approaches is 'fluid' in its acceptance of the symbol's own evanescence. As well as relating Jung's own observation that 'to be effective, a symbol must be by its very nature unassailable' (*C.W.*, Vol. 6: para. 401), Hockley adds:

> Sign is an image which is understood by consciousness; by contrast, a symbol is an image which is currently not understood by consciousness. While the ego is attracted to the symbol, and is able to grasp part of its meaning, total comprehension eludes its grasp.
>
> (Hockley 2001: 91)

With the suggestion that 'the ontogenesis of the individuation process is also phylogenetic' (Hockley 2001: 172), Hockley also hints at the potential relevance of a developmental Jungian analytical psychology to a study of film and of symbolic images in their relationship to a culture's own evolutionary development. The application of a Jungian developmental perspective to the study of film, derived from the insights provided by Erich Neumann (1954) and Anthony Stevens (2002), is an important part of this work.

While Hockley's work is an example of a Jungian screen theory equipped to leave the analytic setting in order to participate in an interdisciplinary scholarly discourse, *Jung and Film* (Hauke and Alister 2001), published in the same year, seems to shift its focus to an exploration of the healing potential of film fulfilled through an understanding aided by a Jungian perspective. Nevertheless, the presence of contributions centred on the appreciation of film's therapeutic function (Berry 2001: 71–72) or on the use of film as an analytical tool which can, when working with women 'allow for the articulation of [their] gender identity' (Dougherty 2001: 206) is counterbalanced by a number of essays more directly preoccupied with the construction of an alternative approach to the traditionally psychoanalytic theorization of film. Christopher Hauke, Lydia Lennihan and John Izod propose, in fact, a perspective that inspires this book's methodological direction: they recognize the presence of symbolic imagery in film as the manifestation of a layer of the unconscious not previously defined by Jung; the cultural unconscious. Izod in particular suggests that, without specifically describing a layer of the unconscious as cultural, Jung had nevertheless argued for the possibility of the emergence of certain symbols or clusters of symbols in the collective consciousness as a manifestation of the specific pressure of the time. From this standpoint it becomes imperative to re-evaluate the images not only within the narrative context of the individual film but within the film's own historical and cultural context. This is an attitude fully embraced by Izod who concludes his analysis of Kubrick's *2001: A Space Odyssey* with the extraordinary suggestion that a film like this 'can bring to consciousness, and then leave latent in the cultural unconscious for years afterward, a trace which modifies the culture by seeding a new image of great potential' (Izod 2001b: 149). Lydia Lennihan's reading of *Pulp Fiction*, through a Jungian understanding of the alchemical motifs manifest in the film imagery, points to the same conclusion. She sees the film's images as symbolic markers of American society's psychological status, as reminders of a potential to be recognized not only individually but culturally (Lennihan 2001: 67). Christopher Hauke's chapter adds a specific methodological dimension, already exploited by Izod's in his study of Roeg's oeuvre (1992), as he chooses to analyse a selection of Spielberg's films. Hauke intends to demonstrate how, through a Jungian understanding, it is possible to trace not only the director's own developmental journey but also changes in the approach to 'reoccurring themes [which] echo changes in the collective culture.'(Hauke 2001: 153–154) This perspective represents a breakthrough not only because it motivates film analysis beyond the clinical confines but also because of the relevance given to the comparative method, allowing for a refreshing incorporation of the film texts (and the plural here is essential) within the collective which participate in shaping as much as it does in receiving them.

John Izod's book *Myth, Mind and the Screen: Understanding the Heroes of Our Time* (2001a) represents the most complete and engaging example of the theoretical potential of a Jungian approach to the moving image. The clear presentation of Jungian concepts such as synchronicity, amplification and coincidence runs parallel to a dialectical approach to existing classical psychoanalytic approaches to film. Izod explores more directly the relationship between screen images and culture and his field of study extends to include cultural icons such as Madonna and Michael Jackson as well as televized sport events. While enlisting the weaknesses and limitations of past psychoanalytical approaches to film, Izod also prepares the way for an understanding of screen images that is to be, rather than a contrasting alternative, a compensation for those limitations. Insisting on the passivity attributed to the spectator by Freudian and Lacanian film theory, Izod refers to the nature of the unconscious which, by these schools of thought 'is not conceived as having the power to overthrow or remake elements of the symbolic order and rewrite cinematic and spoken language to meet the insistence of hitherto unvoiced desires' (Izod 2001a: 6). Unconscious contents are the product of repression and their expression suffers the distortion of displacement. Jungians, on the contrary see dream imagery as the most direct means of communication between the unconscious and the conscious mind and such images, rather than shielding repressed, feared or shameful meaning, are to have the effect of compensating 'for the biases of conscious drives' (Izod 2001a: 7). Moreover, because of the hypothesis of a link between the individual's dream and the emergence in myths, legends and cultural artefacts of images arising from a collective unconscious, a Jungian perspective can justify and benefit from a reading of the film text set against not only such images but also against the specific cultural moments that mould them.

The concept of the collective unconscious has inspired much suspicion on the part of film and media theorists as it is 'at odds with sociological theories that represent human beings as subject to ideological pressure exerted on them through every social and cultural channel' (Izod 2001a: 9). However, Izod suggests, the recent development of a post-Jungian perspective, with its awareness of the importance of the interplay between psychological and social and cultural factors in the formation of the individual psyche, opens the way, within the limitation imposed by its own incompleteness, to a possible integration of the Jungian perspective within the academic discourse on film.

Izod introduces an interpretation of the process of viewing a film which, in his probably unintended similarity with most recent studies on the manipulation of dream material by the waking mind, seems to hold exciting potential. He suggests that 'when the action on screen greatly excites spectators, it seems probable that their emotions set in train the affective process which alters the configuration in the memory of the images even as they are being screened' (Izod 2001a: 17). While watching a film, the spectator temporarily suspends the unfolding of his own fantasy material, only to resume it at the end of the film as 'active imagination' through which cinematic images will be merged with the individual's own repertoire (Izod 2001a: 17). The consequence of the emotional engagement set in motion by the cinematic images is the activation of the unconscious mechanisms of projection and introjection, processes which, in Jungian analytical psychology are considered as aids to the process of integration. When distinguishing between the processes of projection and introjection as they happen naturally throughout the life of an individual and as affect in the interaction with screen images, Izod points to the intentional, predetermined direction of the latter which is a consequence of the sapient manipulation of the filmmaker. The maybe too obvious ideological weight of this suggestion is swiftly bypassed in favour of an interpretation that sees in such a selective input a demonstration of the dependency of cinema's success on 'shared subjective experience' (Izod 2001a: 20).

The symbolic film's potential is the same as that of the symbol as it appears in dreams or active imagination: it activates a process which, by enhancing the development of a more direct dialogue with the unconscious, leads towards integration. And if the exposure to symbols in the cinema, because of the publicity of the encounter, would generally have a diluted effect, Izod reinstates the possibility of a symbol's more powerful resonance with the 'energy of an archetype seeking to compensate for a bias in collective consciousness' (Izod 2001a: 21). The effectiveness of the symbol seems to depend on the conscious attention dedicated to it by the individual or, more specifically, by the textual analyst. This attention translates methodologically into the practice of amplification and of active imagination. Yet, Izod admits, the very limitation of amplification is that it tries to ascertain meaning. If this is acceptable to classical Jungians who believe in the benefits of interpretation, archetypal psychoanalysts such as James Hillman believe in the importance of suspending interpretation in order to allow for the symbolic material to fully resonate with the energy that generated it (Izod 2001a: 23). In line with this perspective Izod proposes that, in order to respect the integrity of the symbol, it is necessary for the textual analyst of film to bring 'their own subjectivity consciously and methodologically into play' (Izod 2001a: 24). While amplification provides a direct, objective mode of reading a text, it is important to insist on the structure so obtained by adopting the constructive method which will help, through elaboration, to bring to light the specific purpose of the symbol. Active imagination is the technique to be used by the analyst who, in response to the resonance of the symbol within him or her, will then become able to incorporate an objective, rational analysis (amplification) with his or her own subjective intuitive, emotional response. The next step is that of external amplification consisting of cross-referencing the symbolic material with related images or stories found within the same or other narrative genres and art forms (Izod 2001a: 29). In particular, the technique of external amplification seems especially suited to a comparative method, to a form of engagement with the film text that seeks to return the analysed image to the pattern drawn by adjacent texts within a specific cultural background. This is, indeed, the methodological direction this work follows.

The sample analyses of film texts such as *The Piano, The Silence of the Lambs, Diva, The Passion of Darkly Noon* and *2001: A Space Odyssey* draw the clear lines of a Jungian methodological approach, where concepts such as synchronicity, coincidence and numinosum become valuable aids in the construction of a theory of film that finally renounces any indulgence into a language heard and dismissed by academics as 'mystical', without, however, renouncing an understanding of the importance of the sacred and of religion in moulding human experience.

Izod's book occupies a solid mediating ground between most recent developments of post-Jungian thought and classical psychoanalytic approaches to film theory. He introduces the reader to an updated understanding of the archetypes, insisting on the difference between form and content and between archetype and archetypal image. The theorization of the presence of a 'cultural unconscious' provides a valid point of reference as well as direction for a more in-depth research which has certainly inspired the development of this work.

Conclusion

Jungian analytical psychology, notwithstanding its great emphasis on the importance of the emergence and understanding of images as means of communication from the unconscious, has managed to remain relatively absent from the academic arena where a psychoanalytical discussion of film has characterized the past three decades. This chapter has explored the field of analysis and the differences in approach between the theoretical position founded on a Freudian/Lacanian perspective and that constructed on a Jungian paradigm.

Consistent with the Freudian 'hermeneutic of suspicion' psychoanalytic film theory's purpose has been that of uncovering the concealed function of the cinematic text and of revealing the hidden but purposeful organization of the viewing process according to the needs of dominant ideologies. The revelation of the subject's passivity in relation to the image requires, according to the theorist considered in this representative analysis, a resistance affected as 'passionate detachment', 'rejection of film pleasure' (Mulvey 1975: 6–17) and the deconstruction of the desire which impedes 'the subject's progress' (Copjec 1989: 452). The goals, if abstract, are nevertheless explicit, yet a coherent programme of action does not follow. The undoubtedly necessary awareness of the potential for manipulative conditioning inherent in the process of film viewing naturally leads to the question of resistance. The question, however, remains unanswered and, like desire, it maintains its existence as a consequence of its unattainable resolution. The psychoanalytic approach has then succeeded in describing the subject/spectator's vulnerability to the subtle power of subjugating ideologies without offering clear enough suggestions for the possibility of his or her re-emergence as agent.

The Jungian approach to the unconscious, rather than constructed around the need to uncover meanings hidden behind the deceitful image, is founded on the trust in the image's positive purpose. Symbols are then the best expression of an unconscious content that, by definition, can never find adequate representation, but which serves the purpose of a process of psychic development that Jung had called the process of individuation. Within this perspective the Jungian approach to film is one that, in interpreting the film's symbolic content, reveals the outlines of a process which is characteristic of individual as well as of collective development. The questions emerging from this approach are, indeed, very different. If, however, throughout the scant history of the Jungian contribution to film theory questions were asked they have certainly not solicited much response. Neither the suggestion of the therapeutic function of film nor that of using film narratives as arenas for the practice of clinical interpretation could in fact justify the Jungian intervention within an academic discussion on film. Indeed, if some of the most recent contributions provide more solid ground for the forming of a Jungian film theory, too often the clinical voice has overtaken the ideological, structural and culturally analytical reading of films.

The tendency to maintain the theoretical exchange within the limits of the Jungian clinical community is only one of the reasons for the academic indifference discussed in this chapter. As well as little evidence of a willingness to establish a direct dialogue with existing theoretical constructs, what emerges is also a sense of self-imposed limitation in the voices of some theorists who seem to consider the Jungian approach ill suited to the task of uncovering the ideological function of film.

More recent publications, such as John Izod's *Myth, Mind and the Screen* (2001a) are, however, testimony to a definitive shift and to a willingness to more readily engage with psychoanalytically informed academic discourses. The post-Jungian introduction of the concept of the 'cultural unconscious' not only as 'repository of cultural experience' but, more interestingly, as 'the means, already existing as a potential, by which the human psyche gives birth to cultural difference and then reinforces it' (Samuels 1993: 328) more directly justifies the participation of analytical psychology in the study of the relationship between the unconscious and culturally specific modes of expression.

The discussion of the limitations and potentialities of the most respected Jungian contributions to date forecasts new possibilities for a dialogue between Jungian analytical psychology and the academic community. The scope of this book is that of supporting and advancing the possibilities opened by such dialogue. Jung himself believed that the amalgamations of 'opposing hermeneutics of causal and teleological perspectives' would lead to a more complete understanding (Marlan 2002: 60). This work encompasses the view that the symbol 'has a prospective and a retrospective meaning' and that the conflict between the two interpretations (as Ricoeur also suggested) is 'provisional'. 'The standpoint beyond the conflict is achieved through dialectic, a dialectic between the differing moments of symbolic reality' (Marlan 2002: 60).

Benefiting from the possibilities opened by such a dialectic, this book tests the hypothesis that sees film as a manifestation of a cultural unconscious communicating with an audience at once recipient and agent of the transformations required to sustain a collective process of individuation. A comparative study of films emerging from a selected cultural context provides the field of analysis. External amplification, informed by an awareness of the film's historical origins, brings to focus clusters of recurrent images that, dotted along a temporal line, suggest a traceable pattern of archetypal themes.

The theoretical framework to this project derives from the integration of traditional Jungian texts with recent post-Jungian rewritings. The analysis of analytical psychology's central concepts provided in the next chapter is an example of the wide-reaching possibilities of this approach.

Chapter 2

Archetype and complex
The paradox of dynamic structures

> The pattern needs no interpretation: it portrays its own meaning.
> (*C.W.*, Vol. 8: para. 402)

Introduction

The intention of this chapter is to offer a condensed introduction to the aspects of Jungian analytical psychology most relevant to the study of film. While terms such as *archetype*, *complex*, *shadow* and *active imagination* have, in varying degrees, become part of everyday language, the theory from which they emerged has either remained the domain of the analyst or has been subject to reinterpretation often inaccurate and diluted. Admittedly, the idea of revising and presenting a fair synthesis of the whole of Jung's writings would represent a task disproportionably cumbersome for the scope of this book, yet a general grasp and a familiarity with some central ideas is indispensable, as is a discussion of the contemporary interdisciplinary discourses which explore their suitability and application. An essential analysis of both the origin and development of certain aspects of Jungian thought will be at the heart of this chapter.

The differences between the Jungian and the Freudian approach, although more complex than would be necessary to describe here, are essentially to be found in the nature of the unconscious and, as already discussed in Chapter 1, in the purpose of analysis. Freud's unconscious stores repressed memories that through analysis and its retrieving techniques become available to consciousness and can then be revisited and revised within the supporting environment of the analytical process. Jung postulated the existence of a collective as well as of a personal unconscious. He described the content of the personal unconscious as complexes and that of the collective unconscious as archetypes.

Although only an aspect, but certainly a central one, of Jungian analytical psychology, archetypal theory, with its emphasis on images, is crucial to a Jungian understanding of film. This chapter outlines a brief history of the concept of the archetype in order to demonstrate not only how the misunderstandings often associated with it can be linked to Jung's own early inconsistent definitions, but also to introduce the most recent intersections of Jungian theory with neuroscientific studies, an interdisciplinary exchange which both enriches and expands the scopes of an already fascinating concept.

This chapter also introduces a concept that, especially in its latest development by post-Jungian analysts such as Thomas Singer (Singer and Kimbles 2004), Andrew Samuels (1985) and John Beebe (2000), has become essential to an understanding of culture and its products within a Jungian perspective: the concept of the 'complex'. The relevance of Jungian complex theory to the analysis of film is evident in Jung's paper on the relation of analytical psychology to poetry which, proceeding from a criticism on the inadequacy of a Freudian approach to artistic production, calls for a comparative analysis and a critical synthesis. Searching for points of convergence as well as discussing those of departure which motivated Jung's development of his own perspective on a psychological understanding of artistic production, this part of the chapter introduces an approach to film that hopes to complement and enrich, rather than replace, others.

Archetypal theory: with Jung, before and after

The publication of Freud's *The Interpretation of Dreams* in 1900 had a definite influence on the development of Jung's own theory. Working at the Burgholzli mental hospital in Zurich, Jung had the opportunity to put Freud's theory of the unconscious to the test. What emerged from his experimental studies was, however, an awareness of how the dream imagery produced by his psychotic patients seemed to 'fall into patterns', and of how 'these patterns were reminiscent of myth, legend and fairy tale'. The images seemed to Jung to reflect universal human modes of experience and behaviour (Samuels 1985: 24). But it was only in 1919 that he finally introduced the term archetype to describe a specific content of what he described as the collective unconscious. This content would make itself manifest through the images, ideas and recurrent motifs of dreams, myths, fairy tales and, as he added later on, of active imagination. Jung then suggested that 'there are present in every psyche forms which are unconscious but nonetheless active-living dispositions, ideas in the Platonic sense, that perform and continually influence our thoughts and feelings and actions (*C.W.*, Vol. 9i: para. 154).

In this attempt to explain the nature of the archetype Jung himself directly refers to and draws parallel with early formulations of what seems to be the same concept. Plato's definition of ideas, Kant's categories of reason, St Augustine's descriptions of ideas 'which are themselves not formed . . . but are contained in the divine understanding' (*C.W.*, Vol. 9i: para. 5) and Schopenhauer's 'prototypes' are presented as precursors of Jung's own theorization of the archetypes as contents of the collective unconscious. However, in contrast with former descriptions, Jung's own insists on the dynamic, functional and psychological nature of these 'identical psychic structures common to all men' (*C.W.*, Vol. 5: para. 224), these 'inherited thought-patterns' and 'forms not personally experienced'

(*C.W.*, Vol. 7: para. 219, 118) which somehow shape and promote what Jung will call the *process of individuation*.

In 1912 Jung first introduced the idea of *primordial images*, described as material not immediately recognizable as deriving from personal experience and rather characteristically resonant with recurrent images in myths, fairy tales and legends. He adjusted the term to *dominants* in 1917 in order to emphasize the attractive, dynamic and active function of what was to finally become in 1919 the *archetype*. As he developed a clearer understanding of the origins and functions of archetypes, Jung came to articulate an essential distinction between archetype-as-such and archetypal image and from 1946 onwards he insisted on maintaining and emphasizing such a distinction. The archetype is an 'unconscious content that is altered by becoming conscious and by being perceived' (*C.W.*, Vol. 9i: para. 6); it is the potential for the image rather than the image itself and it can also be defined as a 'functional disposition to produce the same, or very similar ideas' (*C.W.*, Vol. 5: para. 154). The mythological or legendary figure, dreams and some film images are giving an 'approximate description of an unconscious core of meaning', a meaning which may be 'circumscribed, but not described' (*C.W.*, Vol. 9i: para. 265).

It is the insistence on this difference between form and content that justifies the possibility of inheritance which is central to the functionality of the archetype, and it is the flexibility of such a concept that has, in recent years, rendered possible an interdisciplinary approach which has called physics, biology and neuroscience as witnesses to its applicability. Unfortunately, failing to maintain a sharp distinction between archetype and its manifested content is a frequent mistake, leading to forceful reductionism and a flattening of psychic material into a two-dimensional parade of well-drawn characters.

A reading of the *Collected Works* is in itself confusing because of their thematic structure which somehow hides the chronological development of Jung's own ideas that consequently appear, at times, as contradictory. Jung himself has used the words archetype and primordial image interchangeably after introducing the word 'archetype' in 'Instinct and the Unconscious', a paper first published in 1919 and appearing in the *Collected Works* in *The Structure and Dynamics of the Psyche*. It is nevertheless here that Jung, when describing a layer of the unconscious beyond the personal, states that 'in this "deeper" stratum we also find the a priori, inborn forms of "intuition", namely the archetypes of perception and apprehension, which are the necessary a priori determinants of all psychic processes' (*C.W.*, Vol. 8: para. 270). This suggestion implies an understanding of the archetype preceding the image and, because of its location beyond the realm of the personal unconscious, of its inaccessibility through consciousness. It is in the same paper that Jung finally and explicitly defines the distinction:

> The archetypal representations (images and ideas) mediated to us by the unconscious should not be confused with the archetype as such. They are very varied structures which all point back to one essentially 'irrepresentable' basic

form. The latter is characterized by certain formal elements and by certain fundamental meanings, although these can be grasped only approximately.

(*C.W.*, Vol. 8: para. 417)

By the time it appears in consciousness as a describable image, an archetype has, in fact, passed through a process of adaptation to our realm of comprehension, a process through which it has dressed its 'irrepresentable' nature with a visible approximation of its meaning.

In *The Archetypes of the Collective Unconscious* Jung warns of the elusiveness of the archetype as the subject of empirical study when he insists that one should not 'succumb to the illusion that an archetype can be finally explained and disposed of'. If this might seem disheartening, a positive methodological direction is provided within the same paragraph where Jung suggests that 'the most we can do is to *dream the myth onwards* and give it a modern dress'[1] (*C.W.*, Vol. 9i: para. 271). While explanations and interpretations are nothing but a 'dress' woven with words (in the same paragraph Jung suggests that 'language itself is only an image'), the dream becomes the agent that renews those narratives supportive of the emergence of archetypal images. Although the dream, once described, has already been manipulated by consciousness and somehow partially explained through its narrativization, it still provides an access to unconscious content, explorable with the aid of specific methods.

If Jung, in his suggestion, might have intended to expand the narrow meaning of the word 'dream' to the apparently more conscious activity of a yielding to the process of individuation, his proposition still makes sense as far as this work is concerned. It inspires, in fact, the hypothesis of the possible function of film as 'the modern dress' a culture uses to 'dream the myth onwards'. As the dream is 'a spontaneous self-portrayal, in symbolic form, of the actual situation in the unconscious' (*C.W.*, Vol. 8: para. 505), then films can symbolically describe the unconscious state of a culture at a specific time in the history of its development. The theoretical framework that will allow interpreting and analysing films within such a perspective will derive from a clearer understanding of the characteristics of the archetype and from the discussion and critical analysis of past and recent debates on its significance, meaning and effect.

Archetype and its characteristics

It will have become evident by now how the concept of archetype seems to continually slip from clear definition. It is in fact only defined by its effect. As a content of the collective unconscious it shares its most salient characteristic: its existence 'can be inferred only from individual phenomenology' (*C.W.*, Vol. 9ii: para. 278). As a 'purely formal, skeletal concept' (Samuels 1985: 25) an

---

1 Italics are Jung's.

archetype is available to perception once 'fleshed out with imagery, ideas, motifs and so on' (Samuels 1985: 25). Its irrepresentability, the irreducible distance from the volatile reality of perception, is bridged by a content, by the visual consequence of falling into consciousness. It is this 'consequence', the image, that carries the traces of its origins. As the choice of manifest content is filtered through individuals it becomes more difficult to isolate back the unadulterated collective, skeletal origin but it is nevertheless the image's analysis that reveals the characteristics of its originating mould.

Archetypal images appear in mythology, pictorial art, religious iconography, dreams, films and legends with a recurrence that becomes evident through comparative research, a method which alone reveals constancy in the emergence of such images and allows for classification and isolation of their characteristics. Because of the insistence of certain mythological motifs across cultures and historical periods Jung concluded that somehow their psychological origin had to be found in basic, inheritable patterns of psychic behaviours. The salient dynamic qualities of such patterns are, according to Jung, to be described, in psychological terms such as 'autonomy' and 'numinosity' (*C.W.*, Vol. 18: para. 1273).

Numinosity, unlike autonomy, is a characteristic directly and exclusively derivable from the image but it is the numinous character of an image that in turn supports the hypothesis of the archetype's autonomy. Jung explains that the archetype can be said to have a numinous character as 'it enters into active opposition to the conscious mind, and may be said . . . to mould the destiny of individuals by unconsciously influencing their thinking, feeling and behaviour' and by 'asserting itself with or without the co-operation of the conscious personality' (*C.W.*, Vol. 5: para. 467). It is a characteristic, again, descriptive of the effect. Numinosity is described as the specific energy that attracts to itself the contents of consciousness and therefore accompanies the perception and conscious realization of the presence of archetypal material. The subjective nature of 'numinosity' is emphasized in a passage where Jung suggests that the 'passing over into consciousness' of the archetype is 'felt as an illumination, a revelation, or a "saving idea"' (*C.W.*, Vol. 5: para. 450). By describing the archetype as numinous Jung was not necessarily investing it with that aura of mysticism so often guilty of shutting fast the academic ear. He was instead describing a sense of inexplicability and, as it emerges from his writing, he was using the word numinous in its wider signification of characterizing something which feels greater than oneself, something with a power to produce effects outside of our own will. In this sense the adjective 'numinous' serves to expand the scope of the other adjective 'autonomous'. Jung, in one of the many instances in which he merges image with archetype, suggests that the primordial image 'is a "pattern of behaviour" that will assert itself with or without the cooperation of the conscious personality' (*C.W.*, Vol. 5: para. 467).

Although autonomous and independent from consciousness, archetypes are believed to exert a specific effect, to fulfil a function, somehow guided by the unconscious. The function is one of compensation and correction, with the ambitious goal of pursuing the 'integration of conscious and unconscious, or better, the assimilation of the ego to a wider personality' (*C.W.*, Vol. 8: para. 557). This process of integration is what Jung called the *individuation process*, a process which, through assimilation of unconscious contents, facilitates a development which, although apparently irrational, seems to strive towards the formation of the individual, differentiated personality (*C.W.*, Vol. 7: 155n). If in their autonomy and skeletal inheritability instincts and archetypes are analogous, the overall function of the archetypes as agents of a psychological process of development sets them apart. In fact Jung distinguishes how 'over against the polymorphism of the primitive's instinctual nature there stands the regulating principle of individuation' (*C.W.*, Vol. 8: para. 96), acknowledging the power of what, in the same passage, he calls 'integrative unity'. However, although insisting on archetype and instincts existing at 'the most polar opposites imaginable', Jung manages to re-establish a correlation between the two and indirectly between psychology and biology by affirming that archetype and instinct 'belong together as correspondences . . . they subsist side by side as reflections in our own minds of the opposition that underlies all psychic energy' (*C.W.*, Vol. 8: para. 406).

Jung spent most of his working life concentrating on the aspect of the archetype most alien and most dissimilar to instincts: the spiritual aspect. Yet some of his writings clearly point to the potential for a research that eventually became a practical possibility with the advent of a technology supportive of neuroscientific findings. He suggested that archetypes are:

> the equivalent of the 'pattern of behaviour' in biology. The archetype represents a mode of psychic behaviour . . . it is an 'irrepresentable' factor which unconsciously arranges the psychic elements so that they fall into typical configurations, much as a crystalline grid arranges the molecules in a saturated solution.
>
> (*C.W.*, Vol. 18: para. 1158)

This affirmation does indeed find resonance in the most recent scientific research which in turn has found approval in certain post-Jungian circles.

Archetype and dynamic systems

The analysis of the work of some contemporary Jungian analysts who embrace the psycho-scientific perspective reveals, at times, the not-so-hidden agenda of reclaiming the empirical basis of archetypal theory through scientific accreditation. The intersection with physics, neuroscience and evolutionary psychology defines a field of research that is relevant to this book not because of a supposedly required scientific validation but, instead, because of the clearer, more accessible and in some ways more widely functional definition of archetype which emerges from these studies.

Michael Conforti in *Field, Form und Fate* (1999) examines the possibility of considering the archetype as 'the psychological parallel to the scientific theory of self-organizing dynamics in nature' (Conforti 1999: xiii). At the heart of his research is the exploration of the relationship between archetypes and instincts in connection with their possible role in the emergence of form. By constructing parallels with other disciplines directly focused on investigating such phenomena he hopes to come to a clearer understanding of the nature and role of archetypal structures and in so doing he does, indeed, bring together promising and original perspectives.

Jung himself had made a connection between archetype, instincts and the 'compelling' nature of both: 'Just as instincts compel man to specifically human modes of existence, so archetypes force his ways of perception and apprehension into specifically human patterns' (*C.W.*, Vol. 8: para. 270). Conforti reviews Jung's understanding of archetypes as organizers of 'perception and apprehension' in order to find support for its acknowledgment as a scientific claim. To this end Conforti briefly introduces the perspective of Sheldrake (1988) Goodwin (1989) and Waddington (1972) on morphogenetic processes and on the relationship between organisms and the informational fields that direct their development and growth. Deriving from these perspectives Conforti draws the analogy between an informational field's ability to 'rearrange and reconfigure matter' and the effect of what he calls 'archetypal fields' (Conforti 1999: 43). If the ability to 'rearrange and reconfigure' and the idea of a 'field' suggest a division between a functional and a structural role, Conforti invests the symbol with the task of mediating between the two. Symbols, in fact, stand as orienting markers 'serving to draw the individual into alignment with the particular archetypal field' (Conforti: 1999: 28). The dynamic that governs this process of 'alignment' is further explored by Conforti. From the work of system theorists he extracts the suggestion that in order 'to insure for the specificity of form and that each new form remains consistent with its ontological core, each individual system proceeds from potential to form by traversing through its phylogenetic history' (Conforti 1999: 20). If the 'form' Conforti refers to is understood, psychologically, as the individuated personality and the 'potential' as the archetype, then the proceeding from one to the other describes the process of individuation. The idea, indeed already explored by Erich Neumann (1954), of the consistency between the ontogenetic and phylogenetic development of human consciousness is presented by Conforti as a fundamental characteristic of the emergence of matter in nature.

The danger inherent in making of the archetype a scientifically identifiable agent of the organization of matter in nature is that of falling into the inescapable rigidity of determinism. Moreover, by splitting the archetype or at least the grasping of its existence from the relativity of its representation in consciousness, Conforti is bypassing the essential quality of inaccurate representability which justifies the varied modes of the archetype's emergence. Should the archetype not rely on the inconsistent, or rather, creative mediation of consciousness, individuation would be unavoidable and wholeness would be an achievable goal. Jung seemed to perceive it otherwise: 'the complete realisation of our whole being is an unattainable ideal. But unattainability is no argument against the ideal, for ideals are only signposts, never the goal' (*C.W.*, Vol. 17: para. 291).

If the generalization that aligns archetypes with morphogenetic promptings in nature seems at times to go too far, it must be said that Conforti's attempt to systematize scientifically Jung's central idea also leads to some fascinating parallels. Conforti describes the image as 'a representative of a specific archetypal field' which 'carries with it its own inherent morphology and information, and when accessed works to entrain the individual or culture into that archetypal field' (Conforti 1999: 17). This statement might indeed become extremely relevant to a research into the relationship between cinematic images and the development of a culture once it is freed from the subtly implicit determinism which sees that culture as passive object of the archetype's inevitable agency.

The potential and scope of a research that attempts to find the point of convergence between Jungian archetypal theory, neuroscience and biology is taken further in the writings of Maxon J. McDowell (1999, 2001), Jane M. Knox (2001) and Anthony Stevens (2002). The most interesting development in McDowell's analysis is his study of dreams and his discussion of the archetypal images that at times appear in them. First, he reiterates Jung's belief that dreams seem to be messages from the unconscious (McDowell 1999: 7) and then explains the numinosity of the archetypal images encountered in them by confirming their belonging to 'another realm', that of an unconscious that the conscious mind can never 'know'. The numinosity might be the result of the realization of the incomprehensibility, to the conscious mind, of the archetype (McDowell 1999: 8). Building on the belief he shares with Jung that specific dreams seem to have a purpose, McDowell introduces the suggestion that the conscious personality, like a biological system, grows according to the principle of 'self-organisation' and, as self organisation 'leads spontaneously to an *emergent* level of order . . . more complex than the level that preceded it' (McDowell 1999: 9), consciousness develops through the interaction with the internal environment of the collective unconscious. The interaction is clearly mediated by archetypal material. The archetypes, in this perspective, are specific aspects of the central potential, encompassed by the archetype of the *self*, for a unified, whole personality. The potential directs towards a fulfilment that, as described by the definition of the process of individuation, is in the process itself and it requires the willingness to 'relate consciously to the incomprehensible', an activity which, according to McDowell, needs to rely on a 'standpoint in the rational' (McDowell 1999: 11).

McDowell's overall argument is that 'relatedness is a goal of individuation' (p. 13). Individuation, however, is still considered by McDowell as the tendency to integrate new resources from the unconscious. Relatedness seems more accurately described then as a means rather than a goal. The specific description of it as 'a' goal perhaps clarifies its recognition as a necessary achievement, as a fundamental step towards the overall goal of integration. Having emphasized the importance of relatedness, McDowell is adamant that in order to fully relate to an archetypal image it is necessary to adopt an approach which integrates both a reductive and a prospective analysis, opening the way to a balanced understanding of the relationship between environment, collective unconscious and consciousness.

Some of the concepts that McDowell explores in his more recent paper 'The Landscape of Possibility: A Dynamic Systems Perspective on Archetype and Change' (2000) are of particular value as they represent the integration of the most updated results of research in the field of dynamic systems theory and neuroscience with an unadulterated, pertinent reading of Jung's archetypal theory. In this paper McDowell uses cognitive neuroscience models to achieve a clearer understanding of the dynamics of an archetype's influence on change in the personality. Having mentioned Jean Knox's (1999: 524) suggestion of the parallel between the concept of implicit memory in cognitive neuroscience and that of the Jungian complex, McDowell relates her suggestion to the purpose of dreams. An implicit memory is understood as 'a memory of a procedure which is not accessible to consciousness but shows itself indirectly' (McDowell 2000: 3) and McDowell derives that maybe 'a dream's "purpose" is to representationally re-describe an image from implicit memory and thus to bring it closer to consciousness' (McDowell 1999: 19–21, 27–29, 2000: 4). This concept does not clash with that which sees the dream as a message from the unconscious when considered within the dynamic of the individuation process. The purpose of the dream then is to 'representationally redescribe an image from implicit memory' in order to fulfil the overall purpose of psychological development, in Jungian terms, the individuation process. The choice of images is influenced by individual experiences. McDowell (2001: 11) points out again that Jung had defined the archetype-per-se as 'an underlying constant, while the archetypal image is a particular image which has been chosen to represent that constant. The image can be replaced by an equivalent image. It is derived from the environment by learning.'

The 'constant', the archetype, is a possibility, brought to life by a chosen image in order to stimulate a movement, to facilitate change. McDowell discusses change as it appears to happen in the evolutionary process and suggests that 'a living creature evolves forms which are pre-existing possibilities'. Having established that a living creature is indeed a 'dynamic system', McDowell adds that 'in a dynamic system a pre-existing possibility is not a static form like a triangle. Rather it is a dynamic, an ordered way for energy to flow' (McDowell 2000: 8). Moreover, however complex the dynamic system might be, the number of pre-existing possibilities called to guide its organization proves to be limited. In a similar mode, the personality tends to organize itself in accordance with a set of pre-existing possibilities. Jung had suggested that the personality is organized by archetypes and within this perspective it is easy to see the similarity between their function in relation to the development of personality and that of pre-existing possibilities in the organization of dynamic systems. McDowell further defines this similarity by describing the personality as existing only while energy (both chemical and psychological) flows through it: a determining trademark of a dynamic system. But what is most relevant in McDowell's argument is his referencing to evolution as 'an emergent process in which structures self-organize'

(McDowell 2000: 8) and his introduction of Stuart Kauffman's 'landscape model' of biological evolution (1995). This model suggests that an evolving creature moves spontaneously into a 'fitness valley' (fitness of possible forms) towards a settling position, a stable attractor, a 'stability landscape'. A fit form, the chosen mutation that characterizes evolution, emerges from the interacting of self-organization and natural selection. Having selected the fittest, most stable form, the process of evolution would come to a halt if it were not for the presence of adjacent systems, other creatures, other systems. McDowell points out that a living creature 'co-evolves in an ecosystem of other creatures', it is part of what can be defined as a 'higher order dynamic system' (McDowell 2000: 14).

The transposition of this model to the development of the personality is consistent with clinical evidence and with the core concepts of analytical psychology. In isolation our 'fitness landscape' would not change. Association pressure generated by the environment pulls the personality into a 'fitness valley'. McDowell suggests that each 'valley' represents a complex which then resists change as it is formed around an archetype, a pre-existing possibility for order (McDowell 2000: 15). A relationship with another person in changing my 'fitness landscape' would pull towards change and, most interestingly, the relationship between conscious awareness and complexes, by weakening the pull of the complex, also supports a movement; it allows for the personality to evolve.

The experience of a conscious relation to a numinous dream image might represent a suggestion, the powerful, visual indication of a potential for movement and change. The image's numinosity confirms its origin, it is testimony to the characteristics of the archetype (or, as McDowell has discussed, to the principle of organization we call archetype) it is called to represent. It is an image that comes first to disrupt, then to bring new balance and finally to aid integration. As well as in dreams such images also appear in literature, art, legends and myths and, naturally, in films. Here, their emergence is mediated by an artist whose work is described, by Jung, as the product of an autonomous creative complex, a concept he specifically discussed in his analysis of the relationship between analytical psychology and poetry, but which needs to be understood within the wider development of his Complex theory as complementary to that of the archetypes of the collective unconscious.

The complex: to have or to be had

Jung described complexes as a collection of ideas and images 'linked together by a common affect'. The common affect Jung refers to is the emotional consequence, the specific feeling tone the complex becomes associated with and which makes it recognizable. Anthony Stevens in his updated sociobiological and evolutionary analysis of the archetype suggests that complexes can be treated as 'archetypes actualized in the mind' (Stevens 2002: 74). Stevens's description of the direct relationship between archetype and complex is further elaborated by 'archetypal sociologist' Richard M. Gray who highlights how the close relationship between the environment, the individual and the archetypes of the collective unconscious becomes evident as the archetypes, encountering the world, associate themselves to specific feeling tones which will become characteristic of the complexes associated with them from then on (Gray 1996: 19). Because of their archetypal origin and colouration by personal experience, the complexes can be considered as the all-important bridge between the collective unconscious and the individual's personal psychological experience of interacting with the environment (both natural and of human relations).

A characteristic which is emphatically highlighted by Jung is that of the complexes' autonomy, both as their ability to form themselves independently of consciousness and as that of remaining unconscious to the point of not being recognized by the ego as 'belonging' and therefore treated as projections. This characteristic allows for the suggestion of a natural fragmentation of the individual psyche exposed by Jung himself when he described complexes as 'splinter psyches' (*C.W.*, Vol. 8: para. 202), a concept that in descriptions less charged with pathological connotations has been elaborated as both the psychoanalytical organization of ego, super-ego and id in structural theory and in the importance allocated to the clinically supported dialogue between different, autonomous selves both in gestalt and transactional analysis (Samuels *et al.* 1986: 35).

Indeed, Jung would consider the complex pathological only in the case of a splitting from the central ego-complex which would lead to its dominating the personality either in the form of psychosis, should the complex override the ego, or in forms of inflations and/or possession in the case of identification of the ego with the complex. Healing and a consequent weakening of a complex's hold on the personality is not achieved merely through intellectual reasoning and understanding, the complex being so closely associated with emotions. Jolande Jacobi, a Jungian analyst who worked closely with Jung himself, stresses this point when she indicates that 'only emotional experience liberates' (Jacobi 1959: 14) because, as Jung wrote in his analysis of the archetype of the Self, the complex 'consists not only of *meaning* but also of *value*, and this depends on the intensity of the accompanying feeling tones' (*C.W.*, Vol. 9ii: para. 52). Indeed, it is through 'affect' that the complex makes itself known and influences behaviour, and it is through affect that it can be grasped and dissolved.

More specifically, in his updated presentation of Complex theory, Jung describes the 'feeling-toned complex' as 'the image of a certain psychic situation which is strongly accentuated emotionally and is, moreover, incompatible with the habitual attitude of consciousness' (*C.W.*, Vol. 8: para. 201). The control of the conscious mind over the complex is, according to Jung, only relative as the complex is a psychic factor that seems to possess an energy value which, at times, overrides that of any conscious intention. It is the complex's ability to disrupt the 'unity of consciousness' independently and with disregard of will that led Jung to suggest that rather than 'having complexes' (a concept that has now entered common language) complexes can be said to actually 'have us' (*C.W.*, Vol. 8: para. 200).

Notwithstanding their autonomy and individuality, complexes, as pointed out earlier, still have an archetypal rooting. Yet, unlike symbols, which are the manifestation of a content of the collective unconscious, the complex, because of its association with feeling-toned images drawn from the pool of personal experience becomes a symptom, an individual's response to the entering of archetypal content into consciousness. The feeling tone might, in fact, be described as 'the emotional shape of the complex and of the underlying archetype or archetypes' (Gray 1996: 19). Jung specifically suggested that complexes are 'characteristic expressions of the psyche' (*C.W.*, Vol. 8: para. 209), a definition which encompasses both their archetypal matrix (characteristic) and the individual colouring which distinguishes them (expressions of the psyche).

Complex theory becomes more clearly relevant to film analysis as Jung describes the creative process that brings a work of art to life as the manifestation of an autonomous complex.

A complex('s) relationship with art

Jung's discussion of the 'relation of analytical psychology to poetry' appears in the collection of essays and lectures dedicated to the analysis of the work of outstandingly creative individuals: *The Spirit in Man, Art and Literature* (1966). Jung begins his lecture on poetry by introducing the Freudian psychoanalytical approach to artistic production. While reinstating his appreciation for the clinical value of Freud's reductive method, Jung finds that in its approach to art the Freudian standpoint fails to acknowledge the fact that a true work of art 'has escaped from the limitations of the personal and has soared beyond the personal concerns of his creator' (*C.W.*, Vol. 15: para. 107).

In 'Creative Writers and Day-Dreaming' Freud indeed compares the creative writer to a child who, while playing, 're-arranges the things of his world in a new way which pleases him' (Freud 1907: 143–144). Freud continues by describing how, once 'play' becomes inappropriate in adult life, it is substituted with phantasies and with the construction of daydreams, a kind of play devoid of relationship with real objects. To establish the relationship between the daydreamers and the writer of novels or poetry, Freud applies to the work of art the principle of strict relation to a threefold time frame he had proposed when analysing the nature of phantasy. Daydreaming and phantasy, as well as creative inspiration, are stimulated by a situation in the present which has the power to 'arouse one of the subject's major wishes' (Freud 1907: 14). This stimulus brings to the foreground a memory of an early situation where the wish was fulfilled. The work of art and the daydreaming are the new situations the subject/artist creates in the present to guarantee, at their completion, future satisfaction of that same wish.

Jung's criticism of a Freudian approach seems to insist on what he perceives as an unacceptable shift, one that makes of a method a doctrine. It is against this 'rigid dogmatism' based on an 'arbitrary assumption' that Jung feels the need to make a stand (*C.W.*, Vol. 15: para. 106). And yet, by failing to acknowledge the previously mentioned Freudian contribution to a psychological understanding of art and literature, Jung has not only bypassed the possibility of finding points of convergence rather than discord but has also unwittingly substituted one 'doctrine' with another.

Freud suggested that the creative phantasy, because of its characteristic three-temporal dimension, represents 'past, present and future . . . strung together . . . on the thread of the wish that runs through them' (Freud 1907: 147–148). This is, in fact, a characteristic that could be transferred to the complex, the thread being the archetype it is connected to which guarantees the complexes' relationship to a collective timeless possibility of manifestation. A pool of personal images and emotions from a personal past clusters around an archetypal nucleus, personalizing the complex and allowing for activating situations in the present to bring it to life as specific and individual. The imperative of the complex is in its call for consciousness and, if the call is answered, the ensuing dialogue is a furthering of the process of self-actualization, a projection towards the future goal of integration. But the most relevant point of convergence with a Jungian perspective to be found in Freud's essay on daydreaming and creative writers is in his suggestion that myths might be 'distorted vestiges of the wishful phantasies of whole nations, the secular dreams of youthful humanity' (Freud 1907: 152). The artist who in his creative work uses familiar, refashioned material, finding inspiration in myths, legends and fairy tales, is still maintaining a level of creative independence by infusing his artistic creation with changes and choices originating from his own personal pool of memories and images. This description is certainly in line with a Jungian understanding of archetypes and of the complexes associated with them. However, if Freud is satisfied with the admission of a field of research too vast, and possibly not necessarily worthy of priority, to be included in his analytic work, Jung makes of mythology, religious iconography and artistic production the empirical, validating support to his theory, as deserving of an analysis and as rich in symbolic content as dreams and active imagination. The starting point remains, nevertheless, the individual, and so it is in the case of Jung's more detailed analysis of the working of the creative complex.

When discussing the work of art as the product of an autonomous complex, Jung indeed begins by generally describing the latter as a 'psychic formation that remains subliminal until its energy-charge is sufficient to carry it over the threshold into consciousness' where it is perceived rather than assimilated and remains independent from conscious control (*C.W.*, Vol. 15: para. 122). The energy necessary to activate the complex, thus allowing it, in Jung's own words, to gain 'ground by activating the adjacent areas of association', is drawn from consciousness. This absorption of energy in favour of the complex leads to a degree of apathy and/or regression. And if, as Jung adds, at this point 'the instinctual side of the personality prevails over the ethical, (and) the infantile over the mature' it might be possible to suggest that something of the process similarly described by Freud is at work.

While the mode of movement of the complex into consciousness is described as contained within the parameters of individuality, Jung's attempt to define the creative complex's content leads to the suggestion of the symbolic nature of the work of art, a characteristic which confirms its origin in the sphere of the collective unconscious. It is important to specify at this point that a distinction is made between a work of art which, born out of conscious intention of the artist, remains a loyal reproduction of such intentions and does not 'extend beyond the limits of comprehension' and the artistic product which, originating from the collective unconscious, 'transcends our understanding to the same degree that the author's consciousness was in abeyance during the process of creation' (*C.W.*, Vol. 15: para. 116). Jung provides examples from literature: he suggests that Schiller's plays derive from a conscious mastery of material by the author while Goethe's *Faust* and Nietzsche's *Zarathustra* are the products of an admitted subordination to unconscious inspiration.

While Jung does not specifically mention the visual arts in his essay, it is certainly possible to extend his distinction to an analysis of cinematic material. Having become familiar with mass-produced symbolism in films, it is difficult at times to single out conscious manipulation from unaware unconscious inspiration. However, Steven Spielberg's ever-increasing use of images supposedly rich in symbolic significance stands out particularly in his 2002 release *Minority Report* where the *noirish*, sci-fi driven plot is almost overridden by continuous reference to mythology (Oedipus in particular) and by a use of images so obviously intended as symbolic to be completely devoid of symbolic function. In the much discussed film *The Piano* (Campion, 1993), on the other hand, the conscious mastery of material, as Jung would describe it, is also juxtaposed to images whose symbolic, archetypal significance overlaps the desired, intended psychological study of characters. At the end of the film, for example, Ada, now living with Baines, is learning to speak, but while practising to do so she wears a dark veil over her face. Easily explained as the manifestation of Ada's shame and embarrassment at her childish first uttering of words and also interpretable (and interpreted) as an act of surrender to patriarchy, Ada's veil is, nevertheless, a symbolic necessity. The willing loss of the piano to the depth of the ocean, an image immediately preceding that of Ada with the veil, was also a loss and surrender of a no longer needed identity. Ada's mask, the persona she had previously chosen is now deleted and the process of forming a new identity has begun, developing behind the veil. Her anonymity, guaranteed by the veil, is symbolically elevating Ada to the mythological state of Virgin (in its meaning of anonymous), a sacred being not 'known' to men.

As Jung points out, from the finished work it is possible to recognize the imprint of the archetype. At this point in the elaboration of his theory, he almost allows for the concept of archetype to overlap with the idea of the mythological image. While it is only later that he develops the idea of 'archetype per se' and clears the confusion, this description of the function of mythological images deserves a mention and his final comments on the social value of art are directly relevant to the analysis pursued in this book.

Archetypal images constantly recur in history and appear whenever a particular set of circumstances seems to conjure their emergence. These images are described by Jung as 'psychic residua of innumerable experiences of the same type. They present a picture of psychic life in the average, divided up and projected into the manifold figures of the mythological pantheon' (*C.W.*, Vol. 15: para. 127). The creative process allows for the elaboration and shaping of the archetypal image into the finished work of art. The artist is able, because of his relative lack of adaptation, to follow his own yearning for what seems incompatible with the general attitude, thus finding expression for what is lacking. By giving shape to the archetype, by bringing it to the foreground clothed with the attributes of the present, art then fulfils, according to Jung, its social role of educating 'the spirit of the age, conjuring up the forms in which the age is lacking' (*C.W.*, Vol. 15: para. 130).

The seemingly ideological implications in Jung's statement must be read against his description of the archetype's autonomy. If art has, like dreams, a function in the overall process of individuation of a cultural community, it will be that of hosting the emergence of much needed symbols, images whose unconscious heritage will have the power to communicate to the unconscious of that culture, present whole and in fragment, like in a broken mirror, within its individual members. An analytical reading of the work of art, again in a similar manner to the reading of a dream, has to maintain an active awareness of both the artist's own personal environment as well as the dialectical relationship of art with economic and social forces. The relationship between the work of art, history and the society it emerges from is considered, somehow, one of compensation and response: the work of art is seen as capable of having an impact on the collective, powerful enough to bring a realization of the need for a shift. According to these suggestions it should be possible to retrospectively individuate the specific images, collectively shared through pictorial, photographic and cinematic productions, which suggested, sensed and possibly supported change. Changes in political attitude, in the degree of religious tolerance, in the organization of society, in the relationship to the 'other' both within and outside the confines of a nation are rarely sudden and the images leading to the transformation are testimony to the gradual but consistent movement towards it. The overlapping of the two, image and shift, only becomes evident through an analysis of a relatively extended and turbulent period in the history of a country or society, supported by an understanding of the inevitable distance, no doubt filled with significant images, between the first manifestation of the archetypal image expressed by the artist as 'the unspoken desire of his times' and the subsequent fulfilment of the archetypal predicament culminating in the manifest events of human history (*C.W.*, Vol. 15: para. 153). In the essay 'Psychology and Literature' Jung reinstates his belief in the close relationship between the collective unconscious and the work of art and in the importance of an understanding which, although acknowledging the influence of personal factors contributing the motivation and the individual shaping of the final product, perceives and recognizes the transcendent, collective nature of some of the most powerful and enduringly moving examples of art. In the same essay Jung suggests:

> Whenever the collective unconscious becomes a living experience and is brought to bear upon the conscious outlook of an age, this event is a creative act which is of importance for a whole epoch. A work of art is produced that may truthfully be called a message to generations of men.
>
> (*C.W.*, Vol. 15: para. 153)

This book proposes, indeed, a reading of specific cinematic images informed by an understanding of their close relationship to the cultural context they address.

Conclusion

As well as presenting a synthesis of Jung's own descriptions of the concepts of archetype and complex, this chapter has introduced some updated reviews derived from the intersection between analytical psychology and contemporary neuroscientific, evolutionary and developmental perspectives. Reinforcing the dynamic and process-marking nature of the archetype, Conforti's view on the emergence of form and of 'archetypal fields', McDowell's suggestion of the analogy between archetype and dynamic systems and Stevens's idea of the complexes as 'archetypes actualized in the mind' (Stevens 2002: 74) offer a good theoretical springboard to an understanding of the dialectic relationship between archetypes and cultural change.

In order to more clearly appreciate the extent of this relationship, part of this chapter has engaged with a discussion of artistic production as originating from what Jung called the autonomous creative complex. As the Jungian theorization of artistic inspiration and production is presented parallel to the Freudian explanation of daydreaming and phantasy, the possibility of finding points of convergence between the two becomes plausible. The Freudian wish and its threefold temporal evolution throughout the production of artistic material becomes the Jungian autonomous complex which, while emotionally anchored to the individual's personal past, thanks to its archetypal core, projects the work of art towards its future function of re-establishing balance.

According to Jung there is, in fact, a type of work of art which, responding to a 'lack' perceived unconsciously by the artist becomes 'a message to generations of men' (*C.W.*, Vol. 15: para. 153). Such a message is a response, it describes a situation, the psychological state of a culture, but it also suggests the need for a shift. While Jung's own theorization of the presence of archetypal material in art is centred on the emergence of such material in literature and poetry, the application of his insight to the visual arts is certainly justified by the tendency of the archetype to become manifest through images.

The Jungian participation in the academic debate on the nature, function, impact and influence of cinematic images in their relationship to the culture which harbours their manifestation is relatively recent, yet the dynamic and collective aspects of the Jungian collective unconscious, as described in this chapter, bring analytical psychology to the foreground as a flexible theoretical framework on which to construct an interdisciplinary discussion. The film texts can be considered as the place of intersection between historical, psychological, political, cultural and religious forces, and a greater understanding of their message must be mediated by an interpretative tool capable of negotiating between such forces.

Robert Romanyshyn suggests that 'film portrays the mythology of an age', it is 'a shared myth, a cultural daydream' (Romanyshyn 1989: 19, 2001: 68). What emerges from his insight is the fascinating possibility of reconsidering the Freudian interpretation of artistic inspiration as consistent with a Jungian analysis of the function of art. If film, like myth, is to be considered a 'cultural daydream', then it would be the daydream of the Freudian artist, but a daydream which becomes myth because, as well as being dreamt 'for' a collective cultural conscious who will 'remember' it within the darkness of the auditorium, it is also a response to the compensatory needs of the 'cultural' unconscious who demanded and shaped its emergence.

In the next chapter this possibility will be discussed in more detail with particular reference to national cinema, its role in expressing, through images of archetypal significance, the development of a national identity and the parallel between such a development and that of ego consciousness in the individual and in humankind as a whole.

Chapter 3

Jung, film and nation
Image as witness of a process of becoming

Introduction

Jung wrote that 'the activity of the collective unconscious manifests itself not only in compensatory effects in the lives of individuals, but also in the mutation of dominant ideas in the course of the centuries' (*C.W.*, Vol. 18: para. 1161). With this statement he took the relevance of his work out of the intimacy of the analytical situation, pointing to the possibility of extending the use of the analytical theoretical framework to an understanding of the history of ideas.

Without the pretence of directly pursuing such an ambitious analysis, this chapter introduces the possibility of exploring the relationship between historical context and cultural product, in particular the relationship between recurrent cinematic images and the construction/reconstruction of national identity understood as a process of collective psychological development akin to the development of ego-consciousness. The traceability of this process should be signalled by the recognizable emergence of images of symbolic value and the relationship between the consistency of their appearance and the obviously traumatic or decisive events that mark the history of the culture of which they are born.

This chapter begins with a discussion on the Jungian definition of symbol and of its emergence and function in art. The analysis of the possible application of the idea of the Jungian complex, traditionally used to describe the contents of the personal unconscious, to the discursive unity of a group or nation follows, together with the inclusion of the post-Jungian formulation of the idea of the 'cultural unconscious' as an intermediate layer between the personal and the collective unconscious. It is within this updated, socio-psychological Jungian analytical perspective that film, and in particular the already controversial nature of national cinema and its much questioned role in the shaping and development of a national identity, is reconsidered and redescribed.

The chapter follows the debate around the origin and purpose of the idea of nation and of national identity. Still much influenced by Benedict Anderson's theorization revolving around the concept of 'imagined communities', such a debate has evolved to include perspectives which bind the abstract idea to an individual, emotional experience related to a rather personified collective

(Hayward 2000: 89). This opening of historiographical perspectives to a sociological approach provides an apt point of departure for a Jungian, developmental analysis of the relationship between cinematic images and the forming of a collective identity which can be described as national.

The work of developmental Jungian analyst Erich Neumann is presented as an example of the possibility of transferring the personal to the collective through a comparative reading of mythological material. Neumann's insight will provide a useful reference for the analysis of recurring cinematic images within the context of the development of the community they address and from which they originate through the artist's medium.

An exploration of the relationship between myth, film and politics is supported by the critical discussion of the analysis, by the post-Jungian John Beebe, of the film *The Wizard of Oz*. Beebe's suggestion of the role of cinema as the place where the collective psyche's[1] mediation between archetypal reality and politics finds expression, leads to the introduction of Andrew Samuels's definition of politics as a channel through which specific psychic energy becomes manifest.

Samuels's description of political energy as closely related to creativity seems to naturally frame the introduction of Italy, a country as prolific in art as it is in nuances of political expression, and a decade of the work of the most representative directors of Italian neo-realism as the preferred site for this book's intended analysis of archetypal material in film.

Art as symbol at its best

In *Symbols of Transformation*, a collection of essays first published in 1912, Jung makes a reference to the construction of concepts as a way not only to render 'the object harmless' but also to incorporate it 'into the psychic system thus increasing the meaning and power of the human mind' (*C.W.*, Vol. 15: para. 201). The process leading to the construction of concepts, described by Jung as corresponding to the *magically powerful name* which gets a grip on the object, is, supposedly, one of 'analogy-making'. More specifically, it is from the activity of reflecting energy-charged contents (feeling-toned complexes) into analogies that synonyms are produced which are more easily incorporated into the psyche. If this appears, at first, as a superficial analysis of the formation of language as canalization of libido (a term which for Jung is synonymous with energy), it offers an indirect insight into a Jungian understanding of the process of art. In the same paragraph there is, in fact, a reference to Sabina Spielrein's suggestion on the origins of symbols:

> Thus a symbol seems to me to owe its origin to the striving of a complex for dissolution in the common totality of thought . . . the complex is thus robbed of its personal quality . . . this tendency towards dissolution or transformation

---
1 As Jung had defined it.

of every individual complex is the mainspring of poetry, painting, and every form of art.

(Spielrein 1912: 399)

Eager to find confirmation of his own presuppositions, and possibly still feeling the effect of the unprofessionally handled affair he had with his former patient Sabina Spielrein, Jung seems to willingly ignore her clearly envisioned relationship between art, the collective unconscious and the production of 'symbols' as they are understood in analytical psychology. Jung suggests that his own theory of the construction of analogies (words and ideas) as the tools to 'handle' reality in the psyche finds support in Spielrein's writings once the idea of 'energy value' replaces that of 'complex' (1912: 399).

Indeed the complex's characteristic of providing a bridge between the personal and the collective and its specific relevance to art, is beautifully reinstated within the original integrity of Spielrein's sentence. The personal elements of the complex are easily individuated: the relationship between the feelings and the images from the individual's past form the 'symptom' of its presence, making the pull towards consciousness a manifest possibility. And yet 'the striving of a complex for dissolution in the common totality of thought', as Spielrein describes it, gives birth to the 'symbol', the tip of the largely submerged iceberg of the unconscious, the very core and 'mainspring' of all artistic productions, testimony of both the impossibility of this 'dissolution' (if intended as disappearance) once the complex 'reaches out into the domain of consciousness' (Jacobi 1959: 24), and the equal impossibility for 'knowledge' because the conscious view of unconscious contents is, by definition, forever barred.

What Spielrein is describing is the complex as a point of dual attraction, a 'nodal point' as Jacobi likes to define it, between a collective unconscious from which universally recognizable material is drawn and an environment which stimulates this material's emergence. Stripped of the contents originating from the personal unconscious, the complex's nucleus may be revealed and its relationship to the collective unconscious brought to the foreground. Having established, for example, that certain manifestations in dreams, active imagination or art do not describe the individual's personal relationship with his personal father or mother, it will become possible to infer that the images are symbols, archetypal, collective material, related to the archetype of the Mother or the Father, rather than personal symptoms.

Jolande Jacobi, in *Complex/Archetype/Symbol in the Psychology of C. G. Jung* (1959), also clarifies that while 'most complexes of the personal unconscious must . . . be interpreted as signs or symptom' it is also true that 'a certain number of symbols from the collective unconscious lie hidden behind the individual manifestation and can be divested of their "individual covering" . . . an interpretative action especially fruitful in the case of the artist'. Jacobi agrees, in fact, that for the artist 'complexes and symbols are not material to be exploited for his own psychic development . . . they are the occasion and substance of his process of artistic creation' (pp. 122–123). Indeed, the pioneering suggestion in Spielrein's words is in the idea that, in the case of artistic productions, the 'dissolution in the common totality of thought' does not happen as a retreat into the subterranean waters of the unconscious, nor does it take the form of an intimate form to contemplate within the constraint of individual dreams or active imagination (though it would probably normally appear first as such). The symbol enters the common totality of thought thanks to its outward expression in that common totality via the selected artistic means of communication. The artist himself becomes the bridge; it could be said that he or she becomes a personification of the complex, the complex's own expressive device responsive to the urge for balance and compensation in the society which the artist inhabits.

Symbolic expression in art escapes the artist's will and interpretative skills, thus recalling an autonomy characteristic of the complex. It emerges regardless of intention and often as an accidental occurrence, as a mode or a style which, at first incongruent with the currently accepted, is the foretelling of new, revolutionary perspectives descriptive of a deeper change in cultural attitude. The more detailed and rigorous the dictated stylistic modes in its surrounding, the more troubled and often imperceptible will be the emerging symbolic production. The symbol itself, before its encounter with consciousness, will have travelled through levels of the psyche which will have transformed its characteristics accordingly.

After re-emphasizing the Jungian definition of 'symbol' as 'the best possible description or formulation of a relatively unknown fact' and reproposing his suggestion that 'there are undoubtedly products . . . so constituted that they would lack any kind of meaning were not a symbolic one conceded to them' (*C.W.*, Vol. 6: para. 814–818), it becomes more pressing to ask what are the conditions and influences which make of a description or formulation the 'best possible' one and of symbolic meaning one that is received or 'conceded' collectively enough to be effective.

Personal complexes are somewhat tailored to and fed by the individual's own memories and emotions. Even as the archetypal core from which they originate is traceable, it remains the signpost to a development which, although characteristically human (collective), remains dependent on the individual's own choices and actions. The artist does indeed become such only during the process of creation of his artistic product: individual scenes from his film, the strokes of his paintbrush, the first layers removed by the chisel will all carry the weight of his presence as an individual and tell a story which is only his own. And as a dream, populated by the familiar faces of our dear (or less dear) ones, becomes, at times, the vehicle for the emergence of material of collective nature, so will the work of art. The creative autonomous complex, as Jung named it, becomes activated by specific, uncommon conditions within the practice of art: not every dream is pregnant with archetypal content and, equally, not every painting or film has the characteristics of transcendence that would suggest its role as 'message to generations of men' typical of 'art' as Jung understood it.

The 'expression' of the complex is indeed dependent on the 'analogy-making' process Jung described when discussing the formation of language as canalization of libido. The work of art is the language of the artist's unconscious, and yet it is a language implicitly understood by many, spoken with nuances both unique to the individual, trademarking it as his, and familiar to the receptors who understand it and interpret it but cannot reciprocate the communication (or so it seems). Words, images, colours and certainly musical notes carry a message that wants to be received and thus are structured accordingly. The receiving audience, sharing in the cultural substratum of non-verbal filters and intuitive means of identification which differentiates it, responds with recognition, effectively manifest as consumption. The degree of resonance can often be exponentially related to the degree of familiarity of the message carriers (images, words) and to the identity values implicit in the message. The familiarity will be primarily based on the contents that Jung described as deriving from 'the sphere of conscious human experience – from the psychic foreground of life' (*C.W.*, Vol. 15: para. 140), from the communicating of the artist as individual with other individualities, or more specifically from the artist's consciousness to the consciousness of his audience. The modes of this level of communication will have in common with subsequent, gradually deeper levels of unconscious communication the traits which will make of the latter 'the best possible description or formulation of a relatively unknown fact'. These traits are the 'dress' selected by the symbol amongst the objects available within the cultures it needs to inhabit.

The cultural unconscious: skin deep

When discussing the epistemological viability of the archetype, Jung suggested that one should not 'succumb to the illusion that an archetype can be finally explained and disposed of ... the most we can do is to *dream the myth onwards* and give it a modern dress'[2] (*C.W.*, Vol. 9i: para. 271). Somehow it is the archetype that realized its own need for modernization by allowing for the layers it needs to push through to leave a signifying mark. The layers are the unconscious strata between the collective unconscious, individual unconscious and consciousness and have been specifically discussed by the post-Jungians as the cultural and group unconscious. At the lower border of it are the unconsciously shared traits of ethnicity; deep within it are cultural and religious specifications, and probably closer to the individual unconscious are the unconscious suggestions that maintain a sense of national identity, suggestions characterized by the fluidity and flexibility sustained by a dialectical relationship with an environment which globally describes itself in real time though the most technologically advanced media channels.

William R. Clough (2002) suggests that 'religious and cultural identities ... are the lenses through which we view the world. They are the grammar of patterns and potentials that structure the data we perceive.' But this 'grammar of patterns',

2 Italics are Jung's.

these 'lenses through which we view the world' become 'identities' through a bipolar process that needs an external reference (real or perceived) with which to identify. Through images and sounds organized into a specific language the world is first experienced, perceived and incorporated until an ego emerges capable of relating. The relating will rely on an understanding of the communicated effectiveness of certain objects of exchange, an effectiveness specific to the relationship between communicators: mother–child, child–family, family–clan (possibly class), clan–nation, nation–cultural group, cultural group–others. As communication extends to wider groups the ego stretches its boundaries and the margins become blurred. The variations in the use and shape of the tools of communication exchange are learnt together with the need for continuous redefinition of the boundaries, both enclosing and excluding, of one's identity. As both an individual and a member of various, increasingly larger groups, one's ability to recognize the nature, limits, rigidity or flexibility of such boundaries becomes a skill important for the sustainability of psychological health.

Brian Feldman (2004) emphasizes the fundamental importance of the experience of the skin as a container for the development of the capacity for symbolization from infancy. The functioning of the skin as a 'delineator of boundaries' is what he calls the 'primary skin function' and it is related to 'the evolution of a psychic container within which thought, affect and symbolic experience can be held and reflected upon' (Feldman 2004: 256–257). Feldman suggests the possibility of extending this concept to social groups that also need definition through the imaginary container of a 'group skin function', maybe better described in a previous paper where Feldman points out that 'the self and other in their diverse dialectics give shape to individual and group identity, to a kind of cultural skin as 'a container of collective experience' within which 'one can experience social containment' (Feldman 2003). It might be possible to take this concept further and to suggest that, as in a paradoxical Russian doll, each layer of identification (family, clan, national or regional, cultural/religious) provides a skin granting a relative/temporary inclusion which not only does not exclude but actually specifies the need for individuality.

Although useful when considered as a metaphor for an extensive surface of exchange and interaction, Feldman's use of the word 'skin', with its powerful visual association with a compact, protective container, can become problematic as it seems to fail to address the fluidity and relative instability characteristic of the definition and maintenance of a group's identity. The layers of identification described above might then be redefined as fluctuating boundaries, as porous materials subject to pressure and susceptible to change. These layers are projected inwardly as an unconscious anchoring to the specificity of communication (what Feldman described as the capacity for symbolization), allowing for responses, language tonalities and skills, body language and unconsciously shared rituals to form, develop and remain accessible whenever the outwardly projected boundaries, manifest as nationality, status, sexual role, political stance call for dedicated modes of interaction.

In a sense it is then possible to re-evaluate Clough's definition of religion and cultural identity as lenses through which other realities are perceived. But they work both from within and from without, and only as lenses which enlarge a reality already constructed and unconsciously understood. These lenses, or skins, are maintained, transmitted and transformed as a consequence of changes in the relationships within the community they describe; these changes and developments are often described in the recurring images of art and mythology.

Striving for wholeness from myth to art

The idea of drawing a parallel between the development of individual consciousness and that of human consciousness as a whole has been exploited by Erich Neumann, a student of C. G. Jung, whose developmental approach coupled with an interest in the psychology of consciousness and creativity greatly contributed to the expansion of the Jungian perspective. Neumann's most significant contribution to psychology is considered to be the empirical concept of 'centroversion' as a synthesis of extraversion and introversion, together with his theory of feminine development which somehow compensates for a recognized gendered onesideness in Jung's own theory. It is, however, his painstaking search in mythology, throughout history, for the evidence of parallels between the development of consciousness in the individual and in society as a whole that makes his work relevant to the analysis pursued in this book.

In *The Origins and History of Consciousness* (1954) Neumann describes how the first 'dimension' of the development of personality is a progress towards adaptation to external factors (the world and things), the second is a time for inward adaptation to the objective psyche and to the archetypes and the third will be self formation, 'individuation within the psyche itself' (1954: 219). He defines these moments in development as the processes of respectively extraversion, introversion and centroversion. What is important to remember is that Neumann's stages, notwithstanding the association with the physiological stages of growth such as embryonic, infantile and pubertal, are intended as structural rather than chronological or historical. Indeed, he insists:

> 'Stage' refers to a structural layer and not to any historical epoch. In individual development and perhaps also in that of the collective, these layers do not lie on top of one another in any orderly arrangement, but . . . early layers may be pushed to the top and late layers to the bottom.
>
> (Neumann 1954: 42)

External factors which become personal or collective history influence the shifting from one stage to the next and become the trigger for either the emergence of archetypal imagery suggestive of the need for change or for symptoms indicative of the powerful hold of a complex, leading to regression, the discomfort of neurosis and, if the ego identifies with the complex, to psychotic phenomena.

Gray (1996: 194) writes about the 'relative salience' of the emergence of specific symbolic material within a culture 'as an index of its general applicability to the needs of that group. But the needs of the group change with external circumstances and with them the relative salience of various symbolic elements of the group mythology also change.' Again he insists on mythology as the elected vehicle for the expression of symbols. Mythology's dependence on the visual arts has allowed for the transmission of its message, a message which needed to be maintained whole throughout its passages to younger generations, only to be changed by a power equal to the one holding it in place, that of an archetype. Group mythology has, however, been somewhat incorporated within other narrative systems, bearing possibly lower degrees of transcendence and affording an impact not as directly powerful as that of mythology.

Gray views myths and fairy tales as 'the average representation of the patterns of psychic life common to humankind' (Gray 1996: 89), while for Jung myth, like great art, is the product 'of an unconscious process of symbolization which continues through the ages and, as the primordial manifestation of the human spirit, will continue to be the root of all creation in the future' (C.W., Vol. 10: para. 585). Neumann sees in mythological images the place where traces of humanity's (as much as of individuals') journey towards consciousness are to be found in the form of archetypal sequences (Neumann 1954: xvi). Notwithstanding the undisputable universality of the archetypal core which is shared across the mythologies of distant continents, what distinguishes mythology from fairy tales remains the national or cultural specificity of its expression: 'myth is always deeply intertwined with the cultural expressions of specific people' (Gray 1996: 89).

Religion, with its abundant iconography and its narrative insistence on the duality of man (human and of divine origin, capable of evil and created in the image of God), has somehow inherited the 'explanatory' and the ritualistic functions of mythology as well as the powerful effect of specific imagery (Great Mother, Divine Child, Creation as Light, Sacrificial Offering of Son, etc.) which, like characteristic 'mythologems',[3] emerge consistently throughout disparate religious practices. And so, the variation in the frequency of certain symbolic elements within the group mythology that, as Gray pointed out, reflects the change in external circumstances, needs to be searched for within the pictorial narratives which have taken the place of myths: religious iconography and visual arts.

Jung himself had described how 'the mythological figures appear as pale phantoms and relics of a long past life that has become strange to us' while 'the religious statement represents an immediate "numinous" experience' (C.W., Vol. 11: para. 450). That numinous quality is a consistent trademark of the archetypal experience which certainly finds in art a suitable, ever-contemporary venue while preserving recognizable evidence of its past encounter with more directly mystical, more authoritatively transcendent modes of representation.

---

3 A single, fundamental element, or motif, of any myth.

The relationship between ego and self as template

The second part of this book explores, through the analysis of significant recurrent film images, the possible analogy between the individual and the collective development of an 'ego-consciousness' manifest as a sense of a national identity.

A simple template of the relationship of ego to self is provided by Jung himself in *The Structure and Dynamic of the Psyche* (*C.W.*, 1969). Here Jung describes ego-consciousness 'as a synthesis of the various "sense-consciousnesses", in which the independence of each separate consciousness is submerged in the unity of the overruling ego' (*C.W.*, Vol. 8: para. 614–615). He continues by suggesting that as 'ego-consciousness does not embrace all psychic activities' it might be possible to conceive the existence of a 'higher or wider consciousness in which the ego would be seen as an objective content'. And, as Jung concludes that 'our ego-consciousness might well be enclosed within a more complete consciousness like a smaller circle within a larger', Feldman's analogy of skin as physical precursor of an invisible psychic container maintains its validity only coupled with an acceptance of its multilayered, maybe porous structure.

If the development of an invisible 'psychic container' is reducible to the beginning of the construction of an ego-consciousness, the question arising will be one regarding the emergence of the antagonistic container of the 'self'. Indeed, the process of individuation as a 'coming to be of the self' does not require a merging of the ego with the self. Jung actually suggests that conscious wholeness is a union of ego and self which allows for the conservation of the intrinsic qualities of each. The striving towards wholeness is a process that requires for the ego to act as mediator between emerging unconscious contents and their inclusion into consciousness, between the all-devouring wholeness of the unconscious (Jung also describes it as preconscious wholeness) and an individuated self which 'comprises infinitely more than the mere ego'. In Jung's own words 'individuation does not shut one out from the world, but gathers the world to oneself' (*C.W.*, Vol. 8: para. 432). The process of individuation has, indeed, a positive outcome, and yet it is an outcome which, as suggested earlier, subsists as a goal paradoxically never achievable. It is a drive towards wholeness that holds the tension at the border where the negotiations between ego and self continue to hold the individualities which name our lives.

When considering the relatively young history of the Italian nation, the struggle to achieve and maintain a sense of individual identity, co-habiting with a restless internal political pluralism as well as with a drive towards a merging with the wider community of European nations can be understood as a succession of developments in the process of individuation of a young community.

The images recurring within a selection of films will, in the second part of the book, be set against the events that shape and reshape the country's political balance. If archetypal significance can be attributed to such images it will be possible to discuss whether their presence somewhat marks the shift from one stage to another and work as both symptoms of collective (or cultural) complexes and as symbols suggestive (as archetypes are in dreams) of the need for change.

Theorizing the nation

> We always were English and we always will be English, and it's just because we are English that we're sticking up for our right to be Burgundian!
>
> (H. Cornelius, *Passport to Pimlico* 1949)

A Jungian reading of cinematic images as the product of national cinema calls for a clarification, for a revisiting of the concepts of nation and national cinema within both the framework of Jungian analytical psychology and that of the most recent, often controversial, academic debates.

In *Nations and Nationalism* (1983) Ernest Gellner considers nationalism as 'the consequence of a new form of social organization, based on deeply internalized, education dependent high cultures'. Gellner insists on the constructed nature of nations by pointing out how 'nations are not inscribed into the nature of things . . . nor were national states the manifest ultimate destiny of ethnic or cultural groups. What do exist are cultures'. Gellner's emphasis on the relationship between nationalism and high culture is reiterated in his comment which sees nationalism as:

> the general imposition of a high culture on society, where previously low cultures had taken up the lives of the majority . . . of the population. . . . It is the establishment of an anonymous, impersonal society, with mutually substitutable atomized individuals, held together by a shared culture of this kind, in place of a previous complex structure of local groups, sustained by folk culture reproduced locally and idiosyncratically by the micro-groups themselves.
>
> (Gellner 1983: 57)

In *Culture, Identity and Politics* (1987) Gellner traces the origins of nationalism in the development of industrial societies. He believes that 'agrarian civilisations do not engender nationalism, but industrial and only industrial societies do'. More specifically Gellner points out how 'we live in a world in which the new type of division of labour engenders a powerful, and in most cases, successful nationalist groundswell' (Gellner 1987: 18–19).

Gellner's position somehow seems to find direct evidence in the parallel emergence of nations and of industrialization as well as provide a perspective particularly suited to the specific situation of the developing Italy across the first part of the twentieth century. However, it is difficult to envisage, especially in Italy, a situation where high culture, whether imposed or otherwise, would not run alongside the maintenance of low cultures, where the 'previous complex structure of local groups' would not be redescribed as the 'shared culture' which holds together a group within its new role of fragment of a wider, if 'anonymous' and 'impersonal', society.

In *Imagined Communities: Reflections on the Origin and Spread of Nationalism* (1991) Benedict Anderson tries to demonstrate how 'nation-ness, as well as nationalism, are cultural artefacts of a particular kind' (p. 4). Anderson's definition of nation as 'imagined political community – and imagined as both political and sovereign' (p. 6) has become the obligatory point of departure for theoretical discourses involving an understanding of the meaning and origin of a sense of nationhood. He directly questions Gellner's suggestion that nationalism 'invents nations where they do not exist' (Gellner 1964, cited in Anderson 1991: 6) as this statement would imply the existence of other, real communities juxtaposed to the constructed nation. For Anderson the nation came into being after the dissolution of important cultural systems which preceded it. In particular he analyses the importance of the religious community and of the dynastic realm as 'the taken-for-granted frames of reference' (Anderson 1991: 12), the decline of which (only on the temporal plane as far as the Church in Italy was concerned) becomes a participating factor in the subsequent emergence of the concept of nation. Interestingly, Anderson points to the relevance of the spreading of what he calls 'two forms of imagining . . . the novel and the newspaper. For these forms provided the technical means for re-presenting' the kind of imagined community that is the nation (Anderson 1991: 25). Anderson's reference to both an ability to collectively imagine a collective and to the role the media play in the perpetuation and sustenance of this imagining places his theory at a point of intersection between an understanding of the idea of nation reliant on an acknowledgement of what the Jungians call the cultural or group unconscious and the most recent developments in the debate around the relationship between national cinema and national identity.

Anderson's influence on the latter debate is evident in most of the contributions to *Cinema and Nation* (Hjort and Mackenzie, 2000) which provides a wide spectrum of perspectives and a more extensive context for the consideration of national cinemas. Andrew Higson, in his contributing chapter, summarizes Anderson's perspective and moves it forward by stating that 'it is public debate that gives the nation meaning, and media systems with a particular geographical reach that give it shape' (Higson 2000: 64). And if Higson's statement describes the specification and development of a, supposedly, pre-existing notion of nation, his quoting of David Morley and Kevin Robins who see 'the idea of nation' as working as 'an inclusive symbol which provides "integration" and "meaning"' (Higson 2000: 64, citing Morley and Robins 1990: 6) also suggests a function and an origin understood within the context of the implicit existence of a kind of group subconscious. The role of nationhood is then that of providing a sense of belonging and to fulfil the need for a 'rooted, bounded, whole and authentic identity' (Morley and Robins 1990: 19, cited in Higson 2000: 65); an idea which, again, lends itself to an understanding of the development of a sense of national identity as a process describable within the psychological parameters normally reserved for the emotional growth of the individual.

The words *symbol, integration, meaning*, whole and *authentic identity* are not, therefore, alien to a modern understanding of the idea of nationhood. Moreover, Susan Hayward points out that as nation 'comes to stand for/in for lost issues/

concepts/realities of kinship and family obligations' it easily becomes personified as a 'collective (female) individual that one dies for'. What Hayward calls a close circle leading to nationalist discourses actually 'bounds the notion of nation to the individual and has an embodied ideal (the maternal body)' (Hayward 2000: 89). The emotional language ('one dies for') Hayward uses suggests a relationship between the manifestation of the 'imagined abstraction' masquerading as 'grounded reality', as she describes it, and individual feelings experienced as tied to a personified collective (the motherland or fatherland). It is a similar relationship which, as pointed out earlier, describes, in Jungian analysis, the complex. Taking this analogy further, it might be possible to argue that the variation in images and feelings and the relationship of this particular complex, manifest as nation, with a specific archetypal nucleus (Father, Mother, Child, Self, Shadow) define, if temporarily, the individuality of a nation within the wider spectrum of the culture it stems from. This is, indeed, a suggestion that the second part of this book will explore more closely.

The mention of 'national identity' within a research based on a Jungian theoretical framework is bound to attract suspicion. Jung's own discussion of the subject, together with that of race and of 'Jewish psychology' has been at the heart of fiery criticism and accusations that have sadly, if in some way justly, marked his name and undermined the wider appreciation of his other work. He anchored nationality to land and defined it as an 'inborn character' which can be connected to specific traits understood as distinguishing differences. As Andrew Samuels points out, 'Jung's focus is on the predefining of difference via a classification by characteristics' (Samuels 1993: 315). Moreover, organized in lists of complementary attributes, national differences, for Jung, define opposites (and he actually used them to describe the complementarity between Germans and Jews) which will tend to complement each other in some idealized 'wholeness'. The dangerous underpinning is in the fact that 'this fantasy of "opposites" is presented as something factual, as if revealed by an empirical, psychological method' (Samuels 1993: 316). When describing all outer events according to archetypal dynamics Jung in fact neglected the influence of historical, economic, social and political factors, attempting to produce a 'psychology of nation' (Samuels 1993: 313). In synthesis Jung was 'a psychologist who lent his authority to nationalism, thereby legitimizing ideas of innate, psychological differences between nations' (Samuels 1993: 313).

This aim of this book is certainly neither that of establishing a 'psychology of nation', nor that of explaining the influence of national background on individual psychology (Samuels 1993: 334), but simply that of demonstrating how the emergence of a sense of national identity in a group can be considered vis-à-vis the process of emergence of ego consciousness. Samuels points out that 'the nation has a kind of oneness to it – and the nation itself is also part of a kind of manyness' (Samuels 1993: 334); a relationship between individuality and plurality, between the part and the whole which also describes the process of negotiation between ego and self. The necessary distancing from Jung's political and ideological standpoint does not detract, however, from the appreciation of the Jungian perspective on the unconscious which inspired this work. Benefiting from an approach strongly anchored in a historical and political context, I intend to transpose the Jungian theoretical framework, as applied to the understanding of individual psychological development, to the development of a sense of nationhood in its relationship to the wider cultural community and as relatively contained within negotiated political and/or geographical borders.

In particular, stemming from Jung's description of the relationship between ego-consciousness and Self, and Neumann's detailed analysis of the mythological descriptions of such a development as both personal and collective, it should be possible to theorize the manifestation and emergence of a national community as the expression of a 'collective ego-consciousness', separate from, yet dependent on an originating, wider culture, and yet striving towards integration within increasingly wider layers of self-describing larger communities.

Film and national identity

The relationship between national identity and national cinema is, because of the controversial nature of the adjective 'national', the locus of much academic debate. Anthony Smith ascribes to the artists the responsibility of supporting, with their work, the project of nationalist intellectuals who 'seek to rediscover and authenticate pre-existing collective myths, symbols, values, memories and tradition of "the people", and to locate the "old-new" nation they seek to recreate within its evolutionary ethnic framework' (Smith 2000: 48). Smith's suggestion presupposes both the artist's conscious manipulation of mythological and symbolic material for the benefit of the construction of a nationalist discourse as well as the origin of a constructed sense of nationhood in a 'pre-existing sense of ethnic community' and in the presence of ethnic ties whose variable intensity facilitates or impedes the artist's representational task.

Symbolic material does, however, lose its symbolic value under conscious manipulation and becomes a sign whose impact is predictable and descriptive rather than constructive. Myths, on the other hand, if acknowledged as pre-existing the idea of nation, will resonate back with the collective they originate from which will remain 'ethnic' even if addressed as 'national'. Smith, however, does ascribe the nation within an *evolutionary* 'ethnic framework' and, in that, it is possible to find the possibility for a flexibility and movement which can be recognized as characteristic of the idea of nation.

Film and art are, in Smith's ethno-symbolic approach, responsible for the forming and shaping of national identities. But if the cinematic language of a national cinema was to be ethno-specific and directing, it would fail to address the needs for national inclusion of ethnic minorities. In the case of Italy, in particular, the emergence of a post-war cinema sensitive and responsive to the differences in myth, traditions and values across the politically unified peninsula corresponded to a new popular definition of cinema as 'national'. Here the passivity of the audience, supposedly vulnerable to the propagandistic attempts of art to superimpose the Andersonian image of community, is questioned. As Higson points out, 'the "imagined community" argument . . . is not always sympathetic to what we might call the contingency or instability of the national' (Higson 2000: 66). The case of Italy is exemplary as that very instability has been attributed to a lack of a national popular culture. According to Gramsci, this was the consequence of both the Italian intellectuals' inability to 'imagine' a community besides the 'transnational (Catholic Christendom, Humanist Latinity, Enlightenment rationalism)' and of the extensive influence of non-Italian popular culture on the masses, measured in the volume of consumption of imported fiction in the form of novels, music and films (Forgacs 2000: 149). If an image of Italy was suggested on screen (and it certainly was during the fascist regime), it served the purpose of communicating the existence of a national community outside its own borders. In Jungian terms this was a fictional 'persona', an actor's mask, finding little resonance with the reality experienced by the very people it supposedly represented.

In revisiting Smith it would then be possible to accept that the artist might participate in a project of construction of a national image but his or her effectiveness in creating an image imaginable as national by the 'national' audience it addresses remains questionable. Moreover, Higson suggests that considerations of national cinema need to take into account the fact that the effectiveness of borders containing political and economic development, cultural practice and identity, as well as their very existence, cannot be taken for granted (Higson 2000: 67). If the idea of national identity is, then, negotiable, the images which respond to the need to define it will be representative of this active negotiation. In other words, what is represented is a process. Within a Jungian perspective, the images that can be isolated as symbolic will, then, serve the purpose of describing (when representative of complexes) or preceding (when archetypal) the changes leading to the transformations that characterize the process of negotiation of an identity which can be 'temporarily' recognized as national.

Film, myth, politics and Italy's new beginnings

In *The Vision Thing: Myth, Politics and Psyche in the World*, Thomas Singer (2000) explores the relationship between mythological or archetypal reality and politics and suggests that the tension between the two is mediated and, most interestingly, 'transmitted by a psyche that is somehow shared by all of us and articulated by a psychology that we hold in common' (2000: 5–6). This is what Jung had described as the 'collective psyche'. The book's engagement in an analysis of leadership, rituals and of a country's psychological profile is not so much a source of comparative material as it is an inspiration to consider the sociopolitical development of a nation from the perspective of Jungian analytical psychology.

It is John Beebe's contributing chapter '*The Wizard of Oz*: A Vision of Development in the American Political Psyche' (2000) which introduces the idea of a collective cultural medium such as cinema as a means of expression of that collective psyche's attempt to mediate between archetypal (collective unconscious) reality and politics. Beebe's discussion is worth consideration as an example of an interpretative attitude which, while leaning on a solidly Jungian theoretical framework, seeks to continuously place the film back within the context of its reception.

Beebe's analysis begins with the introduction of the original story, *The Wonderful Wizard of Oz*, a best-selling children's book written by L. Frank Baum in 1900, and reveals Baum's support for the Populist Movement and for the Democratic Senator William Jennings Bryan who, as a measure against inflation, sustained the idea of using silver as well as gold to back America's paper currency. As Bryan stood against the Republicans' vision of maintaining a currency only backed up by gold, Baum's allegory was told with the warning that the Republican approach was to be considered as a 'fairy-tale Yellow Brick Road leading to an impossibly affluent Emerald City, where McKinley (Republican favourite) would preside as humbug Wizard' (Singer 2000: 63).

As if peeling off compatible and complementary layers of meaning, Beebe reads the history of the 'Free Silver versus Gold Standard' debate as founded on the symbolic value given in alchemy to gold and silver respectively. So, gold as 'the earthly counterpart of the sun' stands for the patriarchal, masculine attitude of self-reliance, while silver, symbolic of the Feminine Principle, as the matriarchal stance, supportive of the 'economically less fortunate' (Beebe 2000: 64). Yet the tale, made into a film only in 1939, seems to regenerate its impact on the American psyche outside the constraints of the events which inspired it. Beebe suggests that as *The Wizard of Oz* 'derives a good deal of its energy from a primary concern for the political health of the nation' it is destined to resurface and rekindle its success as that concern becomes more acutely felt. Before World War II it spoke of the anxiety about America's interventionism; in the 1970s, responding to feminism and its questioning of gender roles, it carried the symbolic meaning of 'a triumph of matriarchal values' over patriarchy, and for contemporary viewers it works as a warning, reminding of the dangerous inflation inherent in becoming not only a leading world power but in believing in America's inevitable destiny as 'destroyer of all world wickedness' (Beebe 2000: 65).

Beebe finally suggests a Jungian reading which is political but, somehow, is so from the point of view of the unconscious. Beginning from the end scene in *The Wizard of Oz* that sees Dorothy back from her nightmare surrounded by the seven significant people who populated her dream, Beebe points out how the interaction 'of eight characters is one way to visualize the differentiation of consciousness in an individuating psyche' (Beebe 2000: 65). Harmony will be achieved thanks to a process which Beebe calls *political* because 'it involves alliances, contending parties, and struggles for audience and power, all revealed by the way the characters in a film play out their psychological roles – their different consciousnesses – in relation to each other' (Beebe 2000: 66). The roles played are metaphors for the actual transformations taking place in America at the time of the film's release.

But the metaphor works both retrospectively (in relation to the original story's function) and when projected into America's future. Dorothy is the mediator, the positive feminine who will try to mend the split: first the historical, later the deeper emotional one which underlines American politics' search for purpose. Dorothy represents the extraverted feelings which a country like America, 'whose dominant consciousness is extraverted thinking', finds difficult to individuate. Her ability to reach beyond the selfish justification of her own standpoint is a necessary hope, the hope of becoming able to, like Dorothy, find 'a common ground for the continuity of value' (Beebe 2000: 78).

While Beebe makes a point of finding an internal parallel to external politics, Andrew Samuels expands on Jung's belief that psychic energy is expressed through a variety of channels which include but are not limited to that of sexuality. Jung had mentioned the biological, the spiritual, the psychological and the moral channels and Samuels suggests the possibility of a political channel, specific to the expression of an energy he calls political. Samuels describes such energy as 'the capacity to bring creativity, imagination and effort to bear on seemingly intractable problems and to try to solve them in ways that reflect concern for social justice' (Samuels 2000: 85).

Political energy is to form the voice of the individual as a member of the *polis* (city), driving him to speak for and from the community he identifies with. The 'creativity, imagination and effort' that Samuels attributes to political energy are specifically directed at the collective both in purpose and in effort: political change might begin with the voice of an individual but it is actualized collectively. Jung, when describing the origin of change in society, beautifully defines this relationship:

> Social, political and religious conditions affect the collective unconscious in the sense that all those factors which are suppressed by the prevailing views of attitudes in the life of a society gradually accumulate in the collective unconscious and activate its contents. Certain individuals gifted with particularly strong intuitions then become aware of the changes going on in it and translate these changes into communicable ideas
>
> (*C.W.*, Vol. 8: para. 594)

He than continues by suggesting that 'if the translation of the unconscious into communicable language proves successful, it has a redeeming effect' (para. 595). *The Wizard of Oz*, both in its literary origin and its visual representation, can be taken as an example of the efficiency of this translation through channels such as literature and visual art, and if the effect is not necessarily 'redemption' it might be more acceptably seen as supportive and aiding of change.

Italian cinema has certainly provided such a support throughout the profound transformations in the young history of a nation which is close to being its contemporary. In her introduction to *Italian Film* (2000) Marcia Landy points out how, from its very beginnings, Italian cinema has served the purpose of defining a dialectic between a developing national community and an international cinematic culture, a dialectic eliciting a response which required a stronger sense of unity than that provided by novel political borders. Landy (2000: 1) outlines how 'the national community is forged through the assumed common bonds of unitary language, the nation as a family, conceptions of gender and ethnicity that rely on an identity of "origins, culture, and interests," and geographical (and sacrosanct) borders'.

Rather than 'describing' the 'national community' that hosted its emergence, early cinema might have had to work hard at constructing one. Perceiving itself as a participant in nationhood thanks to the interpellation of a text demanding of identification with motifs, characters, moral stands and a vaguely audible 'unitary language' (silent cinema relying on written text met with widespread illiteracy and with the prevalence of regional dialects), the 'new' Italian spectator might have struggled to find a consistent match in the reality outside the walls of the cinematic auditorium. Landy seems, at this point, to be wittingly bypassing the importance of religion/Catholicism in the construction of a sense of national identity, but she later points out how, in the films depicting World War I for example, an element of religiosity is evident. Nevertheless she insists that 'this religiosity . . . is not that of the church but appears to be of a secular religion, wherein the state assumes the exalted position normally reserved for divinity' (Landy 2000: 66–67). This statement is certainly suggestive of the need for a deeper understanding of the relationship between national community, religion and state.

The next section of the book will engage with an analysis of a decade of Italian cinema with the intention of finding the images which best represent the archetypal nature of this relationship as well as mark, as symptoms and/or as symbols, the psychological stages in the growth and transformation, in Italy, of a sense of national identity.

Conclusion

Helen Morgan describes how 'as the archetypal moves through the social, cultural and personal filters of the unconscious . . . [it] is filled out into an image or an idea that emerges into consciousness' (Morgan 2004: 220). Therefore the analysis of archetypal images as they appear in cultural products should allow a retracing of their contamination by the 'social, cultural and personal filters' as well as their placing within a developmental discourse specific to each unconscious layer.

This chapter has traced the movement of archetypal material through such filters and, while questioning their rigidity, has considered the specific role of art in the deliverance of images symbolically significant and effective in the maintenance and shifting of unconscious layers of social inclusion such as ethnicity, culture and nationality.

Erich Neumann's developmental extension of the Jungian perspective considers mythological images as the place where traces of both humanity's and individuals' journey towards consciousness are to be found in the form of archetypal sequences (Neumann 1954: xvi). It is possible to suggest that as the journey is an ongoing developmental path, traces of its extension into the contemporary history of humanity might have to be searched for within the shared narratives which have replaced and integrated the 'explanatory' function of mythology. The relationship between mythology and art was sealed by the wide impact afforded by the image when mass response and understanding was felt to be essential to the maintenance of the deep structures supportive of cultural order. If mythology and the transformations of its core messages across the ages testify to the evolution of consciousness as a whole, that role had to be inherited by other narrative forms which, as mythology did, still rely on symbolic imagery for their expression and transmission. Religious iconography and visual arts have then become the manifest expression, the witnesses and heralds of a culture's need for transformation.

John Beebe, in his analysis of *The Wizard of Oz*, describes this function as it is fulfilled through the specific vehicle of cinematic images. Moreover, he describes the film as mirroring the political state and needs of a nation through its discussion of the political relationships between the characters who themselves represent aspects of one personality. As a dream would, the film worked at first as descriptive of the unconscious psychological state of the culture producing it (America's anxiety in 1939 at the eve of its involvement in World War II) and it later functioned as an anchor on which to validate the power of profound shifts within that culture (1970s feminism, the weakening of the rigidity of sexual roles and of the moral stand on sexual orientation) and, today, it renews its impact as a psychological tale of the search for a balance between the introverted and the extraverted function, the latter embodied by Judy Garland's Dorothy, across the spectrum of American politics.

Feldman's concept of 'primary skin function', which describes the formation of a psychological container derived from the awareness of skin as both limiting and holding, can be extended, as he himself suggests, to groups. In this light the sense of nationhood as an abstract, intuitive filter of perception, as a limiting as well as containing identity, derives from the external perception of political borders. The development of Italy as a nation begins, historically, with the demarcation of new borders, sanctioned with the unification of 1861 and only partially relieving the fragmentations expressed by regional independence of dialects, by varying subcultural attitudes and by a retained administrative independence. This first attempt at unification provides, however, a new, fragile, delicate skin from which a new, fragile, delicate sense of nationhood struggles to emerge. Italian cinematic production follows this struggle and calls for an 'Italian' spectator; one who at first only exists as a model and an aspiration and soon, during the 20 years of fascist dictatorship, is filled up with a sense of his heroic past, demanding a participation in an equally heroic, if desperately illusory future. Yet there is a moment of truth, a time when the projections fall and, amongst the ruins, where humiliation has taken the place of pride, Italy has a chance to redefine itself.

The next part of the book is an analysis, supported by an understanding of the core concepts of analytical psychology, of a decade of post-war Italian film, directed by those directors who recognized themselves as neo-realist and whose style continued to change together with the historical and political context of the production of their work.

Marie Louise Von Franz (1966), an extremely prolific writer and close collaborator of Jung himself, believed 'that critical comparisons were meaningless outside a developmental context'. Hollwitz (2001: 86) shares her standpoint which sees psychodynamic criticism as meaningless if it is not predominately dynamic: 'Symbolic materials are supposed to move somewhere', or maybe, more directly, are supposed to generate a movement. The following section traces the images, the symbolic material recurring within the films, which lead towards or, when unsuccessful, merely suggested a movement, the next step towards the development of an Italian consciousness.

Intervallo

Chapter 4

Italian neo-realism and the unmitigated darkness of historical truth

Introduction

In *Archetypal Patterns in Fairy Tales*, Marie Louise von Franz talks of her clinical experience as analytical psychologist in relation to her patients' dreams. Sometimes, she reveals, she had the strong feeling that certain dreams should remain uninterpreted. The dreams that are best 'left alone' are the ones that seem to contain 'something of the essence of that person's being and fate' and these are the ones Von Franz would 'prefer not to touch' as within 15 or 20 years their meaning will become naturally evident. 'With such a dream,' she maintains, 'one grows. One goes along, one puzzles, and then bit by bit, by becoming oneself, one also becomes that dream, and then one understands it' (von Franz 1997: 154).

Produced and released between the first years of World War II and the beginning of the economic and political reconstruction of Italy and mostly depicting the true conditions of the country during that period, Italian neo-realist films, like the dreams von Franz prefers 'not to touch', seem to contain something of a country's 'being and fate'. Moreover, the often openly declared desire simply to 'present' reality with minimal intrusion (expressed in voice-overs, superimposed text at the beginning of films, interviews and journal articles) seems an excellent alibi to escape the sieving of interpretation as the message seems to coincide with that of the objective history which the films portray. Nevertheless, neo-realist films have certainly not remained uninterpreted: the generally positive reception by international critics (the French in particular) has insured a constant flow of reviews and analyses of a flexibly defined body of films, a flow which continues to be prolific and increasingly detailed.

The available discussions, reviews and analyses seem to cover a wide spectrum of interpretative directions: aesthetic, ideological, structural, historical, architectural and often psychoanalytical (Bazin 1971, Deleuze 1989, Rocchio 1999; Brunetta 2001; Restivo 2002; Shiel 2006) with a satisfactory presence of monographs and articles which often incorporate more than one framework. Yet, seen through the five decades of history and the changes standing between the present academic discussion and the last of the films considered neo-realist (a contended position claimed by and offered to half a dozen films released between

1951 and 1954), the work of the directors which brought the pain of a humiliated nation to the screens of the world remains open to another reading. The unconscious material emerging through some of the most convincingly real films of the period in question has, in fact, often been bypassed in the name of their obvious significance as the pained self-reflection of a country on its own trauma and sense of loss, achieved through the direct opening of the camera lens on the unstaged drama of reality.

Jung described both dreams and the work of art which carries the imprint of the archetype as messages from the collective unconscious (*C.W.*, Vol. 15: para. 153; *C.W.* Vol. 10, para. 318) and indeed, the message emerging from Italian neo-realist films is one carried by images which, like the dreams to which von Franz refers, often leave the viewer 'puzzled' and almost forced simply to 'go along' with the truth they reveal. A thorough understanding can only come from life itself and from history as it is described and 'documented' by the films. However, a rereading supported by a Jungian theoretical framework and by a contextualization which can now include the development into the future of the films' depicted present, might finally reveal both the impact on and the origin from the collective unconscious of that message as the image will have been translated by history in a shift that has either become manifest or has evidently been repressed.

The choice of Italian neo-realism as the object of a study of film in the light of a Jungian analytical perspective derives from the realization of an unexplored and possibly non-coincidental relationship between a widely acknowledged crisis of an Italian national identity, described by Galli della Loggia as the 'eclipse of the national dimension'[1] (1996: 134), more evident from the end of World War II, and a body of cinematic work which, although seemingly providing the world with the truest and most enduringly remembered portrayal of the Italian people, also documented profound and unresolved divisions, lack of solidarity, loss of direction and a poverty too great to be fed on ideology alone. The timely emergence of a desire, in directors coming from different sociopolitical and intellectual backgrounds, to record and deliver images as witnesses of an era and so create a tangible pool of collective memories of one the most dramatic moments in the history of the young nation, is in itself a symptom of a movement rooted in an unconscious expanding beyond the limits of the personal and into the group or cultural unconscious.

The acknowledgement of the presence, function and impact of archetypal material in the films of the neo-realist period presupposes the support of an understanding pursued through a perspective encompassing both a review of the immediate circumstances from which the films emerge, the cultural and political situations preceding their production, and the relationship between the images and the social, cultural, religious and political changes they forecast. The chapter begins by presenting the method which, in line with the implementing of such a perspective, seems most suited to the analysis of the films. This will be followed

---

1 Translation mine.

by an overview of the historical events and of the political circumstances that, after the complex process of unification of Italy led to the rise of fascism and later to Italy's entry into World War II as ally to Hitler's Germany.

An analysis of the effects of fascist propaganda on the perception and general attitude towards the institution of the family, gender relations and the role of women within and outside the confines of the familial structure will also be developed. This will prepare the way for a more objective reading of the often personified emergence, in the chosen films of the post-war period, of significant archetypes, an emergence which inevitably includes the traits which an ideology has successfully sown, more or less forcefully, into the terrain of a cultural unconscious.

In order to appreciate the consistency of the relationship between the development and/or the weakening of a sense of national identity and the cinematic images which describe the process psychologically, this chapter will also review the advent of neo-realism in connection with the transformation and changes undergone by the cinematic medium, both in modes of production, reception, subject matter, genre and ideological contents, throughout the interwar years.

A methodological approach: from dreams to films

Rather than storing repressed and still censored material, dreams are, for Jung, the way through which the unconscious makes itself known, its own means of communication with consciousness. The process of individuation (as described in previous chapters) which calls all individuals to 'wholeness' is accomplished by confronting the unconscious and striving for a balance between opposites as they become manifest through images in dreams, active imagination, creative art, etc.

As pointed out in Neumann's comparative analysis of mythological material, individuation 'is something that happens not just to individuals but also to cultures'. It is a process through which cultures 'become aware of the diversity and opposition within them, and they come to accept their shared, collective conscious qualities' (Hockley 2001: 43) or rather – remaining true to Jung's suggestion that individuation is a process rather than a goal – strive towards such 'becoming'. In order to demonstrate how this process, first described in mythology, is now traceable in film images it is important to isolate a methodological approach which, consistent with the suggested analogy between dreams, myth and film, will also successfully return the archetypal content back to the films' cultural and historical context of their production.

The selection and analysis of a series of films produced by more than one director across a determined period of time provides a good field of research, but if the reference to important historical events or social and political changes contemporary to the films is an important part of the interpretative process, the review of the history which immediately precedes them is also crucial to the process of understanding. As with psychiatric patients, the collection of an anamnesis, as a revisiting of the relevant case history, is an essential step in the analytical relationship, so extending the film's anchoring in the collective past of the group it addresses offers an essential reference, particularly relevant to the specific, traditionally psychoanalytic method of association. Jung's method of association had the intent of describing the personal 'psychological context in which a dream is naturally embedded' (Samuels *et al.* 1986: 29). Transposed to the analysis of film this process refers to the psychological meaning of relevant past or present historical events. Moreover, association becomes particularly effective in linking the significant recurring material across the films of different directors produced within the same short period of time. This should help isolate the images that demand a closer analytical attention which will take the form of amplification.

Amplification, as described in the *Critical Dictionary of Jungian Analysis*, is an interpretative method which 'involves use of mythic, historical and cultural parallels in order to clarify and make ample the metaphorical content of dream symbolism' (Samuels *et al.* 1986: 16). Amplification, by emphasizing the 'metaphorical (hence, approximate) rather than literal translation of dream content' and allowing for the isolation of what is 'most immediately relevant for the dreamer' points towards understanding 'as a consequence of reflection' (Samuels *et al.* 1986: 16).

Interestingly, this particular methodological approach seems to be consistent with one of the ideological underpinnings of neo-realism. Zavattini, one of neo-realism's most prolific writers, insists that 'the artist's task is not to make people moved or indignant at metaphorical situations, but to make them reflect ... on what they and others are doing, on the real things, exactly as they are' (Zavattini 2000: 50–51). Paradoxically, this suggestion makes sense within a Jungian interpretative approach with the premise that the metaphor as object of reflection is not intentionally represented but is itself a consequence of interpretative readings. As in a play with mirrors, reality is twice reflected. The first time the reflection incorporates the spectator as an internal viewer (the process which, as we will see, Zavattini cherishes and Deleuze points to as a defining attribute of neo-realism). The second reflection points the images towards the collective consciousness which, recognizing its own presence in the reflected reality, can find resonance with the unconscious content (image) thus realizing the image's archetypal purpose.

The success of this second reflection can only be measured with the help of a method that, through the contextualization reinforced by association and the comparative analysis of the contemporary productions of the three directors, proceeds to a sieving of the personal material in search of a collective symbolism consistent in all. Therefore, an understanding of the past and contemporary historical setting, as well as a consideration of the director's own personal involvement and development, should help to distil out the reality they hoped to capture with their camera from the inevitable filters of their own perspective and, finally, distinguish it from the collective material of unconscious origin.

In dream interpretation the meaningful synthesis between the personal association and the historical and mythological parallels revealed through amplification leads to a satisfactory isolation of meaning. The final synthesis in the case of film analysis has to rely on the subjectivity of the interpreter. If this can be considered a limitation when engaging in an academic discourse it is, again, the consistence of the synthesis with the comparative findings across multiple samples of film that provides a degree of relief.

My personal involvement with the history I refer to in this book has certainly had an impact on the process of research as well as affecting the emphasis given to a particular aspect. Interestingly, some of the history with which the book deals has been systematically and successfully kept from entering my field of knowledge by the Italian Catholic educational system. Just as I discovered a cultural history very different from the one I have been taught, so the directors of the films had to work against an official historiography as promoted by the fascist regime. This overlapping has somehow brought my perspective closer to the one of the directors and, more significantly, to that of their contemporary spectators. The strong emphasis I place on history is the result of a desire to find a way of approaching films which could help review a country's cultural movements through the enriched understanding provided by a Jungian analytical reading.

The foregrounding of the films' historical contents coincides with the emergence, across the texts, of important social and political issues. Particularly evident is the exclusion or isolation of women in the neo-realist directors' texts which, although understood archetypically, still demands a perspective capable of acknowledging the images' anchoring in a post-war reality. At this time the threat of women's emancipation was bound to affect the representational products of the three men as they were certainly not immune from pursuing, through their art, their own 'gendered' agenda. In view of this, the reading of the films is also a reading of the history of what Demaris Wehr has described as an 'internalized oppression' (Wehr 1987: 18–22). Wehr describes it as the persistence, within a patriarchal society, of certain symbol sets or pre-verbal images which, supported by means of collective representation such as cinema, has led to the internalization in women of men's images of them (Wehr 1987: 18–22). A thorough analysis of the history leading to the war will help tracing back these images into the rhetoric and policies of the fascist regime.

The birth of a nation time and time again: a brief history of Italy

It is difficult, without fully embracing the complex historical and political debate, to extract a clear line of development that describes and, even less easily, justifies and forecasts the coming to power of Mussolini, the establishment of his dictatorship in the early 1920s and his senseless decision to take Italy to war in 1940. A brief analysis is, however, useful for the purpose of this work as it provides a background to a film analysis that heavily relates to historical and political context in its interpretation of symbolic material. Post war reconstruction in Italy was not simply a question of physical rebuilding of damaged structures but involved a revision of the forms of government and a reflection on past events in order to avoid their recurrence. The contribution of neo-realist films to such revision can only be discussed with the help of a wide-angled view on the construction of the 'national self' which was supposedly crushed and then resurrected throughout the war years. This construction begins with the unification of Italy in 1861.

The unification of Italy and the passive revolution

The unification of Italy was the culmination and the end of the nation-building movement and historical process traditionally known as the Risorgimento. Inspired by the liberal ideals of the French revolution, the Risorgimento can be said to find its origins in the late eighteenth century, at the time when a temporary expulsion of the Austrians from the peninsula seemed to open the possibility for the creation of a new free Italian state. Crushed by the re-establishing of an 'order' based on monarchic and papal leaderships sanctioned during the 1815 Vienna Congress, the first impetus towards the 'rebirthing' of the nation (Risorgimento literally means 'the process of resurrection') disappeared into an active net of underground activities and secret societies. These active nuclei of revolutionary spirit were behind the first uprisings in Naples and Piedmont in 1820–21 which were suppressed with the help of the Austrians. Revolutionary action, however, continued to spread and in 1848 'disturbances in most of the urban centres ... assumed a weightier aspect in relation to the wider national movement'. After the initial gains, those 'disturbances' were contained and the status quo was restored (Haddock 2000: 35–37).

The failure of the nationalist revolution exposed the lack of co-ordination amongst the various political fronts involved in the process and a general weakness of intent deriving from opposing views on the form which the ideal new Italian state should take: the discussion of the possibility of a unitary against a federal, of a republican against a monarchic state as well as the differences in interests and objectives between regions and classes contributed to the initial disappointing result. The time of dissatisfaction and unrest that followed was also an opportunity for the only monarch in Italy to have kept a Constitution (granted as a consequence of the revolutionary efforts) to offer much needed leadership: Carlo Alberto of Savoy, King of Piedmont, declared war on Austria in 1849.

The King of Piedmont's half-hearted effort was unsurprisingly unsuccessful and he soon abdicated in favour of his son Vittorio Emanuele II who, helped by the diplomatic ability of his Prime Minister, Cavour, prepared the ground for a new attempt at unification, both through internal policies aimed at the reinforcement of the parliament's powers and economic stability, and through a new attitude in foreign affairs with the binding of strategic alliances. During the period of his ministerial vocation Cavour's tactics, his strategies and the treaties he subscribed exposed his own as well as the House of Savoy's true ambitions which were expansionistic more than patriotic (Duggan 1994: 122–123). Nevertheless, a partial unification was finally achieved under the governing hand of Vittorio

Emanuele II in 1861, the result of a combination of military, diplomatic and revolutionary efforts. At first Rome and Venice were excluded from the unification and remained under the role of the papacy and of Austria respectively. Italy obtained Venice after joining Prussia in a war against Austria in 1866 and when the French withdrew from Rome in 1870 during the Franco-Prussian war, the Italian troops could finally take the practically defenceless city. The unification was effectively complete and Rome became the capital of the new kingdom of Italy although the Church only officially recognized and accepted the new territorial and governmental arrangement in 1929 (Haddock 2000: 42–45).

The very process that led to Italy's unification becomes relevant to an understanding of the post-war events which inspired the neo-realist movement if considered as the precursor of a weakness in the sense of national identity which World War II exacerbated. Luchino Visconti, one of the recognized fathers of Italian neo-realism, suggested a parallel between the Resistance movement in World War II and the Risorgimento in his 1954 film *Senso*, set in 1866. The film is a clear revisitation of historical events in the search for analogies and for a new understanding of the failure to transform Resistance values into a sustainable political activism. Visconti supports, with his film, the Gramscian suggestion that the Risorgimento was in fact a 'passive revolution' which deprived popular masses of agency, leaving leadership to the already powerful 'ruling classes'.

In his *Prison Notebooks* Gramsci, in fact, discusses the function of Piedmont in the Italian Risorgimento as that of the 'ruling class'. Rather than a social group 'leading' other groups it was 'a State which, even though it had limitation as a power, "led" the group which should have been "leading" and was able to put at the latter's disposal an army and a political-diplomatic strength' (Gramsci 1971: 105). In order better to judge the long-term effect of the limited involvement of the popular masses in the liberation of the country, it is worth citing in full Gramsci's comment (as found in one of his *Quaderni*[2]) on the 'passive revolution' as first intended by Vincenzo Cuoco[3] when describing the 'tragic experiment of the Parthenopean Republic in 1799', a description which can be easily transposed to the events unfolding several decades later:

> One should study the way in which the critical formula of Vincenzo Cuoco on the 'passive revolutions', which when it was formulated . . . was meant as a warning, to create a national mood of greater energy and popular revolutionary initiative, was converted in the minds of the neo-Guelphs[4] and Moderates, in their state of social panic, into a positive conception, into a political programme . . . the determination to abdicate and capitulate at the

---

2 'Il Materialismo Storico e la Filosofia di Benedetto Croce' (1948).
3 A Neapolitan conservative thinker, 1770–1823.
4 Members of a liberal Catholic movement in Italy in the first half of the nineteenth century. Their aim was an Italian federation under the Pope (Gramsci 1971: n58).

first serious threat of an Italian revolution that would be profoundly popular, i.e. radically national.

(Gramsci 1948: 184–185, in 1971: n59)

More than the result of a national revolution the unification under a 'constitutional monarchy' became, then, a well-piloted diplomatic solution to foreign exploitation and, at the same time, the means to control anarchic and republican rebellions which, although successful on a local scale, seemed to lack the co-ordination and political unity necessary to drive the process to completion. The first 'seeds' of a national sentiment were then rejected in the name of the growth of the state with profound consequences for the stability and healthy development of both.

From Crispi to Mussolini: the state looks for the nation

If the process of transforming the geographically defined peninsula into a politically contained single state was a complex one, the actual building of a national identity, which was certainly not a direct consequence of, nor, obviously, the single motivational force behind the unifying effort, was to prove a true challenge. A policy of centralization, implemented as a desperate attempt to contain the internal fragmentation which tended to disperse political energy, actually worked to enhance already profound regional differences and reinforce the division with the south.

When Crispi became prime minister in 1887 he found both a country weakened by an ongoing agricultural crisis caused by increasing unemployment which led desperate 'day labourers' to strikes and revolts, and a government devoted to protecting the interest of the ruling class to the point of willingly surrendering 'principle to short-term expediency' in the process known as 'trasformismo' (Duggan 1994: 161). Trasformismo is 'the process whereby the so-called "historic" Left and Right parties ... tended to converge in terms of program ... The two main parties disintegrated into personal cliques and factions which characterized Italian political life until Fascism' (Gramsci 1971: n58). Trasformismo was also the result of uncertainty, 'a feeling that Italy's ruling class needed to close ranks in order to face the growing challenge of Socialism' (Duggan 1994: 161).

Realizing the inability of parliament to 'subordinate private or local interest to those of the nation' and aware of the problem of a lack of national identity, Crispi set out a programme of reforms: he invested his energy between the founding of a system of political education and the reinforcement of Italy's military power as he believed in war as a good generator of a sense of nationhood. He also believed that Italy needed a strong government to the point of accepting the idea of a dictatorship should it serve the national interest. His African campaigns were disastrous failures and his repressive measures against the threat of socialism only led to a re-evaluation of leftist revolts, inspired by his attempts at limiting liberties, as a defence of the constitution. As the country begun to move out of recession by the end of the century a 'new breeze of liberal optimism begun to stir' (Duggan 1994: 170).

The first two decades of the new century are traditionally known as the Giolittian years: under the almost uninterrupted government of Giovanni Giolitti (1842–1928) the country experienced a period of modernization and economic growth. The 'boom' in industry was not, however, paralleled by an equal change in the conditions of agriculture and, notwithstanding the significant exodus of peasants overseas during this period, the Italian countryside remained overpopulated (Duggan 1994: 175). The majority of Italians hardly felt the impact of the new affluence that seemed to benefit mainly the middle classes.

Angela Delle Vacche offers, as a background to her analysis of the way Italian culture is translated to the screen, a review of the events and conditions that prepared for the advent of Fascism. In her description of Giolitti's Italy she suggests that the difficult transition to modernity which Italy experienced at the beginning of the twentieth century saw 'the industrial groups of the Turin-Genoa-Milan triangle' as major protagonists with an increased distancing and abuse of the rural and urban proletariat, particularly in the consistently exploited areas of the South (Delle Vacche 1992: 22). In fact, although Giolitti believed that the way to counteract the socialist tendency towards revolution was to improve the conditions of the working classes and to adopt a neutral policy towards strikes and workers' revolts, his benevolent strategy, rather than social justice, had at its heart economic stability and the strengthening of the state (Duggan 1994: 180–181). Eventually, Giolitti attracted both the scepticism of those old school industrialists who believed in the government's duty to protect their interests rather than those of the workers and the resentment of the workers who soon realized that the government's neutrality would not hold when put to the test and that violence would be (and was indeed) used against strikers. Moreover, Giolitti's pragmatism and lack of ideals and the liberal parliamentary system he represented were considered 'symptomatic of the failure of Italy's ruling class' by a group of dissidents known as the Nationalists (Duggan 1994: 184).

The Nationalists' view that Italy needed a much more authoritarian government and their idea of war as a necessary tool in the creation of a sense of devotion to the nation were particularly suited to the industrialists who saw the benefits of a more containing approach to Socialism and the positive financial gains in the prospect of war. In the hope of gaining the support of the Nationalists and to clarify the position of the socialists in relation to the government, Giolitti decided in 1911 to invade Libya. The success of the campaign did not translate into the support he hoped for and in 1913, when facing the first election with universal manhood suffrage, Giolitti turned to the Catholics, intending to use to his advantage the Church's general view that Liberalism was, in relation to Socialism, the lesser of two evils. When news of a scandalous 'deal' between Giolitti and the Church began to spread, his government collapsed. Succeeding Giolitti in government was Antonio Salandra who, parading the ideal of a liberalism which found its essence in patriotism, led Italy into World War I in May 1915 (Duggan 1994: 184–188).

Alexander J. De Grand maintains that 'the war took on the character of a revolt against the past which aimed at the creation of a new political system'. De Grand not only adds that 'during the crisis over intervention and the long war that followed, liberal Italy died', but he also sustains the importance of the campaign for intervention in uniting the efforts and political agenda of the Nationalists with those of Benito Mussolini, thereby providing a platform for the future development of Fascism (De Grand 1971: 394). The declaration of war in May 1915 was the result of economic, strategic and expansionistic considerations, with the government hoping to acquire the Trentino and Trieste as a result of a victory alongside Britain and France, and the Nationalists pushing their territorial ambitions as far as the whole of Istria, Dalmatia and the islands of the Adriatic (De Grand 1971: 402); and both expecting financial support from their wealthier war allies at the end of the conflict. The Nationalists, through their publication, the *Idea Nazionale* and their participation in the large interventionist demonstrations only days before the entry into war, had expressed their belief that only unlimited territorial expansion would be a valid measure of the country's success. Moreover, they had 'furthered the synthesis between conservative ends and revolutionary direct action which was to result in Fascism' and, finally, had managed to link Giolitti, both his neutrality and his corrupt activities, with parliament, thus weakening the 'very idea of parliamentary rule' (De Grand 1971: 412).

'Far from healing the rifts that had so threatened the stability of liberal Italy before 1914, the experience of 1915–18 served to fragment the nation more than ever' (Duggan 1994: 191). The war did, in fact, leave behind a climate of disorientation that would prove to be fertile soil for the 'seeds of discontent', planted by Giolitti's paternalistic and often opportunistic administration (Delle Vacche 1992: 22) and nurtured by the feelings of humiliation and disappointment which followed the negative response to the absurd requests made by Italy during post-war territorial negotiations. Ready to take advantage of the difficult and extremely unstable post-war economic and political situation was Benito Mussolini and the movement he started in 1919, a movement that would later become the fascist party (Mack Smith 1983: 41).

Mussolini the chameleon

Mussolini's political orientation was, at first, surprisingly leftist. As editor of various socialist papers in the early teens, he would condemn Giolitti's colonial enterprises, advocate a socialist revolution and passionately attack the Church, until his personal ambition became the driving force in the name of which ideals were to be reviewed and often betrayed.

The beginning of World War I saw Mussolini's shift from the socialist policy of neutrality in a war considered 'a purely bourgeois concern' to the nationalist admission that 'Italy had to show the world she was capable of a "really great war"' (Mack Smith 1983: 31–32). Expelled from the socialist party because of his interventionist declarations, he started his own newspaper *Il Popolo d'Italia*, nominally socialist but funded by industrialists and, partially and indirectly, subsidized by the government itself (Mack Smith 1983: 30).

In 1919 Mussolini founded the movement Fasci di Combattimento with a programme still similar to that of the socialists, an association which threatened to end Mussolini's political career when in the 1919 general election he failed to gain a single seat even in his home town in Romagna. At that point, the only option left to guarantee political survival was a shift towards the right, a move which would not only attract the conservative section of Italy into the ranks of fascism but, because of the unfolding of events outside Mussolini's control, transformed fascism into a party with enough popular support to justify a revolutionary seizure of power. The factors which led to such a transformation were the economic depression and high unemployment which characterized the immediate post-war years, the workers' occupation of factories in 1920 and the government's apparent willingness to negotiate in favour of the workers, paralleled by the lack, among Italy's working classes, of cohesion and revolutionary determination. Moreover, the split within the socialists, which ended with the founding of the Italian Communist Party led by Antonio Gramsci in 1921, not only weakened the general electoral impact of the socialists but provided another, clearer negative catalyst for both the Catholics and the industrialists who saw in Gramsci's new party the embodiment of their fear of an Italian Bolshevik revolution. Paramilitary groups knows as *squadristi* also begun to form with the intent of using violence in order to destroy the 'national enemy' represented by the socialists, now perceived as the origin of the economic crisis and made to bear the burden of the recession (Duggan 1994: 1998–204).

By 1921 the fascist movement had become a party and in the elections of 1921 gained a number of seats in parliament which allowed for Mussolini's manipulative ability to have more significant effects. Pushed on one side by the *squadristi* who urged him to seize power though a demonstration of violence, and on the other courted by a government now hoping to avoid a revolution by welcoming him into a coalition, Mussolini managed to respond positively to both. On 28 October 1922, responding to the threat of a march on Rome, forecast by a gathering of blackshirts (*squadristi*) around the capital and local insurrections in the north, the declaration of a state of emergency was demanded by the government, but the king, seeing in Mussolini the last hope to re-establish order, declined to sign the decree and Mussolini was appointed prime minister (Mack Smith 1983: 61–65). Although his rise to power had officially happened within the rules of the Constitution, the march on Rome was functional to the establishment of a myth of invincibility and violent determination and, as it happened on 29 October, rather than a proof of military superiority it became a celebratory demonstration where some 30,000 men (not enough to amount to a real threat) paraded across the capital, effectively 'overtaking' an enemy who had surrendered before the battle.

Nevertheless Mussolini was now in power and, realizing that his own party had neither a constructive programme nor homogeneous values, he organized his government accordingly, with the participation of liberals, of the Popolari[5] and the Nationalists attempting to form a broad base to complement the inconsistencies and weak ideological stand of Fascism.

A 'creative' dictatorship

Quite certainly aware of the instability of a relatively young party reliant on an ideologically fragmented electorate, Mussolini worked to enhance his chances at maintaining power by managing to obtain the approval of a Bill that guaranteed two-thirds of the seats in parliament to the party with the majority of votes, provided that party also obtained a quarter of all of them (Duggan 1994: 208). The elections of 1924 placed his government in power as well as demonstrating the now drastic containment of the 'threat' of Socialism with only a small percentage of votes going to either the Partito Socialista Italiano (PSI) or the Partito Comunista Italiano (PCI). Yet, although Mussolini had, seemingly, achieved his position without a clear revolutionary act, the pressure from the *squadristi* who asked to be led into a revolution which would finally destroy the liberal state reached a peak in 1924 with the murder of Giacomo Matteotti, a socialist deputy who had dared to expose the extent of fascist violence and corruptibility. Torn between supporting the *squadristi*'s action and losing respectability or condemning them and losing their support, Mussolini not only took personal responsibility for the events that confirmed the descent into violence of Fascism but, taking advantage of the boycott of the opposition which had effectively left parliament in disgust, he offered to single-handedly take control. It was the beginning of his dictatorship.

The official abolition of the opposition came in October 1926 when opposition parties were banned and made illegal. Censorship was reinforced, the police given greater power of arrest (Duggan 1994: 214) and the ideals of democracy considered negative as they would 'stamp out all beauty and interest and individuality from life' (Mack Smith 1983: 161). Mussolini now set about addressing the problem of 'doctrine' but never resolved the inconsistencies which he declared part of the spontaneity, intuition and impulse which characterized the 'genius' of fascist ideology (Duggan 1994: 211).

At the beginning of the 1930s, however, a definition of Fascism appeared in the *Enciclopedia Italiana* and, under the section discussing 'doctrine' the fundamental ideals were summed up by the regime's philosopher Giovanni Gentile who provided 'the theoretical foundation of Fascism as a socio-political system, based on the notion of the "ethical state"'. For Gentile 'in the ethical state the good fascist citizen is the individual who embodies the nation, while the nation represents a moral law binding together individuals and generations to come in a tradition and mission'. Gentile was against individualism and envisaged 'the state

---

5 The Catholic party.

as a totality' while considering Fascism as the natural development of the unifying efforts of the Risorgimento (Delle Vacche 1992: 95).

The totalitarian spirit of the regime was synthesized by Mussolini himself in his 'Doctrine' when he described Fascism as:

> definitely and absolutely opposed to the doctrines of liberalism, both in the political and economic sphere. . . . The State lays claim to rule in the economic field no less than in others; it makes its action felt throughout the length and breadth of the country by means of its corporate, social, and educational institutions, and all the political, economic, and spiritual forces of the nation, organised in their respective associations, circulate within the State.
> (Mussolini 1935: 41)

Indeed the fascist state did make 'its action felt' by absorbing the *sindacati* (unions) into corporations, controlled by the state, to which membership was compulsory for both employers and workers; by forbidding strikes and lockouts; by abrogating the article of the Constitution which allowed for the chambers to initiate legislation; by passing a new electoral law which restricted the eligibility to vote to 'men over twenty-one who paid contributions to the corporations . . . and men between eighteen and twenty-one who were or had been married' (Wiskemann 1969: 22–26).

Moreover, in order to ensure the 'circulation within the State' of 'all the political, economic and spiritual forces of the nation', associations were founded allegedly to benefit but practically to exert greater control over every aspect of individual life. When the Balilla (Fascist youth organization) was founded, the clash with Catholic youth organizations led to the abolition of the Catholic Scouts and it was at this point that an agreement with the Vatican became a necessity which would provide Mussolini with the control over the last spiritual stronghold and the Vatican with a vehicle of reinforcement of Christian values (as well as a substantial financial settlement). The Lateran Agreements were signed in 1929 and with it the Papal State was re-established, a financial settlement offered to the Pope and Catholicism was confirmed as the state's religion (Wiskemann 1969: 26–27).

If Mussolini successfully managed to settle the Roman question (the refusal of the Church to recognize the Italian state) his attempt at resolving the question of the South was less successful, with the *latifondisti* (landlords) rebelling against any policy aimed at reducing their complete power over the peasantry and at giving the workers a chance to voice their discontent deriving from unfair wages and unsuitable working conditions.

Notwithstanding the campaigns aimed at making Italy a self-sufficient nation and the government's intervention when at the time of the 1930s' depression the Bank of Italy faced collapse, Fascism's first priority was not economic growth. Fascism's main task was to forge a new Italian man and the Duce was to become the idealized model integrated within a regime supported by myths, symbols and leadership cults (Duggan 1994: 222). The cult of the Duce and that of ancient

Rome and its empire became a seemingly effective propagandistic move towards the attainment of solid consent. Spectacular parades and well-choreographed celebrations offered a façade of uniform intent and the safety of apparent mass approval. Moreover, leisure organizations offering after-work cultural activities, cheap children's holidays and family day trips became extremely popular and succeeded in 'penetrating the working classes', at least in the north and centre (Duggan 1994: 225). Yet the task of building the spiritual backbone of a national community required first a spiritual focus that Fascism could not or did not care to cultivate and second the lifting of the daily struggle for dignified survival faced by much of the population.

War and consensus

At the beginning of his second decade in government, aware of growing discontent both amongst the disillusioned intellectuals and the financially distressed working classes, Mussolini hoped to resurrect nationalistic spirit and awaken a sense of political purpose by leading the country into a war aimed at expanding Italian territorial domain and so begin the reconstruction of an empire emulating the greatness of the one built by the Romans. He invaded Ethiopia in 1935 and in 1936 he sent forces to Spain in support of General Franco against the Republicans. When the League of Nations imposed sanctions against Italy in disapproval of the Ethiopian war, trade towards Germany became more significant but, more interestingly, the now deeper incompatibility with democracy-loving Britain and France pushed Italy more confidently towards Hitler's Germany. Returning from his visit to Germany in 1938, Mussolini's political decision became a direct consequence of his admiration and desire to emulate his German role model. As well as a ridiculous 'reform of customs' (the handshake and certain forms of address were banned and the German goose step was adopted by the Italian army), anti-Semitic laws were introduced, censorship was made more effective and foreign policy became more aggressive, leading in 1939 to the signing of the Pact of Steel with Germany which, agreed upon with the understanding of Italy's lack of resources, was nevertheless a consent to Italy's involvement with a war the country was in no condition to fight, let alone win (Duggan 1994: 234–239).

On the assumption that it would only last a few weeks, on 10 June 1940 Mussolini announced to an unenthusiastic nation that Italy was entering the war. Besides the tempting opportunity to participate in the distribution of conquered territories after a victory gained with little effort, Mussolini was eager to emphasize how the war, by bringing some serious hardship to the bourgeois he now despised, would finally strengthen their character and make them worthy of his paternal leadership. The war did bring serious hardship and the expected few weeks of 'defensive' participation lasted five long and tragic years, marking the end of Mussolini's charismatic leadership, the collapse of the façade which held together a still fragile, inarticulate and demoralized national 'self' and the beginning of a search for the identity which Fascism had taken over rather than supported

Women in the fascist imaginary

The positioning of women within the fascist ideology is an apt example of the congruence of the fascist discourse with the authoritative moral guidance imparted by the Church, the latter providing directions and models already 'naturalized' into the collective consciousness throughout a spiritual unification which preceded by centuries the rather young and precarious political definition of Italy as nation.

Adultery, homosexuality, illegitimate desire and its consequences were not part of the imperialistic fascist 'imaginary' which was instead populated by 'prolific mothers and virile men' (Spackman 1996: 34). Already in the early 1920s Mussolini had in fact identified, in the drafting of his domestic policy, the vital contribution of women to the success of the regime. This contribution consisted of providing the country with 'births' (De Grazia, 1992: 41), an imperative which, while supposedly providing an abundance of cheap local labour and a quantifiable justification of the colonialist efforts, was to substitute women's individual identity with that of a biologically functional organ. The perpetuation of a supposedly superior race had thus isolated the purpose of womanhood to the carrying of a sacred womb and attempted to legalize and control its function by banning the use of contraceptives and by prescribing heavy penalties for illegal abortions in 1931 (De Grazia 1992: 58). Supportive of such sanctions the Church, which already offered as the only acceptable female model that of the virginal, all-suffering motherhood of Mary, contributed more specifically to its acceptance with the publication in 1930 of the papal encyclical *Casti Connubi* (literally 'chaste wedlock') in which Pius XI condemned birth control and abortion (De Grazia 1992: 58).

Notwithstanding the regime's measures to increase the number of births, the interwar years saw a definite demographic decrease and a marked increase in the number of abortions. As for other aspects of the dictatorship, 'results were ... incommensurate with intentions' (Mack Smith 1997: 353). The attempted control over conjugal sexuality did not have the desired effect, possibly because of the inevitability of women's emancipation, which had started at the turn of the century thanks to the necessities of industrialization that had taken women and their role out of the exclusively domestic sphere, or maybe because the messages of the regime were (characteristically) inconsistent and created doubts and anxieties in relation to motherhood. According to science (one supportive of the regime) women were, in fact, 'weak and imperfect in their generative apparatuses, intoxicated by voluptuary poisons and professional ambitions' and needed to be prepared for the 'sacred and difficult mission of maternity' (De Grazia, 1992: 54). This belief supported the exclusion of women from the public sphere and from the educational system (as teachers) on the basis of the supposedly dangerously 'sterilizing' effect of their presence (Spackman 1996: 34). Furthermore the ascertained inadequacy of women to fulfil their destiny of a motherhood extending beyond the physical act of giving birth needed state support which became manifest through typically fascist 'mother and baby' organizations such as the Opera Nazionale Maternità e Infanzia (ONMI).

But if statistics seem to provide evidence of a reluctance to deliver (literally) the much desired increase in cheap labour and potential citizens for the newly conquered colonies, the outcome of Mussolini's policies and the attitude of Fascism towards women is certainly reflected in and had an influence on the representation of women both in films produced during the regime and in the neo-realist films of the post-war years.

Italian cinema before neo-realism: images of the nation

The fascist regime's attempts to rebuild a 'national self' produced a temporary appearance of uniformity and a propagandistic image of a country founded on tradition, on a rural way of life and characterized by a grandiosity inherited from the newly mythologized figures of the Renaissance and of the Risorgimento (Forgacs 2000: 153). However, the realization of the revolutionary dream of bringing together the long divided segments back into a unified nation was a rather more complex affair from its origins. The fragmentations enforced through centuries of subsequent foreign invasions would not be painlessly and smoothly resolved neither with the abstract enforcement of new political borders, nor with the homologation of the educational system. As at the time of unification at least two thirds of the entire population was illiterate (Duggan 1994: 154) and only spoke and understood the local dialects, the effectiveness of what David Forgacs describes as the 'vertical communication network' in supporting the forging of a unified national image was to fall more directly on image aided media as well as on more direct forms of communication and propaganda mostly centred around the local church (2000: 152).

While the advent of radio and regular cinema newsreels in the early 1920s was significantly to improve the dissemination of information and have an impact on the emergence of an 'imagined' nation, Forgacs insists on the importance and effectiveness of other channels of communications such as popular songs, nationally established 'cults' (Garibaldi and Anita, Queen Margherita) and mass events (Forgacs 2000: 148) which, during the fascist period, served as unifying rituals (a typical example is the calling of couples to donate their wedding rings to finance the war in Ethiopia in 1935).

Although the influencing power of the moving image was only to be fully realized and channelled into political propaganda during the last few years of the fascist totalitarian regime, Italian silent cinema in the years preceding World War I is described by Marcia Landy as participating in the construction of a world 'which creates the illusion of wholeness and suggests a mastery over environments and opponents through its affective power and its focus on the efficacy of action' (Landy 2000: 7). This was done through an overall visual rhythm which saw 'parts ... continuously reassembled into a whole,' (Landy 2000: 7), by 'grouping actions, gestures, bodies, and decors in a motivated ensemble ... projecting a model of truth in relation to totality' (Landy 2000: 7, citing Rodowick

1997: 152). The historical epics, characteristic of this particular age of Italian cinema, as well as providing the ideal narrative structure to support this subtly ideological aesthetic, might be seen as correspondent, in the words of cinema historian Gian Piero Brunetta, to the manifestation of a 'pedagogic-didactical' vocation which masks the actual longing for international recognition and success through the exported image of an Italy founded on 'culture and past history'[6] (Brunetta 2001, Vol. 1: 146). Brunetta also suggests that in these years (preceding World War I) cinema is used as the place where collective desires, rather than fears, are channelled (Brunetta 2001, Vol. 1: 143), therefore signalling a lack and providing the imaginary, collective yet temporary satisfaction of a longing which remains, for years to come, unfulfilled; the longing for a sense of national unity.

This period in the history of Italian cinema is also characterized by the phenomenon of *divismo*, the early Italian equivalent to the Hollywood star system, which mostly related to female stars. *Divismo*, with 'its roots in the theatre and in operatic melodrama', involved in its translation into cinematic images 'the visualization of the feminine figure as the incarnation of fascination and desire' (Landy 2000: 5). *Cabiria* (1914), a film that traces the life journey of the eponymous heroine as she struggles to survive and maintain her chastity throughout the misfortune of the loss of her parents, her enslaving at the hands of Carthaginian pirates and kidnapping while under the protection of the aristocratic Sofonisba, is a classic example of such a phenomenon. While Cabiria is the 'passive receiver of others' effort to free her and return to her rightful land', Sofonisba, true to the spirit of *divismo* embodies the transgressive, languid, passionate female. Sofonisba, played by the then popular Italia Almirante Manzini, is the typical diva (literally a 'goddess'): she is powerful, passion driven, domineering and often destructive, and yet suffering and tormented (Landy 2000: 33–36).

The diva is forced, in most of the films of the early 1900s, 'finally (to) subjugate heterosexual desires to nationalistic aspirations', providing, according to Brunetta, a form of compensation for a 'prevailing sense of cultural and national inferiority on the part of the bourgeois public' (Landy 2000: 6). Most importantly, the woman's body has already become the site where disruptive desires are both expressed and feared. More specifically, in the historical epics, women stand as a reminder of the danger/fascination of sexual transgression as well as the embodiment of a new 'other', introduced by the colonizing efforts which, beginning with 1890 in Eritrea, continued into the years immediately preceding World War I and towards the end of the fascist period with the expansion in Libya and Ethiopia. The two female characters at the centre of *Cabiria* provide again a fitting example, with Cabiria and her submissive, innocent and passive attitude associated with a safe, weaker femininity, easily controlled and dominated and Sofonisba, who, with her sensuality and eroticism, becomes through her North African origin

6 Translation mine.

associated with a dark and alien world which, as such, needs to 'justifiably'[7] be brought under the dominion of a 'European' civilization (Landy 2000: 36).

After World War I, Italian cinema faced a crisis deriving, amongst other factors, from competition from the United States which was met with the unwillingness to shift to new technological and cinematic forms and narratives as substitutes for the now too expensive and not so popular historical epics. The advent of Fascism in 1923 coincides with the forming of the L'Unione Cinematografica Educativa (LUCE), an organization founded with the intention to serve as an educational and propagandistic medium which was to be nationalized in 1925, becoming a directly influencing tool of the fascist regime. If the Istituto LUCE was clearly bound to express the tenets of fascist ideology, the response of the rest of the cinema industry to the advent of a totalitarian regime was not homogeneous (Landy 2000: 36). As well as the popular 'telefoni bianchi' films (upper class comedies where the white telephones, considered a status symbol of the upper bourgeois, were an evident part of the mise-en-scène), films clearly supportive of Fascism such as Alessandro Blasetti's *Sole* (*Sun*, 1929) and *La Vecchia Guardia* (*The Old Guard*, 1934) were produced alongside others subtly critical of the political situation. Mario Camerini (*Gli Uomini, che Mascalzoni!*, 1932; *Il Signor Max*, 1937) and Ferdinando Maria Poggioli (*Ricchezza senza Domani*, 1940; *Sissignora*, 1942) were able to present audiences with both comedies and melodramas expressive of a growing anxiety and preoccupation with the destructive potential implicit in investing a single individual with unlimited power.

Mussolini did, indeed, order extensive cuts to Camerini's satirical *Il Cappello a Tre Punte* (1934), and yet his policy, with regards to the moving image, was one of active propaganda rather than of strict censorship, if only during the first decade of the regime. In fact newsreels emphatically descriptive of the achievements and grandiose projects undertaken by the fascist government were produced by the Istituto LUCE and projected before the screening of every commercial film. Italy is here presented as a country immune to crime and corruption and a haven where a rural way of life, aided and encouraged by the all-accomplishing fascist state, becomes the safeguard against the contaminating moral decay spreading across the western world (Landy 2000: 49–50).

Notwithstanding a growing nationalist attitude, foreign films were systematically imported and distributed with the imposition, by 1935, of the projection of two Italian films for every foreign screening, a strategy which, together with one of more direct financial support, helped boost the indigenous cinema industry. From 1938 production began to steadily increase while, thanks to new legislation which gave state monopoly to the importation of film, foreign films almost disappeared from Italian screens (Gundle 1990: 205).

---

7 In the perspective of the colonizer.

Censorship, more direct and severe with foreign films, where cuts, alternative endings and the shameless abuse of translation in dubbing were systematically requested, was, on the other hand, rather preventive with regard to national productions. The revision of screenplays before their shooting, as well as protecting the finished work from the knife of the censors, worked as an incentive for the filmmaker to act as self-censor and read his or her work in view of the possible anxieties deriving from any more or less overtly political message (Brunetta 2001, Vol. 2: 33–35).

Yet, as with other aspects of the dictatorship, the efficacy of control was inconsistent and the filtering often lax. As the journalist Ranieri Polese (2002) suggests in an article on the Italian newspaper *Il Corriere della Sera*, 'until 1943, Fascism was an imperfect dictatorship and even the cinema took advantage of it'. Indeed, it seems plausible to infer that, rather than using the media to directly impose a political ideology, the regime was instead preoccupied with presenting the country with an image of itself which, acting as a believable reflection, would work to reinforce or maybe create an easy to internalize self-image, an image of an empire reliant on the maintenance of delicate yet rigid class divisions and on the high moral stature of its people. Therefore, if censorship was not always sensitive to political satire, it would not tolerate suggestions of adultery, homosexuality and moral depravity as belonging to the limpid landscape of a virile, courageous, honest and industrious country. Moreover, the propaganda's emphasis on ritual, choreographically spectacular mass celebrations and ceremonies and on the mythologizing of history had to be ideally reflected in the films of the period.

It is thanks to the often obtuse choices of the fascist censors that Visconti's submission of a script for a film based on Verga's novel *L'amante di gramigna* was rejected while his adaptation of the American novel *The Postman Always Rings Twice* (which became his debut film *Ossessione* in 1942) unexpectedly passed. The inconsistency of the censors is also evident when considering the films by Mario Camerini of this particular period. Camerini, notwithstanding the cuts to one of his more directly satirical films, was somewhat able to insistently deliver a message subtly critical of the fascist ideology: although pervaded by an attitude of resignation to the rigidity of class structure, Camerini's films often stress the superficiality of the gains derived from indulging in 'the game of appearances, the game of social masks' (Brunetta 2001, Vol. 2: 256). His characters' typical attempts to borrow an identity from an upper class layer are systematically defeated with an emphasis (which in itself can be read as satire) on the potential happiness residing in the acceptance of one's inherited, if static, place in society.

Camerini's films, and his increasing desire to depict the reality of working-class life in Italy, although perhaps suffering from the economically necessary influence of Hollywood, prepare the way for the bolder approach of a more radically realist mode of filmmaking which will characterize post-war Italian cinematic production: the approach of neo-realism.

Neo-realism

Vittorio De Sica, Luchino Visconti and Roberto Rossellini are known as the undisputed 'fathers' of the Italian neo-realist movement, yet the term 'neo-realism' has become increasingly controversial and its use to describe a definitive body of work remains debatable. While stylistic uniformity was neither consistently attempted nor achieved, the films traditionally recognized as neo-realist were produced between 1942 and 1952 (however, these signposts are also frequently questioned) and are the expression of a genuine desire for a cinema committed to representing the truth. Indeed, the stylistic attributes as listed by Millicent Marcus – unlikely to all cohabit within the same piece of work – cannot alone determine a film's belonging to the 'movement':

> location shooting, lengthy takes, unobtrusive editing, natural lighting, a predominance of medium and long shots, respect for the continuity of time and space, use of contemporary, true-to-life subjects, an uncontrived, open-ended plot, working class protagonists, a nonprofessional cast, dialogue in the vernacular
>
> (Marcus 1986: 22)

On the other end both 'a deep ethical component that leaves its imprint as an openly stated pedagogical intent' (Torriglia 2002: 33), the 'active viewer involvement, and implied social criticism' (Marcus 1986: 22) and the directors' desire 'not just to record post-war society, but to suggest that events had a meaning' (Wood 2005: 89) are often considered to be the attributes from which the specific stylistic choices derived.

Cesare Zavattini, 'central theoretician of neo-realism', author of the scripts for the most famous neo-realist films and close collaborator of De Sica for most of his neo-realist adventures, confirmed the social/humanistic vocation of neo-realism when in 1953 he shared his belief as follows:

> The most important characteristic, and the most important innovation, of what is called neorealism . . . is to have realized that the necessity of the 'story' was only an unconscious way of disguising a human defeat, and that the kind of imagination it involved was simply a technique of superimposing dead formulas over living social facts. Now it has been perceived that reality is hugely rich, that to be able to look directly at it is enough; and that the artist's task is not to make people moved or indignant at metaphorical situations, but to make them reflect . . . on what they and others are doing, on the real things, exactly as they are.
>
> (Zavattini 2000: 50–51)

Taking into consideration the time frame within which neo-realism emerges, experiences its golden era and then declines, Zavattini's comment on a newly perceived richness in reality and the value he attributes to the unmediated reflection on the real can be understood as part of a 'reaction against the rhetorical insincerity and inhumanity of the fascist regime' (Shiel 2006: 13); a reaction which also motivates neo-realism's dedication to 'exploring and exposing the rhetorical lies of the fascist period and to confronting the social reality of the present' (Overbey 1978: 10).

In 1954, in an interview with Eric Rohmer and François Truffaut, Rossellini actually defined neo-realism as 'primarily a moral position which gives a perspective on the world. It then becomes an aesthetic position, but its basis is moral'. This 'moral position' is translated in a conscious refusal to indulge in the analysis of character or to focus on the fragmented exploration of action, privileging instead a documentary and unobtrusive style hoping to so capture a naturally 'narrativized' real and to provide a message emergent from the interaction of an active spectator with a cinematically reproduced social and physical environment which is the natural extension of his surrounding. Neo-realism's 'search for authentic human experience and interaction' and the interest of its directors in 'the visualization of the ordinary events and environments of Italian life' (Shiel 2006: 12–13) lead, paradoxically, to increasingly 'structured' attempts at minimalizing or eliminating any trace of classical narrative structure, focusing instead on chance motivations for movement and thematic development.

Nevertheless, the directors' attempt at defictionalizing their films in order for them to become 'documented' stories, to provide a clear, unmediated and objective view on history is, in these terms, ultimately flawed. Both the stories, the protagonists and the landscapes become visible to the spectators from within the director's field of vision and are selected at the expense of what he excludes. Indeed, the screen can at its best become the site where the inevitably subjective nature of representation offers the intermediate ground where a relative truth is negotiated between the projected and the perceived image of reality. Yet it is this unwilling 'subjectivity' that provides the most accurate historical documentation of a time as it is the unaware mediation of the artist that, as discussed in the previous chapter, allows for the emergence of a complex collective symbolism, affected by events and by political and philosophical currents. André Bazin did, in fact, describe neo-realism as 'a global description of reality by a global consciousness' as its 'realism is directed not at the choice of subject matter but at the process of awareness' (2000: 159), a process that both characters and spectators enter through 'seeing'.

Gilles Deleuze indeed suggests that what 'defines neo-realism is this build-up of purely optical situations . . . which are fundamentally distinct from the sensory-motor situations of the action-image in the old realism' (Deleuze 1989: 2). It is this fundamental change in the 'motivation' for movement which transforms the relationship of the viewer to the images: as the character becomes 'a kind of viewer' and 'records rather than reacts' (Deleuze 1989: 3), the spectator is also asked to just 'see'. Deleuze maintains that 'the identification is actually inverted' (Deleuze 1989: 3), yet it would be more accurate to say that identification(s) 'converge' in the act of seeing, of recording or viewing. The film becomes a journey across time and space rather than a pursuit of action: a search rather than a finding (*Ladri di Biciclette*, 1949),[8] a wandering rather than a going (*Germania Anno Zero*, 1948, *Europa '51*, 1952),[9] an elliptical journey of return rather than an outward projected arrival (*Bellissima*, 1951).[10] Deleuze describes the action as floating 'in the situation, rather than bringing it to a conclusion or strengthening it'. Despite everything remaining real, 'in this neo-realism between the reality of the setting and that of the action, it is no longer a motor extension which is established, but rather a dreamlike connection through the intermediary of the liberated sense organs' (Deleuze 1989: 4).

It is this 'dreamlike connection' between the reality of the setting and that of the action which brings the insignificant details of the surroundings into focus, often to elicit questions of meaning which the action itself cannot and is not meant to answer. The directors' choice to abstain from offering stabilizing if narrowing interpretations is possibly rooted, as Zavattini would have liked it, in their trust in the inherent power of an inquiry-inducing real, or, quite likely, in a belief that the questions 'had' to be moved out of the cinematic text and answered back in the context which produced it.

Because of this conscious surrender of the directors to the communicating power of an image that borrows its forms from reality to ask rather than gratuitously offer meaning, neo-realist films can be seen to represent, within a Jungian theoretical construct, a collective equivalent to personal dreams, and it is with an understanding of this analogy that they will be later analysed.

The directors

Luchino Visconti's career as film director begins in 1942 with *Ossessione* and it had its origin in his passionate work as a stage director, an activity which influenced his perception of background space and fuelled his desire to experiment with the moving image. In fact, theatrical productions filled the years between the releases of *Ossessione* (1943), *La Terra Trema* (1948) and *Bellissima* (1954). Although Visconti's personal insight into the effect of the political transformations taking place in Italy between the end of Fascism and the beginning of the process of reconstruction emerges as increasing disillusionment and 'scepticism about the value of progress', his interpretations of European and Italian history are founded on the translation onto the screen of a perspective which is essentially Gramscian. The Gramscian understanding of history as 'a process which remains external to men even when they are involved in it' is, in Visconti's oeuvre, somewhat balanced by the influence of the German-Hungarian philosopher Lukacs

---

8 *Bicycle Thieves*, Vittorio De Sica.
9 Rossellini.
10 Visconti.

with whom Visconti shared a belief in the function of the artist as 'interpreter of the world' and as capable of offering the 'most profound critique that could be made of bourgeois society' (Nowell-Smith 2003: 216).

Visconti's realism was from the outset – before he had read any Gramsci (published in Italy only in 1948) or Lukacs – more 'than a passive reflection on the world it surveyed but a way of entering into its very heart' (Nowell-Smith 2003: 217). Indeed, the director's belief in the value of 'a cinema of which Man (capital M) would be the measure' was already expressed in the article 'Anthropomorphic Cinema' which he wrote in 1943, and the attitude to realism as 'a critical enterprise' (Nowell-Smith 2003: 217) was certainly present in his early films.

However, the critical attitude together with Visconti's aristocratic, classical education and his proverbial attention to detail interfere with the free emergence of images of symbolic value in his films. Visconti's tight control over the construction of the image and of the film's structure makes it difficult to isolate elements inspired by an unconscious of either a collective or personal nature. As Nowell-Smith acutely pointed out 'it is not true that everything in Visconti is all there on the surface. Quite a lot is hidden. But it's there because he put it there and hidden because he hid it' (Nowell-Smith 2003: 222). Yet it also becomes evident, once the material of obvious personal origin is decanted (the homosexuality, the closeness to his mother, the dialectical relationship between his aristocratic origins and his Marxist ideals), how Visconti's 'work is far more revealing about the culture to which he belonged than of him as an individual artist' (Nowell-Smith 2003: 221). Indeed, this qualifies a search for collective unconscious material in his early work as relevant to the scope of this work.

Vittorio De Sica's directorial career also had its roots in the theatre. He formed his own theatre company in 1933 and never completely gave up his acting which brought him to fame in the 1920s both as a 'rivista'[11] performer and as protagonist in other directors' films. Although his first films as director may be understood as 'a natural outcome of his success on the music hall stage and in Camerini's film comedies', it was De Sica's desire to 'assume responsibility for his acting performance' (Armes 1971: 141) that provided him with the real motivation to direct his own films.

Although De Sica dismissed the role of art as an 'expression of political commitment' (Chiarini 1978: 145), there is in his work as director in the years from 1943 (which saw the beginning of a harmonious collaboration with screenwriter Cesare Zavattini) through to 1951 a social criticism and a tendency to 'moral pronouncements' (Chiarini 145) that expose a particular sensitivity to historical and political circumstances and reveal the impossibility of political

---

11 Described by Mira Liehm in *Passion and Defiance: Film in Italy from 1942 to the Present* (1984: 47) as a 'particularly Italian type of variety theatre . . . born at the end of the nineteenth century as a "review" (rivista) of political, literary, social, theatrical, and sports news'.

neutrality when adopting a style that is in itself a revolutionary artistic response to the ideological restraint of Fascism.

In an interview with Charles Thomas Samuels, De Sica emphatically insisted that neo-realism was not to be recognized by the authenticity of locales used. He added that neo-realism 'is not reality. It is reality filtered through poetry, reality transfigured' (Curle and Snyder 2000). His statement would indicate an understanding of the effect on reality of the artist's intervention, and the impossibility, at least through the medium of the neo-realist film, to objectively represent it. The only transformation neo-realism will consent to is, according to De Sica, a filtering through poetry, the artist's own language of emotions, which will transfigure the reality he is set to represent. De Sica's suggestion does not contradict the generally accepted description of neo-realism as a cinema 'dedicated . . . to confronting the social realities of the present' (Overbey 1978: 10). Yet it adds the possibility of the effect, on the finished work, of the artist's own emotional involvement with that 'present', an involvement which, because of the nature of artistic production (as discussed in Chapter 3) is only partially conscious.

Between 1942 and 1952 De Sica directed six films. Only four have been selected for a detailed analysis and these have been chosen because of the timing of their production which matches that of the films selected for Rossellini and Visconti, an important detail if the comparative analysis of the films reveals the presence of shared archetypal themes which then need to be related to the context of their emergence.

The almost unanimously acknowledged contribution from Rossellini to neo-realism is his internationally applauded *Roma Città Aperta* (*Rome Open City*, 1945), a film set in Rome during the German occupation of the capital in 1943 and shot soon after the liberation by the Allies. As for the rest of Rossellini's rich film production, the critics are often inclined to consider his previous directorial work, supportive of the fascist war efforts, and his shift to a more reflective, more traditionally constructed narrative in the films of the early 1950s, as a betrayal of the values and ideological tenets of neo-realism The spiritual, at times fully religious, essence of Rossellini's films after 1948, and his apparent shift of focus from the 'popular' streets (*Roma Città Aperta*, 1945; *Paisà*, 1946; *Germania Anno Zero*, 1948) to the more comfortable bourgeois interiors (*Europa '51*, 1952; *La Paura*, 1954 and to some extent *Viaggio in Italia*, 1953) created a diffidence in the critics and a lack of interest in the public that in Italy also remained unforgiving of his relationship with Ingrid Bergman at the expense of his previous partner Anna Magnani.

However, as Christopher Wagstaff, in discussing the relationship between Rossellini and neo-realism suggests: 'neo-realism . . . is not so much a matter of choice of subject and setting, as a new dramaturgy in the cinema; it replaces the dramaturgy of "givens" contained in genre cinema with a dramaturgy of search and discovery' (Wagstaff 2000: 40). And so within an understanding that through neo-realism 'the *function* of cinema became enquiry' and considering how 'neo-realist films ask, rather than confirm; they wonder, rather than reassure' (Wagstaff

2000: 40), Rossellini's work begins to show evidence of continuity. His commitment to the real is nevertheless possibly shadowed at times by a pedagogical intention which became increasingly central to his work and eventually led Rossellini to leave the cinema in favour of television, a medium he considered more adaptable and wide reaching as an educative tool.

Notwithstanding Rossellini's own defence of a consistency in his work confirmed by a developing 'theme of spirituality . . . his interest in human character or his pursuit of documentary enquiry' (Forgacs 2000: 5), judged within the rigid parameters of the critics who unsuccessfully tried to define the limits of neo-realism, he remains different. But it is Rossellini's difference that, while remaining possible in spite of an almost paradoxical belonging sealed by his often misread commitment to the real, provides another perspective, one which, possibly conditioned by a contrasting political vision, has nevertheless given life to images and narratives potentially rich in archetypal significance of precious comparative value.

Conclusion

This chapter has introduced the book's methodological approach. Subsequently, it has endeavoured to search in the history of Italian unification for the origin of the crisis of national identity which, I will argue, becomes visible in the films belonging to the movement universally known as neo-realism.

The seemingly detailed historical account is actually only a relatively brief overview of a process leading to the traumatic events that exacerbated an already weak sense of national 'self'. The 'passive revolution' that virtually excluded the masses from the making of what should have been 'their' country was only the beginning of a complex search for a unity which was obviously not guaranteed by geographical and political borders. The alternating attitudes of government leaders who offered moments of inconsistent liberal benevolence contradicted by actions dictated by economic and class interests might somewhat explain the apparent yielding of the masses to the rhetoric of an individual, capable of imposing authority and of managing the effects of violent control. Mussolini's coming to power, his policies and his confused doctrine will become points of reference in an understanding of the narratives of loss and of ineffective paternal authority of the post-war years.

In particular, this chapter has considered Fascism's attitude to, and the policies drafted in order to control and contain the danger of, women's emancipation. Although not always efficient in their desired effect, such policies remain the manifest expression of anxieties related to the perceived weakening of patriarchal control as a consequence of industrial progress, which asked for women to join the workforce outside of the domestic environment. Fascism's support of a strengthening of the supposedly agricultural vocation of Italy served both to reinforce with it the traditional image of the family and to redefine the nation as 'motherland' and associate its productiveness with the fertility and mothering vocation of its women. If women remained relatively impervious to the demographic demands of the regime, the effect of fascist propaganda on men's unconscious will become more transparently visible in the films supposedly inspired by principles of democracy and equality.

The development of cinema and its relationship to the historical and political transformation that the country underwent in an almost parallel period of growth has been analysed in this chapter in order to contextualize the thematic and stylistic changes which led to the birth of neo-realism. Generic developments and the phenomenon of *divismo* have been considered as reflective of sociopolitical climates and attitudes while Fascism's belated awareness and abuse of the cinematic medium as a tool of propaganda and its final tightening of the rules of censorship are seen as catalysts of a reaction which manifests itself as a new, uncompromising commitment to the real in the films produced during World War II and immediately after.

Neo-realism was, however, more than just a reaction to the totalitarian regime which the movement outlived by at least a decade: its aesthetic was the visualization of an ideology of integration. Undeniably motivated by a 'political will to create an "other" cinema for Italy in the immediate post-war context', neo-realism was also the place that allowed a coexistence of 'variations of the idea of realism and for many variants of otherness' (Nowell-Smith 2000: 9). The seemingly possible cohabitation of various political approaches in the government set up immediately after the war (Communists, Socialists and Christian Democrats) was, indeed, consistent with a cinema which, in reflecting that reality, was the voice of one people rather than of one party. The way that voice became images and delivered both collective conscious aspirations and the unconscious patterns which trace the development of a national consciousness will be discussed in the next chapters.

Secondo tempo

Chapter 5

1942–1945

War and archetypes: an orphan nation with a legacy of murder

> Lady Macbeth: Out, damned spot! out, I say! One; two: why, then 'tis time to do't. Hell is murky! Fie, my lord, fie! a soldier, and afeard? What need we fear who knows it, when none can call our power to account?
>
> (Shakespeare, *Macbeth*, Act 5, Scene 1)

Introduction

Italy entered World War II in June 1940. The expected brief engagement of the previously declared 'non-belligerent' country was to last five long years and it would bring the collapse of Fascism, the humiliation of unconditional surrender and the confusion and uncertainty of unevenly shifted loyalties in the difficult transition to new Allies and to a new form of government.

The events leading to Mussolini's dismissal and subsequent arrest in July 1943 provide the context of production for three of the five films discussed in this chapter, a context which is profoundly transformed by the delayed signing of the armistice on 8 September of the same year. As the Allied invasion brought the fighting to Italian soil, the films produced between 1943 and the end of the conflict reflect the changes in both the political and physical landscape as the directors' lens is finally set to 'objectively'[1] document the extent of the confusion, suffering and destruction experienced by a people who struggled to retrace and rebuild a worthy definition of nationhood.

For this reason the chapter is divided, according to chronological criteria, into two parts each with a conclusion that, drawn from the detailed analyses of the films of the period, reflects on the possible translation of the symbolic and mythological content of the films into the meaningful dynamic of a psychological process which, akin to the one leading to the emergence of individual ego-consciousness, suggests a direction for the development and/or reconstruction of a national identity. A description of the fallacious strategic choices that gradually

---

1 Here understood as the directors' claim.

isolated Mussolini, alienated him from his own government and attracted the resentment of the people who found themselves reluctantly fighting a war in the name of his personal ambitions, precedes the analysis of the films produced by the elected directors during these years.

In the period between 1939 and 1943 Rossellini directed three films thematically linked by a war subject and supportive, to a certain extent, of the fascist ideology. The film selected for a detailed analysis is *Un Pilota Ritorna* (*A Pilot Returns*, 1942), chosen because of its context of production close to that of Visconti's *Ossessione* (1943) and of De Sica's *I Bambini ci Guardano* (*The Children Are Watching Us*, 1943) released in close succession. Both Rossellini's and De Sica's films, although still suffering from the fascist legacy of sentimental rhetoric and idealized gender relations, display the unequivocal pull towards a realism which will become increasingly central and more consciously committed in the years immediately following the fall of Fascism. *Ossessione*, on the other hand, is recognized by most critics as the cornerstone of neo-realist production and, although based on the American novel *The Postman Always Rings Twice* (James. M. Cain, 1946) and undoubtedly influenced by French realism and by Visconti's Marxist ideals, it actually dared to bring to the screen the reality of an Italy that Fascism had long tried to negate.

While all three films deal with the difficulties or impossibility of heterosexual (as well as homosexual) relationships, the children's presence, central in De Sica and only brief in Visconti's and Rossellini's films, acquires value in relation to the events contemporary to the films' production. This value and its symbolic significance, together with that of the father's absence and the representation of motherhood, will be discussed in the individual analyses and brought together in the first conclusion.

The second part of the chapter, after a brief discussion of the difficult shifting of loyalties and of the rising and function of the Resistance movement during the last two years of the war, introduces the two films produced in this period: *La Porta del Cielo* (*The Gate of Heaven*, 1944) by De Sica and *Roma Città Aperta* (*Rome Open City*, 1945) by Rossellini. If the latter has become one of the most widely appreciated and discussed films of the Italian director, the former is often omitted from De Sica's filmography and rare available copies are only found in specialist archival collections. Nevertheless, the unwillingness to single out and dedicate privileged narrative attention to a central character, the running theme of solidarity and the focus on the vicissitudes of the working classes, on their poverty and on their true aspirations together with a predilection for non professional actors, should certainly identify this film as an example of neo-realism. The relationship between the Church and the Resistance and their attitude towards the past are discussed throughout both films' analyses, while the relevance of the images of suggested archetypal significance is argued first within the films' narratives and then given contextualized reflection in the conclusion. Moreover, the distinctive centrality of a decidedly Catholic iconography and the seemingly ideological predominance of a Christian perspective will be reviewed within a Jungian theoretical construct in order to then relate their symbolic value to the social substratum which shaped their emergence and to understand their function as catalysts of change.

1942–1943: leaving the Father's house

The immediate historical precedent

On 10 June 1940 Italy entered World War II on the side of Nazi Germany. Partially blinded by the possibility of easy territorial gains and partially misinformed as to the readiness, efficiency and technical competence of his army, Mussolini single-handedly decided the fate of a country clearly unprepared for a conflict of such proportions. Having appointed himself as 'supreme military commander' and ignoring the king's constitutional claims to such position, Mussolini had taken full responsibility and, he hoped, full glory for his impulsive decision. Believing the war would only last another few weeks he hoped to manage a 'defensive war' which, at the 'cost' of a few thousand deaths, would earn him a place at the peace negotiations table (Mack Smith 1997: 403–405). However, as there was not an immediate threat of attack or invasion coming from either Britain or France, Mussolini found himself unable to justify rationally and strategically his bellicose intention. His call to arms became then a supposedly necessary reinstatement of the right to exist as a people as well as an ideological battle against the democratic forms of government he so despised and associated with corrupt capitalism. The words he used in the speech that announced the declaration of war set the scene:

> Fighters of the land, the sea and the air, Blackshirts of the revolutions and of the legions, men and women of Italy, of the Empire, and of the kingdom of Albania.
> Listen – the hour marked out by destiny is sounding in the sky of our country. This is the hour of irrevocable decision. The declaration of war has already been handed to the Ambassadors of Britain and France.
> We are going to war against the plutocratic and reactionary democracies of the West, who have hindered the advance and often threatened the existence even of the Italian people.
> (Benito Mussolini, speech declaring war on the Allies, 10 June 1940)[2]

Yet the fervour of a war fought in the name of class and ideology did not penetrate the spirit of an army which, notwithstanding the depiction in the fascist

---

2 From Spartacus Educational website, available at www.spartacus.schoolnet.co.uk/2WWitaly.htm (accessed 5 June 2007).

propagandistic campaigns of an organized, courageous and well-armed body, was instead badly equipped, unmotivated and confused by orders of questionable military logic. Italian intervention began with the sending of troops to France in the hope of making an entrance before the signing of the armistice France had already asked for. But by the time the armistice with Nazi Germany was signed only a 'slight penetration into Savoy had been made' by the Italians at a disproportionally great cost in lives and equipment with not much to show for it and none of the hoped for territorial gains. The failure of the African campaign, in the winter between 1940 and 1941, added to the disillusionment as the Italian troops were chased out of Egypt, one hundred thousand men were taken prisoner and the colonies of Eritrea, Somalia and Addis Ababa were lost (Mack Smith 1997: 407).

Rossellini's film *Un Pilota Ritorna* is the story of a pilot involved in an air attack on Greece which ends with his capture by the British. Notwithstanding the display of courage and abnegation attributed to the seemingly confident and competent Italian military, the film also represents the British enemy as gentlemanly and humane and the prospect of fighting the Greeks not as palatable as that of returning home. Indeed the Greek campaign was not a proud page of the history of Italy at war: with no other reason to invade than Mussolini's irritation at Hitler's sudden occupation of Romania, the badly timed attack ended within a few days with a full retreat and put Italy in the embarrassing position of having to ask for Germany's intervention (Mack Smith 1997: 407).

By January 1943 half of the armies Mussolini had sent to the Russian front in 1941 were lost and by July of the same year the Allies were finally landing in Sicily. Rossellini's last of the fascist war trilogy films presents an unusual aspect of the failing Russian campaign: the spiritual rescue of a Bolshevik woman who, thanks to the example and guidance of an Italian Catholic priest, is converted to Christianity. It is possibly not coincidental that all three of these pre-armistice films by Rossellini, although intended as supportive of the fascists war, display very little interest in military excellence and rather focus on examples of Italian moral and spiritual superiority: the clear and sacrificial answer to duty, the subordination of personal fulfilment to military economy and the power to redeem souls 'lost' to Communism.

By the time of the Allies' landing, which marked the beginning of an advance on the mainland and confirmed the weakness of the Italian army, general discontent and feelings of disillusionment and diffidence towards Fascism had already materialized in the industrial cities of the north in the form of the 'great strike wave during March 1943'. The strikes, only partially originating from the disappointment with the poor war performance, were also a reaction to more pressing physical conditions – bombing, shortages of food and fuel, inflation – and succeeded in alerting the industrialists to the need to turn to Britain and America and to sabotage war production (Ellwood 1985: 13). Yet, rather than being overthrown by oppositional revolutionary forces, the collapse of the regime was manufactured from within. Increasingly aware of both growing popular discontent and of the irremediable weakness of a practically systematically defeated army, a swelling group of fascist party leaders eventually considered the removal from office of Mussolini as the only hope for survival. When Rome was finally bombed by the Allies in July 1943, realizing that Mussolini would not take a stand to defend the country even at this disastrous stage in the war, the king, who had been quietly awaiting the opportunity to safely return power into traditional hands, made his intentions known to Marshall Badoglio and General Ambrosio, who then acted in his name. After a dramatic meeting of the Gran Consiglio a motion was approved to 'limit' Mussolini's authority, and on 25 July the king quickly appointed Badoglio as premier and had Mussolini arrested (Mack Smith 1997: 413–414).

News of the fall of the regime and of Mussolini's arrest were greeted with unanimous popular rejoicing. Yet the war was not over and the newly appointed prime minister was not an anti-fascist, rather an army marshall who had supported Mussolini's efforts and who did not hesitate to use old fascist laws not only to severely repress subsequent strikes and demonstrations but also to dissolve the anti-fascist committees which begun to form in the main cities of the north and centre (Ellwood 1985: 14).

The fighting continued with Italy on the German side for another six weeks and the king, afraid of taking a clear stand against Hitler, delayed the signing of an unconditional surrender with the Allies who needed the co-operation of the Italians to secure their victorious penetration of the peninsula in order to push the Germans out and finally to eradicate Fascism. However, after signing a 'short' version of the armistice on 3 September, Badoglio tried to disregard the agreed terms and withdrew the military support promised for the landing at Salerno, afraid of having to defend Rome alone. When Eisenhower, in response to Badoglio's change of heart, announced Italy's unconditional surrender – thus attracting a German response – Badoglio and the king fled to the South. On 29 September a full version of the armistice was signed. Immediately afterwards Eisenhower himself described the armistice as the granting of full control and as a 'full capitulation by Italy' (Ellwood 1985: 39).

Change had again come for Italy through an agent different from the people who made up the nation, different from the people who worked, hungered, lived in fear and had, with weak fervour, obeyed a paternal voice whose authority without coherence had manipulated them into a near fatal illusion. The following films were produced between 1942 and 1943.

Un Pilota Ritorna (A Pilot Returns, *1942*)

A mother's darling

Rossellini's *La Nave Bianca* (*The White Ship*, 1941) and *Un Pilota Ritorna* (*A Pilot Returns*, 1942) are part of what is called his 'fascist war trilogy' (completed with *L'Uomo della Croce* (*The Man with the Cross*, 1943): a set of films supportive of Italian intervention and adulatory of a heroic Italian spirit. Each of the films concentrates on a branch of the military, respectively the navy, the air force and the armoured infantry.

Women's presence, in all three films, is peripheral. In both *La Nave Bianca* and *Un Pilota Ritorna* their participation in the war effort is more iconical than practical. In fact, it soon becomes evident how in these first three films of his directorial career Rossellini's policy is one of distancing and it suggests a sexual segregation justified by the practical urge for the specificity of roles required in war.

The first film tells of the wounded sailors of a warship and follows the men as they are transferred to a hospital ship. Before the enemy attacks their ship, the men skip through a photo album, more like a catalogue of women's faces. They are the war-godmothers who write to the soldiers in order to keep their hopes and visions alive. Falling in love with them is a safe concession to a sexuality which would otherwise function as a distraction from the discipline of war. The recognition by one of the men of his war-godmother as one of the nurses on board and the danger of emerging individuality is quickly contained by a reminder of the woman's changed role: 'a nurse is the godmother of all who suffer and we must not make distinctions', a comment which emphasizes an anonymity already granted on both sides by the uniforms.

The comment, by forcing emerging individuality back into an anonymous collective, also transcends the contingency of the narrative and becomes an opportunity to understand an attitude towards women certainly influenced by two decades of insistent, if practically ineffective, demographic policy which had concentrated on singling out childbearing as a woman's destiny. Notwithstanding women's weak response to the regime's demands for intensively prolific marital unions, Mussolini's direct suggestions somewhat penetrated the cultural collective and psychologically conditioned the spontaneity of heterosexual relationship. The extreme emphasis on motherhood would have supported, if effective, a hypertrophy and an intensification in women of the maternal instinct which should lead, according to Jung, to unconsciously identifying man as an 'instrument of procreation' and to regard him 'merely as an object to be looked after, along with children, poor relations, cats, dogs, and household furniture' (*C.W.*, Vol. 9i: para. 167). Despite women's statistically proven unresponsiveness, the powerful propaganda and the public rewarding of mothers of large families would point to men's auxiliary role in the process of procreation and produce the 'effect' of the desired 'hypertrophy' and intensification of the maternal instinct without necessarily finding correspondence in its existence.

In *Archetypes and the Collective Unconscious*, Jung describes how this particular expression of the mother complex has as a consequence the development in women of an 'Eros' exclusively functioning within the 'maternal relationship while remaining unconscious as a personal one', a dangerous outcome as according to Jung 'an unconscious Eros always expresses itself as a will to power' (C.W., Vol. 9i: para. 167). In a country where the Catholic Church could rely on state policies for the support of the maternal model of womanhood as the natural goal of female development, that danger is possibly more readily perceived. The consequences of such awareness will become clear in later films. *Un Pilota*

Ritorna is exemplary of a separation made inevitable by technology and rendered physically visible by a war vehicle, the fighter aircraft, which takes men to heights and eventually to a freedom unavailable to women.

A pilot, captured during a bombing raid in Greece, meets and falls in love with a local girl who assists her doctor father. Her assistance is, however, never portrayed as indispensable: she takes temperatures, wipes sweat, tucks youngsters under blankets and shares comforting words but her refusal to choose marriage and to escape with the man she loves is not justified in reality, except in an acknowledgment of the impediment she would represent to the fulfilment of male duty. Before escaping on a stolen enemy aircraft the pilot gives the girl his father's gold pocket watch, his precious good luck charm (see Figure 5.1).

The remembrance gift she is given is supposedly that of a past to cherish and look after. Yet it also seals her fate to a life of imprisonment in waiting anonymity. It condemns her to the impossibility of choice, having been elected to represent an ideal of chastity, innocence and obedience to a worthy father and of dutiful wife to an improbable husband who has already imposed a limitation by describing her as a 'sensible little woman'.

The watch is delivered to the girl soon after she has promised she will wait 'forever'. Neumann in his analysis of the Great Mother Archetype suggests that 'the Feminine is ... the goddess of time' (Neumann 1963: 226), representing a wholeness which precedes the differentiation brought by consciousness. The response to the suggested timelessness of the girl's waiting is one of containment. The old 'father's watch' forces the borderless maternal, the all-embracing and dangerously devouring feminine (characteristics of the Great Mother Archetype

Figure 5.1 How long is forever? It will be determined by his father's watch. *Un Pilota Ritorna*. Roberto Rossellini (1942). (Thanks to Roberto Rossellini's Estate).

as discussed by Neumann) into the discerning specificity of the masculine. The acceptance of separation as a consequence of an obedience to a father (duty) whose requests can be difficult to understand might signal the imminent solution of an Oedipal journey, yet the offering to a mother figure of what is left of the paternal is forecasting a regression. It works as an attempt at pacifying a possibly castrating feminine (accidentally the girl assists her father in amputating a soldier's leg) before fleeing back 'home' to an unfinished letter to a distant and harmless biological mother.

Symbolically the offering of an instrument of timekeeping which, although described by the young man as 'ugly', has the function of preserving a 'good', longed for past, might also work as a hopeful impregnation. The equivalent is to be found in Greek mythology: Cronos, the Greek god of time, after castrating his father Uranus, eats his own children in order to avoid the fulfilment of the prophesy which would see him killed by one of them in retribution. His wife Rhea gave birth to her sixth son Zeus in secrecy and gave Cronos a stone to eat instead. There is, possibly, in the giving of the watch as a substitute for a fulfilling love story, a desire to preserve that which might otherwise be eaten up. Mussolini's engagement with the Futurist art movement spelt out a passion for modernity and his attitude towards the past was one of reverence rather than of preservation. The inheritance from the past was a destiny of greatness but there was neither longing nor nostalgia for the past in the fascist perspective.

The uncertainty of the war objectives, the failure of fascist propaganda to provide an enemy worthy of hatred is visible in this and in the following film by Rossellini. Both the British and the Greeks are portrayed as human and communicative despite the language barrier, a detail emphasized by a dialogue which remains untranslated. Moreover, the pilot's heroism, rather than a resoluteness to fight, emerges as a willingness to go 'home'. As the girl suggests, it is his duty to go back but it is ultimately a duty to return to a fatherless mother and accept a destiny of son-lover.

L'Uomo della Croce transfers the healing role previously conceded to women to the ministers of the Church. A war chaplain sacrifices his life in order to succour a wounded Russian. Throughout the film his role is that of representing 'Mother Church' as healing, soothing, comforting and reassuring. The impossible coexistence with another motherly presence is confirmed by women's need for redemption as he succeeds in converting a Bolshevik woman to Catholicism. The Church's role as a safer alternative to the dangers of feminine sensuality and to the proven uncertainty of a politically defined Mother country will be more evident in Rossellini's post-war films.

Ossessione *(1943)*

Dying to be a father

Geoffrey Nowell-Smith has described *Ossessione* as 'a film about the destructive power of sexual passion' (Nowell-Smith 1967: 19). *Ossessione*, released in 1942, although generally excluded from the category of purely neo-realist films, marks both stylistically and thematically the beginning of the discussion of politics and participation that neo-realism was to become as well as the beginning of Visconti's career as film director. The film is based on James M. Cain's novel *The Postman Always Rings Twice* (first published in 1934). It is the story of the unhappily married Giovanna who falls in lust (not quite in love) with a handsome tramp Gino who eventually helps her to murder her husband. The substantial insurance she collects at her husband's death could mean a new beginning for the lovers but the shadow of their illicit past is soon isolating them from an unforgiving society and from each other. Both Giovanna's pregnancy and her tragic death serve to reconcile her with Gino and with society.

At the beginning of the film Giovanna is allowed to lead the narrative forward. Her light-hearted song attracts the attention of Gino who stands within the kitchen doorframe waiting for her to notice him. His gaze does not receive subjective authority as the shot positions him, seen from behind, between Giovanna and the camera lens. The counter-shot is a close up of Gino's face, stating his passivity and containment within Giovanna's dangerously sensual gaze. His objectification is complete when she remarks that his shoulders are horse-like (a comment lost in the English subtitles), emphasizing not only the physicality of her attraction but also the wild, primitive and unashamed nature of her desire. Although Gino responds to her gaze he quickly re-establishes her maternal role of provider of nourishment as he comments on her culinary skills. By paying for his food he is, however, stating his independence from the maternal, a dependence she is not prepared to renounce. By telling her husband that Gino hasn't paid for his meal she calls him back to the house.

The image of the 'disorderly woman' has been invested before not only with the power of providing wider behavioural options for women but also with the function of sanctioning 'riot and political disobedience for both men and women' within otherwise oppressive societies (Zemon Davies 1975: 169). While this was most probably Visconti's conscious intention, Giovanna's portrayal is still trapped between the prescriptions of an ideology a lot older than the 20 years of the fascist regime and one too young to understand the necessity for unconditional equality. Giovanna is not a mother and her pregnancy becomes an issue only towards the end of the film, and yet her first moment of rebellion against the institutionalized violence of marriage is marked by a symbolism which, in suggesting the possibility of conception, justifies and dilutes the potential danger of her sensuality. When her husband succeeds in bringing Gino back to the house, Giovanna pulls out a basket of eggs and, while engaging in a sensual and subtly intimate verbal exchange with him, she intently caresses them. Besides the obvious connection between this mindless gesture and Giovanna's subconscious desire and/or awareness of her destiny as mother, the egg is also a reminder of the containing nature of motherhood. In ancient matriarchal symbolism 'the old cosmic egg [is] the universally known symbol of the primordial matriarchal world, which as Great Round contains the universe' (Neumann 1963: 328). Within it the bipolarity characteristic of the archetype of the Great Mother is synthesized by the depiction of both a white and a black half. In Erich Neumann's words:

> Just as world, life, nature, and soul have been experienced as generative and nourishing, protecting and warming Femininity, so their opposites are also perceived in the image of the Feminine. ... For this woman who generates life and all living things on earth is the same who takes them back into herself, who pursues her victims and captures them with snare and net.
> (Neumann 1963: 149)

In calling upon an idealization of woman as essentially maternal, Fascism might have awakened an awareness of the power associated with this image. The consequence of advocating a certain 'hypertrophy of the Maternal Element' is again the possibility of a realization in women of the secondary importance of men. Neumann reminds us of the role 'played (from prehistoric times) by the divine kings, who had either to kill themselves or be killed when ... they could no longer guarantee fertility' (Neumann 1954: 57). This predicament is fulfilled in *Ossessione* when Giovanna's husband is killed soon after his mentioning of a desire for a son. Her willingness to kill and the consequent distancing from Gino have both a psychological and a political meaning.

The newly found courage to face the darkness of her condition is guiding Giovanna towards consciousness, a movement which implies the temporary loss of the beloved. In the well-known tale by Apuleius, Psyche, guided by what Neumann calls 'the cruel militancy of the matriarchate' (Neumann 1956: 78) is prepared to kill the 'monster' (Eros) she believes her husband to be. That 'monster', the one who keeps her captive, must die to allow for a true encounter with the masculine. She is aware that the light of consciousness might mean the loss of both the diurnal safe but lonely domesticity and the nocturnal, secretive sexual bliss. Giovanna's narrative follows this process and she does indeed lose Gino not once but four times until he finally returns when her pregnancy gives them both the illusion of omnipotence and immortality. Her death, unlike the deathly sleep of Psyche which her lover Eros now freed from maternal dependence can restore to life, is a final dismissal which restores the balance that Giovanna had temporarily upset.

Politically, Gino's departures and Giovanna's initial reluctance to leave her husband's house serve as a condemnation of Fascism. Giovanna's first return to her domineering husband exposes the degeneration of the institution of the family to a sort of 'institutionalized prostitution propped up by a capitalist ethos' (Bacon 1998: 21). In a country where poverty and deprivation were the reality masked by the glowing facade that the regime was adamant to maintain, sexual passion was a relatively unproductive commodity easily replaced by 'petit bourgeois aspirations, carping domesticity and avarice' (Caldwell 2000: 135–136). The murder of the husband, which remains visually concealed, is the elimination of a father figure who seems deserving of death because of his stupidity, self-centredness and abusive attitude rather than wickedness. His older age justifies the murder psychologically as it confirms the unfolding of an Oedipal act where, as father, he represents the obstacle to a union which, as the film narrative suggests, is destined to happen. However, it is Giovanna's suspiciously greedy motivation, rather than Gino's redeemable sexual obsession, which calls for the ultimate punishment.

Both morally and politically Giovanna's death takes place early in the narrative. Soon after being denied the blessing of their union by the minister of a Church preoccupied more with 'gossip' than with the salvation of the soul, the lovers are sitting in the kitchen. A presence appears within the doorframe calling Giovanna's name. Occupying the space previously taken by Gino's first appearance is a darkly clad old woman holding a sickle, an unmistakable image of death, so closely related, spatially, to the object of Giovanna's first desiring gaze and, temporally, to the priest's refusal, to suggest a reference to a Catholic association of sexual desire with the death of the soul (see Figure 5.2).

Later in the film, when after collecting the life insurance a jealous Giovanna threatens to inform the police, Gino's reaction is violent. The surrounding crowd seems to come closer in order to watch rather than interfere and then follows Gino's trajectory as he turns to walk away, joining him in an almost ritual abandonment. Demaris Wehr points out that 'the very worst punishment a society can inflict on its members is exclusion' (Wehr 1987: 17), and in a sense this works as an execution, a social death. While legitimized prostitution can be overlooked, legalized theft will be punished (an attitude in full contrast with that of Fascism) not with violence but with indifference. Notwithstanding his violence, Gino represents a country passive and overtaken by events and naively free from

Figure 5.2 Death calling. *Ossessione*. Luchino Visconti (1943). © MARZI Srl. All rights reserved. Courtesy RIPLEY'S FILM Srl.

economic ties. Giovanna is the seductress and the calculator, representing the other Italy, a petit bourgeois accepting and participating in theft and corruption in the name of apparent economic stability. Isolating Giovanna becomes, then, a metaphor for a silent rebellion, a mirroring of a course of action possibly adopted by the intellectuals towards the corruption and greed of the regime.

At the end of the film Giovanna is reintroduced with her pregnancy within the acceptable structure of the family and paradoxically her physical death coincides with the resurgence of the image of the 'good' woman, willingly giving up her aspirations, her independence, her body and her life in order to be a mother. Her death is caused by Gino's inability to 'see', reminiscent of the Oedipal epilogue, as the fatal car accident is a consequence of the thick fog which the lovers encounter in their final fleeing journey. Giovanna's attempt at reforming the nuclear familial structure within an economic stability inherited through murder can only lead to death. It is also a dead end for Gino, who had the opportunity earlier in the film to opt for both the political commitment represented by the homosexual Spanish friend he meets on the train, and the innocent devotion of the 'good' prostitute, Anita, who offers him comfort and shelter. Visconti's message is a warning: the killing of obtuse leaders will not in itself bring change if sexuality and economy remain tied to the petit-bourgeois values which the regime has validated, values which are incarnate in the attractive yet deathly sensuality of a woman who, in line with fascist ideology, is decidedly a 'mother'.

Besides the archetypal attributes of the Great Terrible Mother embodied by Giovanna, the film is also enriched by a clearer personification of an archetype: the archetype of the child. When Giovanna confesses her pregnant status to Gino, a little girl never clearly introduced by the narrative suddenly appears in the corridor. A little girl will appear again at the end of *La Terra Trema* (*The Earth Trembles*, 1948) and throughout *Bellissima* (1951) as a representation of preserved innocence and of a potential spiritual growth. Gino asks the little girl, 'Do you think I'm bad?' – spelling out Visconti's characters' shameful relationship with their future: hopeless in *Ossessione* because of the claustrophobic containment of the fascist regime, ideologically hopeful yet practically fallacious in *La Terra Trema* with the enthusiasm of reconstruction disintegrating against a fear that holds progress tied to negative traditions, and disillusioned in *Bellissima* (1951) at a time when change is only apparent and social structures based on class division prove resilient to change.

The appearance of the little girl is indeed, because of the anonymity and inexplicable belonging of her character to the narrative, of archetypal significance. Jung suggests that 'the essential feature of the child motif is its futurity' and adds that the child 'paves the way for a future change of personality' and it is a 'symbol which unites the opposites, a mediator, bringer of healing, that is one who makes whole' (*C.W.*, Vol. 9i: para. 278).

Indeed, as both Jung and Neumann point out, it is not surprising to find that many of the mythological and religious saviours are 'child gods' representative of development and wholeness, of beginning and end (*C.W.*, Vol. 9i: para. 278). The fact that Visconti's child here and in *La Terra Trema* is a girl is an admission of a presence, of a possibility for redemption antithetical to the one offered by the Church. This possibility rests on a confrontation that in the two films is expressed through rhetorical questioning, psychologically translatable as a need for a confrontation with a Feminine demanding of self-reflection and revision. Her demands, however, are nullified respectively by passivity, lack of solidarity, deceit and later (in *Rocco and his Brothers*, 1960) by murder.

I Bambini ci Guardano (The Children are Watching Us, 1943)

The deadly price of relatedness

If *I Bambini ci Guardano* somehow disrupts 'the unquestioned conflation of women with motherhood and family that was to be found in the policies and statements of Fascism' (Caldwell 2000: 131), it also reinstates the inevitability of a patriarchal order where women's role is subordinate to men's own organization of society. The film is a comment on the fragility of the institution of the family in petit-bourgeois Italy between the wars, with a narrative centred on a child, Prico, who witnesses the breaking up of his parents' marriage and suffers the consequences of their indifference and irresponsibility.

Prico's adulterous mother abandons her family to escape with her lover only to return home in order to nurse her sick child. In a miserable attempt to re-establish the acceptable façade of familial happiness she spends a few days in a holiday resort with her husband and son. While the husband returns to his tedious job she is left behind to enjoy a longer holiday with the child. However, her lover reappears and the two decide to enjoy the last few days of freedom before her return home. The abandonment of the child in the blind search for sexual satisfaction receives full narrative attention and forms the strong emotional lead into the film's tragic conclusion. The child returns home alone and is taken to a priest-run orphanage where his mother will visit him to break the news of the father's suicide. The justification and catharsis afforded to the murderous and adulterous Giovanna in Visconti's *Ossessione* through conception and death find no equivalent in De Sica's narrative resolution, yet the message of the impossibility of the coexistence of motherhood with desire is delivered through the infliction of the equally fatal punishment of isolation.

The opening sequence settles the moral tone of the film. A group of children is watching a puppet show set in the park: the Neapolitan marionettes are violently fighting each other for the love of a girl who only comes to the stage at the end of the fight as the deserved prize for the victorious Pulcinella. One of the children in the audience, put off by the violence, refuses to watch, but the mother insists on him watching what is supposed to be natural and entertaining. The same scene appears later in Prico's delirious feverish dream, only this time the girl standing between the lovers gets the worse of the beating. Not only do the two episodes expose the objectification of the woman and her passivity as she is conquered and possessed through fighting, but there is also the director's preoccupation with the blurred margins between love and violence, desire and death filtered through the innocent eyes of the witnessing children, a theme De Sica will take further in *Sciuscià* and in *Ladri di Biciclette* (*Bicycle Thieves*).

Prico's innocence is a pretext that mitigates his acts of condemnation of a desire which he has learnt to associate with violence and separation from his mother. In the three episodes of physical intimacy to which he is witness his reactions change from the curiosity which leads him to accidentally drop a plant pot on his young auntie's head as she kisses her boyfriend, to the jealousy expressed in a tragic re-enacting of the puppet show saga as he beats his mother's lover, to end with disillusionment and escape meant as a pertinent response to the mother's carelessness and abandonment.

Understood as the materialization of Prico's Oedipal fantasy, the film narrative appears to be built upon the logical chronology of exemplary psychological resolutions which make the solidification of the Oedipal bond not only desirable but indispensable. From the initial voyeuristic episode at his grandmother's house, Prico's delirious fantasy of the beaten girl between the lovers becomes a cathartic reality as it enables him to later project the father's persona onto that of the lover and safely fight for the love of his mother without risking the loss of paternal approval. The mother's 'betrayal' happens at a time when again the father is safely absent, a time of a possible blissful incestual union disrupted by the unwelcome return of the lover. Prico's escape towards the sea, understood by Jung as an archetypal representation of the Mother, suggests the need for symbolic internalization before the inevitable separation from the physical mother. Prico can then turn to his father alone, ready to face the reversal of the journey including the materialization of the homosexual fantasy of being invited to share the father's bed. The father's inability to perform as mother and his failure to contain his wife's disruptive desires drive him to suicide, an act which is an acknowledgement of his inadequacy to mediate the emotional into the social as well as an act of self-alienation from a process of growth. The offering of the child to the care of the Church has then both the function of reassociating the maternal with the divine and that of denouncing the Church's conspiracy with the regime in the political disempowerment of the individual.

In the tailor's fitting room the child stands in front of a mirror to have a new uniform fitted, a uniform that will look just like the one his father wore as a child. As Prico takes the hat from his father's head and puts it on his own the cycle of identification is completed. The subconsciously reassuring narrative transposition of the naturally occurring process of sexual identification is abruptly stripped of its psychological justification as the film's end tragically infuses the Oedipal fantasy with the crudity of reality. The father dies and although he commits suicide finding the loss of object (mother/woman) unbearable, Prico is spared the guilt that the materialization of his subconscious desire would call for and, instead, projects that guilt on to his mother. She is left to stand between the priest and the old maid as her own child walks away. While in Visconti's *Ossessione*, the deserted river bank to which the pregnant Giovanna escapes represented the self-inflicted price of loneliness the adulteress had to pay, in De Sica's *I Bambini ci Guardano* isolation takes the form of rejection and exclusion from past (old maid) and future (Prico) coupled with the burden of the oppressive misunderstanding of the Church, happy to take on the maternal responsibilities together with the powers associated with the role.

In stark contrast to the faint but essential glimpse of hope represented by the understanding of Bruno as he is reconciled with his father at the end of *Ladri di Biciclette*, there is no such narrative solution in *I Bambini ci Guardano*. The film's refusal to investigate the emotions which drove the woman to adultery and escape, and the depiction of a feminine world preoccupied with appearances, gossip and financial wealth, run parallel to the portrayal of a hard-working, pompous, insensitive but sacrificing husband whose suffering together with that of the child receives the privilege of the only extreme close-up of the entire film. Such narrative and stylistic premises disengage the spectator from the possibility of the sentimentalism associated with the maternal, as encouraged by the fascist propaganda, and lead to the impossibility of forgiveness for an act of rebellion against the laws of patriarchy which are seamlessly superimposed over those of nature. The film, in challenging the official fascist propaganda which claimed that unhappy children, adulteresses and suicides were unthinkable within a fascist state' (Liehm 1984: 49), criticizes the complicity of a 'bourgeois society whose agreeable elegance covers a multitude of weaknesses and vices' (Liehm 1984: 49), but most significantly does not hesitate in representing such a despicable society as predominantly female.

The call to realism can be blamed for a shifting of perspectives which, in order to affirm the social over the individual, does not allow ease of identification. However, De Sica's stylistic and narrative choices are also justified in a contextualized psychological analysis. The hopelessness of the film's message coupled with the emotional involvement it elicits, demands in fact a reading that unbinds the characters from their narratives of individual development and understands them as 'images' which work as materialization of a collective drama.

In *The Origins and History of Consciousness* Neumann (1954) describes the development of the ego in the individual as a process parallel to that of the development of consciousness in humankind, a process symbolically described by certain consistent narratives in world mythology. A specific moment in this process of development is described mythologically with the fight which the hero endures in order to free the captive virgin. This fight stands to represents what analytical psychology describes as 'crystallization of the anima from the mother archetype' (Neumann 1954: 198). Within the fight, the relationship of the ego to the female is altered as she, as anima, is freed from the dragon of the Terrible Mother and thus from captivity. This marks the beginning of the ability to relate.

The father in the film lacks the ability to fight. Instead he chooses either escape (returning from the holiday earlier than his family) or suicide, thus demonstrating his unpreparedness and/or an immaturity which prevents him from moving to the next stage of development. Prico, with his well-timed fever first and hysterical beating of the lover later, offers solutions that suggest an unconscious trust in the possibilities implicit in the return of the conflict to the domestic arena where it belongs and where it should indeed be consummated. Prico's presence as a precious potential, as the 'future' and as a possibility for rebirth, is only acknowledged by the objectivity (if relative) of the camera which, choosing him as central, exposes the void created around him by the unconsciousness of the adults. The father's continuous rejection and misunderstanding of his responsibilities and the mother's neglect of her role in the name of the selfish satisfaction of her immediate desires make of Prico an orphan from the beginning of the film, implying the weakness of the presence of the child as a catalyst of reunion. Prico's rejection of his biological mother is announced by his solitary walk towards the sea before his final journey home: the return to the uterine safety of borderless waters is, as mentioned above, the choice of the symbolic over the neglectful biological mother and it is the prelude to a surrendering to tradition which is exemplified by the events that follow Prico's return to the paternal relationship. Back at home the familiar structure is reconstituted temporarily thanks to the reassuring maternal substitute provided by the old maid. The child's uniqueness is flattened by the military uniform he is made to wear, and the Church-run boarding school sanctions the safe transmission of traditional values. Still, returning to the father is a reluctant choice made out of rejection; the sharing of his bed is the unpleasant alternative to an incest now seen as impossible rather than undesirable, and the wearing of a uniform which makes the child father-like is only a superficial acceptance of a masculinity that first because of the father's proven inability to fulfil his role (mirroring Mussolini's and maybe more significantly the king's leadership throughout the war) and then because of an emasculating Church's embrace will only become possible as a reaction to the feminine.

Considering the film as a social critique, it is clear that although alternative behavioural options for women are finally suggested they are all defined by a male presence while its absence or the misrecognition of this point of reference means again social death. In De Sica's supposedly apolitical pictures the greatest sin is not adultery, not even the shameless display of those fear-inducing qualities characteristic of the male-perceived female. It is in taking these powers out of the safe maternal bond that there is unforgivable sin. Even the film's tragic end transforms what would be the subconsciously reassuring narrative of the psychological process of sexual identification into what can be considered, socially, as an exercise of condemnation of women's conscious appropriation of their powers and psychologically as a regression into a state of inclusion within the nullifying embrace of an all-encompassing Great Mother here represented by the Church.

Antonio Gramsci in his *Prison Notebooks* wrote that 'the new industrialism wants monogamy: it wants the man as worker not to squander his nervous energies in the disorderly and stimulating pursuit of occasional sexual satisfaction' (Gramsci 1971: 305). Gramsci highlights the presence in America's new industrial society of a 'moral gap between. . . . the working masses and the ever more numerous elements of the ruling classes', a gap made evident by the spreading of what he calls 'social passivity'. Women, in his view, have a rather important role:

> The male industrialist continues to work even if he is a millionaire, but his wife and daughters are turning ... into 'luxury mammals' ... who seem to have nothing to do but travel and contract marriages which have become nothing but legalised prostitution or 'white slaving'.
>
> (Gramsci 1971: 305)

Antonio Gramsci's *Prison Notebooks* were published in Italy together with *Prison Letters* between 1947 and 1951. It is unlikely that either De Sica or Visconti would have read extracts relevant to women and their relation to industrial progress before they began the shooting of their first neo-realist films, yet the message in their work reflects a perspective certainly coherent with that developed by the Communist intellectual leader and their rather punitive narrative solutions a suspicious attitude towards the possibility for the emergence of a social consciousness shared with an untrustworthy female.

Conclusion

The three films analysed above form a bridge between the cinematic production of the last years of the regime and that of the first years in a 'liberated'[3] country. The search for objectivity and realism has certainly begun although it is still dependent, in the case of De Sica and Visconti, on a narrative structure borrowed from literary texts and suffering at times from the tendency to an emotional involvement expressed by the dramatic weight of the few extreme close-ups which gradually disappear from the neo-realist feature, only to return towards the very end of the decade.

The films are the successful product of a conscious desire to participate in the awakening of a social conscience, achievable, as far as the cinematic medium is concerned, through the production of images and narratives of immediate and recognizable relevance. The stories covered by the three directors range from Rossellini's account of the contrast between the glossy image of a traditional, competent and confident army and its actual ineffectiveness; to the portrayal in Visconti's piece of the dangerous consequences of an impulsive reaction to a repression which, sustained through a collaboration with the Church, cannot be overturned without the support of a clear vision for the future; to end with De Sica's recounting of a familiar drama of incommunicability and hopelessness which, unresolved, produces a lack of direction that dangerously turns the potential for the new towards the safer option of traditional structures.

---

3 A term which, as will be discussed later, is questionable.

The common threads to the three films are the fathers' absence and the presence of children. The first is only implied in Rossellini's film, the consequence of suicide in De Sica's and of murder in Visconti's *Ossessione* (if Giovanna's husband is understood as the representative of a fascist ideal of fatherhood). The presence of a child is only suggested as the inward development of a mother–son relation in Rossellini's piece where the protagonist son is, indeed, first mentioned as 'bambino' by his mother and it becomes central in De Sica's *I Bambini ci Guardano* returning as implicit in *Ossessione* from the forecasting of conception to the actual revelation of the pregnancy materializing in the late little girl's appearance, inconsistent with narrative continuity.

The mothers, in different capacities also ever-present, complete the familial units and offer the possibility for typical Oedipal triangulations. Nevertheless, the thread of an Oedipal trajectory, while certainly valid amongst them, is but one of the mythological narratives suitable for the process of 'amplification'.

The elimination of the father, either absent from the outset, suicidal or murdered, while granting either a temporary (*Ossessione*) or potential (*I Bambini ci Guardano* and *Un Pilota Ritorna*) incestual union with the mother, is a direct consequence of 'mothers' ' desires for new beginnings which clearly involve the destruction of the old tyrannical system. Prico's return to his father results from his awareness of the impossible attainment of a desired union with a mother who is available but not to him and the little boy's conscious choices are punitive of a female emancipation obtained at the expense of a father whose tyranny is only thinly suggested. In *Ossessione*, Bragana's (the husband) authority is only tied to economic advantages, easily reversed by the terms of a 'paternally' benevolent life insurance, and his downfall is brought about by his own stupidity, arrogance and narcissistic complacency. He does not represent an obstacle to either Giovanna's or Gino's sexual satisfaction and his death coincides with their separation rather than final union. In *Un Pilota Ritorna* the father stands (as the gold watch) between the protagonist and the new relationship and its presence as ever-ticking marker of time acts as pacifier of a sexually desiring maternal while the flight to the pre-Oedipal situation is guaranteed by a borrowed identity (enemy's plane) which almost costs the pilot his life.

The sexual character of the relationships described by the films works, thanks to narratives of refusal and death, as a condemnation of women's emancipation expressive of an anxiety related to a belief in the imminent end of the war, and with it the necessity to face the inevitable consequences of women's widened participation in the public sphere during men's absence. However, the transpersonal or archetypal value of the father figures points to a reading more easily related to anxieties of political as well as sociological origin.

If there is a 'death wish' in the films it is directed towards a father who represents a limiting (Rossellini), overpowering (De Sica) or restrictive (Visconti) authority and it is as such, rather than as a sexual rival, that he must be eliminated. That his killing is not perpetrated directly by the hero is as relevant to the historical context of the films' production as are the chosen embodiments of the father figure in the three films.

Rossellini manages to avoid the deadly conflict by literally 'dropping' a token of tradition, containing structures and protection (the gold watch is the pilot's lucky charm) which proved itself useless at the time of capture, into the hands of a virgin who will keep it 'forever' ticking in sterile waiting. His returning home without the 'father's watch' and in someone else's plane points to the cost of a freedom which, obtained individually and through borrowed identities, loses its historical value and can be treated as either heroism or betrayal. The confrontation with the Terrible Father understood as transpersonal is the confrontation with a 'spiritual system' which appears as 'the binding force of the old law, the old religion, the old morality, the old order' (Neumann 1954: 187) and it is a necessary step towards the affirmation of an ego capable of asserting its independence and of bringing change. Neumann describes the possible defeat resulting from this confrontation as 'patriarchal castration' that can take the form of 'annihilation through the spirit', mythologically represented in the Icarus myth, where the flying too high describes an egomania which, failing to recognize the magnitude of that against which the fight is directed, ends in disaster. Rossellini's hero and Mussolini himself can be related to such a figure, the first because of his actual role in the army, the second because of his driven, inconsiderate belligerency. The other outcome of patriarchal castration is 'captivity', which either becomes manifest as 'excessive respect for the law ... or the authority of the old collective father' and leads to sterile conservatism lacking the dialectical struggle between generations; or, if identification with the father is absent, the refusal to become a father and to assume power leads to the neurosis of the 'eternal son', described by Neumann as the 'permanent revolutionary'. Again Rossellini's pilot, who neither questions the authority which took him as far as fighting a war he does not seem to be eager to fight nor is willing to 'own his own kingdom' (described by the potential relationship with the girl), suggests the anxious emerging of an attitude which the events leading to the armistice of 8 September risk crystallizing: the lack of revolutionary spirit and the unwillingness to take charge of the future.

Gino in *Ossessione* displays similar lack and unwillingness and his tendency to passivity is highlighted by Giovanna's contrasting resolute use of deceit and of violence in her search for freedom. Within a narrative where money seems to govern the existence of relationships, Gino's insistent ideological detachment from capital and his scorn for the restriction on movement implied by possessions deprive him of agency at crucial points in the film. His refusal to identify with the father (Giovanna's husband), exemplified by the difficulty in accepting a life which would imitate Bragana's, only fuels weak and temporary rebellions. The reappearance of the Spaniard (the homosexual friend who shares his vision of freedom and independence) after the murder is a chance for reflection but is understood by Gino as an accusation and welcomed with violence. Gino's freedom is in wandering and the fragility of his independence is in unconsciousness. His refusals are passive exits rather than engaging confrontations and his only attempts at reclaiming agency from the events which seem to drive him are, again, actions of abandonment or escape. Giovanna's pregnancy is the catalyst for change and it seems to awake in Gino paternal responsibilities, yet the car journey and Giovanna's death are a revisiting of the murder sequence which indeed finally defines Gino as a killer in the eyes of human justice.

Mussolini's demographic policy had emphasized woman's reproductive role but it also somewhat suggested, with an ideology where men were to find their value in war and obedience, a distancing of the father from the cycle of reproduction. As mentioned before, rites of fertility from prehistoric times involved the sacrifice of the divine king either so that his seed would impregnate the earth (mother) or so that, having fulfilled his function of fathering, his life could be made worthy by offering it in sacrificial blood shedding (Neumann 1954: 57). Bragana's murder on the night he expresses the desire for a son creates an association between fathering and death from which Gino tries to escape by inverting the trajectory and leaving behind the 'old system' Giovanna's husband had created. His destiny is, however, conditioned by his unconsciousness and, consistent with his psychological immaturity, he drives, lacking direction, into a deadly fog. Unprepared for fathering, Gino cannot 'see' into the future and unwittingly he causes Giovanna's death.

As representative of the infantile form of a new national consciousness that can emerge at the end of the war effort, Gino aptly embodies a revolutionary spirit without a programme, a vision of freedom understood as disengagement and an acceptance of the responsibility for the new only when built upon the denial of the past. As a stage in the development of ego-consciousness the successful fight with the tyrannical father should, in fact, end with the individual's acceptance of his central position within the collective on the basis of either the recognition or the rejection of the laws of ethics, religion and social organization laid down before him. Gino's failure and the flight of Rossellini's pilot then describe the forecast consequences of Italy's unwillingness or unpreparedness to take responsibility for the social and political renewal which Mussolini's removal from office would allow.

Finally, in De Sica's piece, the self-exile of Prico's father and, more dramatically, his self-elimination from the possibilities of productive conflict point to Prico not only as the vague representation of the future but also as a competent, precocious (Prico sounds like a contraction of the word in Italian *precoce*) embodiment of an emerging new identity. Aware of the mother's blindness to his needs as she searches for new beginnings elsewhere, the child seems to reconcile himself both with traditional values, represented by his weak father, and with the motherly authority of the Church. Searching back into the history of united Italy it becomes evident how the pull towards an often corrupt and lay liberalism has been counterbalanced by more authoritative, centralized, undemocratic forms of government leading to the violent rise of Fascism. With this in mind, the last scene, still maintaining its negative value as a social condemnation of women's emancipation, can be read psychologically as the positive affirmation of an identity capable of rejecting the negative predicament of both options. The child rejects his mother because her unreliability makes her unsafe and her understanding of freedom has failed him. A return to her is weakly advocated by a reassuringly protective

Church probably because of the support provided by traditional versions of motherhood (the old maid), yet Prico, impermeable to such pressure, resolutely walks away from both, a mindless liberalism and the conflation of tradition with the opportunism of a rigid spiritual system. The Church, deprived of its influencing power, becomes then effective as a temporary refuge, as a safer 'womb' entered with the consciousness of one's immaturity but without the annihilation that an unconscious 'falling' back into the mother would entail.

Mussolini's speech of declaration of war had depicted the conflict as protective of the right to be a nation; a nation described by a collectivity organized within one party, defined by an imperialist dream of extended borders and safeguarded by a rejection of individualism which, at the heart of capitalism, needed to be neutralized in war. The lack of military success quickly deflated a paternal authority he had built upon a rhetoric of grandness and invincibility but it also brought under scrutiny the validity of the motivations which led to the war. The marionettes' fight in De Sica's film is in the name of the unattainable princess, but it soon turns against her in the feverish dream when she, as mother, is no longer worth dying for. Galli della Loggia regards the armistice of the 8 September 1943 as the equivalent of the 'morte della patria' (the death of the homeland), as with the final destitution of Mussolini's nationalistic dream many Italians felt unable to 'think', let alone defend or understand the nation as a unitary and/or unifying concept. Mussolini's castrating paternal tyranny produced disillusioned sons whose fight for new identity had only just begun.

1943–1945: towards the end of the war

Something old and something new: passivity, mistrust and resistance

On 15 August 1943 Marshall Badoglio declared Rome an 'open city', a demilitarized zone, a declaration which remained unilateral and that the Germans only acknowledged after they occupied the city on the 11 September, soon after Italy's reluctant declaration of unconditional surrender on 8 September. In the time between the fall of Mussolini and the armistice on 8 September, the country had remained in a state of chaos, uncertain about its position in relation to Germany and aware of the weakening effects of a war which had continued beyond the realistic military power and economic resources Italy could rely upon.

Nevertheless, amidst the confusion, the seeds of clandestine political activities, reawakened from the end of 1942 by the increasingly clear signs of a crisis in the fascist government, began to germinate and new parties were formed either as a development of already existing groups or as freshly established ones (de Blasio Wilhelm 1988; Katz 2003).

The revolutionary movement known as Giustizia e Liberta (Justice and Liberty), founded in Paris by anti-fascist exiles as far back as 1926, united the efforts of non-communist, anti-fascist, republican forces and in January 1943 a party was formed which after 8 September became the political point of reference for the partisans belonging to that movement: the Action Party.

The Popular Party, originally founded by Don Sturzo and Alcide de Gasperi in 1919, was considered the vehicle for the return to the political arena of the Catholics, previously excluded from the political life of the country by a papal veto only removed that year. The Popular Party was dissolved, together with all other opposition parties, in 1926 and its leaders exiled. In October 1942 de Gasperi founded the Christian Democracy (DC), a party which, as opposed to the aconfessional spirit and independence from the Vatican of the Popular Party, was eager to make of Catholicism the political as well as spiritual unifying force of the nation (Bedani and Haddock 2000: 216–217).

When Resistance activities began in the autumn of 1943, a large number of partisans claimed affiliation with the Communist Party, born from the split from the Italian Socialist Party at the Livorno congress in 1921, and the anti-fascist United Freedom Front, created in April 1943, which had as its leader the ex-Socialist Ivanoe Bonomi.

On the night following the announcement of the armistice, Marshall Badoglio and the king, fearing Hitler's reaction, abandoned Rome and fled to Brindisi from where they established the Kingdom of the South, supposedly giving the Italians a hope for a monarchic future after the war. Their move was quick and unannounced with no orders left to defend the city, no one left in command and the majority of ministers of the government uninformed of the departure (Katz 2003: 32). While the Allies were landing in Calabria and at Salerno the Germans invaded from the north, reaching as far as Naples, and Rome was occupied by Nazis on 11 September. At the same time the United Freedom Front was rebaptized Committee of National Liberation (CNL), an organization which was to become the catalyst for the unification of Resistance efforts across the peninsula. Such efforts were weakened when Mussolini was rescued by the Germans and established as head of a new government in the German-occupied north, with headquarters in Salò on the shores of Lake Garda, the day before Italy finally declared war on Germany on 13 October. Here Mussolini founded the Repubblica Sociale Italian (Italian Social Republic) claiming the loyalty of the few who still believed in the grandiosity of the fascist vision and fomenting civil war.

Although supported by the Allies as an essential means to the achievement of the liberation of the peninsula, the Resistance groups united under the co-ordination of the CNL were also perceived, by the Americans and by Churchill in particular, as a growing political force with a post-war programme not necessarily consonant with theirs. The CNL had in fact proclaimed its independence from Mussolini's supposedly republican state as well as from the king and Badoglio's government and expressed the intention to leave it to the people, at the end of the conflict, to decide on the form of government most appropriate for their country (De Balsio Wilhelm 1988: 199–201).

Despite the landing of the Allies at Anzio in January 1944, the liberation of Rome took longer than envisaged and the Americans only entered the city on

4 June 1944. This delay and the one which made the final liberation of the north a year-long struggle was to affect popular perception of the new war partners. Indeed, between the hopes associated with the arrival of the Allies as liberators and the actual reality of their intervention, a gap was beginning to form and feelings of disappointment and distrust were filling it fast. The feelings were, however, somewhat justified and/or reciprocated and manifested in actions which would qualify the Anglo-Americans as occupiers rather than as liberators. Uncertain about the technical and administrative abilities of an Italian government reduced to little more than a nominal leadership of dubious loyalties (Badoglio and Vittorio Emanuele III), the Allies, fearing revolutionary unrest, established the Allied Control Commission with the intention of supervising political and economic changes and of preventing with all necessary repressive measures the establishment of 'unacceptable' forms of government (Ellwood 1985: 53–55).

In the spring of 1944 the strikes organized by the Communists in the industrial cities of the north proved a success in popularity and participation but also made Anglo-American anxieties about the future establishment of a leftist government more real. If Togliatti (the new Italian Communist Party leader now returned from exile) seemed reassuring when he re-emphasized the importance of unity in government even if under the leadership of the king and Badoglio, after the liberation of Rome the CLN influenced things towards a more uncompromising political choice: the king's reign was brought to an end (at least temporarily) and Ivanoe Bonomi was asked to form a new government which now included antifascist as well as Communist leaders such as Carlo Sforza, Benedetto Croce and Palmiro Togliatti (De Blasio Wilhelm 1988: 204–208).

Vittorio De Sica's *La Porta del Cielo* (*The Gate to Heaven*, 1944) was filmed in Rome during the German occupation of the city. The film was conceived as a credible alibi which would exonerate De Sica from his duty to accept the requests from the Salò government to make his talent available to the new republic. Supposedly commissioned by the Vatican, the assignment worked as a safe cover for actors, scriptwriters and technicians unwilling to support Mussolini's farcical establishment and, most importantly, it provided a significant number of Roman Jews, purposely employed as extras, with an escape from certain deportation. On 16 October 1943, 1023 Jews were arrested in the Rome ghetto and later deported to concentration camps from which only 16 came back (Katz 2003: 100). The film manages to relate, with the regular shifts from the protagonists' flashbacks to their journey of hope towards a miraculous shrine, the tension between a traumatic past and the hopeful movement towards a future which promises change.

Rossellini's *Roma Città Aperta* (*Rome Open City*, 1945) documents the difficult and courageous work of the Roman Resistance as well as presenting the emotional and physical conditions of the population during the German occupation of the city. The film works as the materialization of a desire to finally 'own' a past worth building upon, to represent and immortalize a history of martyrdom and sacrifice as the key to a hard-earned victory and as a vehicle for a future of positive international relationships built upon respect rather than on pity and distrust.

When the advance of the Allies towards the north came to a halt in the winter of 1944, action soon took the place of initial disillusionment with Anglo-American inconsistent support and local Resistance groups managed to free most of the major cities of the north. This final struggle was essential if Italy was to claim agency for its own liberation and indeed most partisan insurrections ended with victory before the Allies' arrival (De Blasio Wilhelm 1988: 210). Mussolini was shot by partisans in April 1945 as he was trying to flee north across the Alps (Duggan 1994: 241). By 8 May when the war officially ended in Europe all of Italy was free. Reconstruction would soon begin.

La Porta del Cielo (The Gate of Heaven, 1944)

The miracle of solidarity

> The spirit and meaning of Christ are present and perceptible to us even without the aid of miracles. Miracles appeal only to the understanding of those who cannot perceive meaning. They are mere substitutes for the not understood reality of the spirit.
>
> (*C.W.*, Vol. 11: para. 554)

Maybe because of its acknowledged function as temporary protection of a number of Roman Jews from Nazi deportation and of friends and colleagues from the demands of the resurrected fascist government, *La Porta del Cielo* remains a 'virtually forgotten film' (Curle and Snyder 2000: 103). Yet notwithstanding its value as a successful means of escape from both Nazi and fascist roundups, with the protection afforded by the extraterritorial nature of the Basilica of St Paul which was the location chosen for the shooting, the film is also another example of De Sica's ability to express with his images the desires, fears and hopes of a country at war, a war fought to this point on the wrong side.

La Porta del Cielo is the story of a so-called 'white train'. A 'white train' would normally travel across the country picking up on its way people with illnesses of both a physical and emotional nature, having as its final destination a sanctuary, a church or a place, in this case the shrine of the Madonna of Loreto, where the pilgrims would hope to ask for and receive miraculous healing. The film is organized in overlapping sections following the conversations and thoughts of groups accommodated in different coaches. Through the conversations and with the help of flashbacks the characters' background and the origins of their infirmities are revealed. As the train approaches its final destination, the unfolding of the connections between them as they share a journey of hope suggests the importance of solidarity as a prerequisite to healing.

Coming from the south, the train's first stop is in Salerno, south of Naples, where it is welcomed by giggling young women, excited at the prospect of travel.

There is a train and there is a journey and yet the individuals' situations within the train make of this journey a peculiar one. As the nurse suggests, 'These coaches are reserved for people who don't feel like laughing.' De Sica, working in the precarious situation of a city (Rome) occupied by the Germans and of an established new fascist government still trying to convince people of the advantages to be gained by remaining loyal to Nazi Germany, is maybe exposing his own anxieties in relation to others' perception of the real state of his country and his belief in the urgent need for an intervention which seemed, at the time, slow in its effect.

Mussolini's incarceration, followed by the confusing events leading to the 'unconditional surrender' of 8 September, was the beginning of a series of disillusionments in the possibilities for alternative forms of leadership. Having lost, with the Duce, its charismatic political leader (a loss of authority and meaning before his physical elimination) and now deprived of the hope for solid alternatives (Marshall Badoglio and King Vittorio Emanuele III), the country was again broken and disjointed and the efforts of the Resistance, although locally effective, were lacking the necessary overall co-ordination. The only point of hope and focus was the Church, not necessarily because of the actual protection it offered but as the remaining common ground, the 'destination' towards which despair could travel in search of a 'miracle'. What was needed was indeed a 'miracle'. It is a recurring sentence in the film and it suggests both a lack of realistic hope in the possibilities already present in one's reality and a desire to surrender to the mercy of a greater understanding.

At Salerno a little boy in a wheelchair boards the train accompanied by a young woman, sister of his now dead best friend. The woman believes in the little boy's intelligence and skills and hopes he will be able to pursue his dreams if he can finally walk. In the same compartment is an old man, accompanied in his travel by his opportunist nephews. At first the man shows intolerance towards the little boy and his friend, but during the course of the journey he comes to realize the potential and skills of both while becoming more aware of his nephews' opportunistic intentions.

In the flashbacks the little boy's life was one of self-sufficiency and loneliness. Orphaned and in the care of an uncle involved in suspicious activities, he found solace in the friendship of the young woman who seems to act as a self-abnegating godmother. Her positive glow is guaranteed by an almost childish innocence, a seal of virtue, as well as by a maternal role acquired without sexual participation: she is a Madonna figure, looking after a special child put by providence in her care. As the Virgin Mary is considered 'the mediatrix', interceding between God and man (*C.W.*, Vol. 11: para. 625), so the young woman intercedes for the little boy both by accompanying him on his journey of hope as well as by creating a favourable ground for the development of a working relationship with the old man, who happens to be a tycoon.

The role of the woman as virginal 'mediatrix' is recurrent in the film. There is the nurse who allows a man to remain on the train without the approval of her superior. She does not intend to perpetrate an act of mutiny but believes in the unending mercy of her senior and trusts in her forgiveness while acting, effectively, on her behalf. And the old maid who travels to Loreto to ask for a resolution of her master's desire for revenge against his now dead, adulterous wife is also interceding, so that the preserved memory of his children's mother will not be soiled by the truth.

The desire to maintain appearances is also traceable across the film. The man who clandestinely boarded the train is a pianist who is beginning to lose the use of one hand. His greatest preoccupation seems to be the humiliation his father will suffer as the whole village where his family lives now knows of his upcoming involvement in prestigious concerts. In his own flashbacks of a recent visit to his parents he instinctually runs to his mother confessing his need for her comfort, yet he won't confide in her and tells her it is someone else's envy that had deprived him of the chance to play at the concert. She suggests that 'we must laugh at our enemies'. The enemy in question is an imagined one and will not be exorcized by laughing. The denial of a personal lack calls for an external justification and the belief in another's envy seems a fitting possibility, which might in truth lead to a paralyzing fear of success. The admission of his own illness would admit to his own and to his mother's (as lifegiver) imperfection, a possibility the mother herself has described as impossible in suggesting invincibility and a self-confidence capable of facing the enemy's aggression. Laughing at the non-existent enemy is, in this case, the equivalent of fighting a war on the wrong front: it will not solve the problem created by a substantial and quite real inadequacy (that of an unprepared and ill-equipped army) while demanding engagement and energy for a battle which can only end in ridicule and defeat. The reference to Mussolini's rhetoric and fatal misinformation is quite direct.

On the train are also two men; one of the two is blind and the other accompanies him in his journey of hope. Through another flashback their story is unveiled. The two men are fellow workers in a factory. Preoccupied with his friend's emotional well-being, the more confident and popular of the two tried to convince his friend of the unworthiness of the woman he was seriously dating. As his friend refused to believe in the negative gossip about the woman's sexual availability, the young man orchestrated a public 'accident' where a large group of fellow workers – his involved friend included – witnessed the girl's yielding to his embrace and kiss.

The woman and her involvement are soon eliminated from the narrative as, now that her intentions are exposed, she flees the scene on a horse-drawn carriage. Her escape and its mode confirm her brief yet well-drawn role of an attractive and fatally dangerous goddess of love. As 'sacred prostitute' she is well integrated within the predominantly masculine environment of the factory and her availability is light-heartedly accepted until one man decides to make of her an individual worthy of love. In mythology the 'sacred prostitute' is the virgin in its meaning of 'unknown' to men and anonymous (Neumann 1954: 52–53). Her identity as human individual is necessarily erased in order to transcend the sexual nature of intercourse and maintain its sacredness. A privileged relationship with such a woman reinstates her individuality, thus creating an unsolvable dissonance with her previous anonymity which guaranteed not only her autonomy but also safe and uncompromising sexual relations for men. The previously harmless availability becomes then a potentially lethal instrument and the friend of the man temporarily 'blinded' by love is eager to help him regain sight. In turn, the wounded lover, now humiliated and searching for revenge, will unwittingly inflict on his friend a physical blindness which he hopes another 'virgin' will reverse.

The inability to see, again following an Oedipal trajectory, becomes a self-inflicted physical blindness as a response, in awareness, to a destructive blindness experienced unconsciously. Yet the two men are but complementary aspects of a masculine damaged by the encounter with an Anima figure (the woman's autonomy and sensuality are confirming attributes) at a stage when they would rather embark on a return journey to the safety of a Great Mother, embodied by the willingly miraculous Madonna of Loreto.

The pain endured by the travellers seems to be in most cases either enhanced or directly deriving from the actions of a woman (one absent as mother of the wheelchair-bound boy, another adulterous yet revered as pure, one sexually available and deceitful, another unable to support a son's despair). The negative causal relationship between pain and woman is, at this point in the film, reversed as a prayer is heard. It is a Hail Mary, part of the reciting of a Rosary and more specifically the sharing of a part of the Rosary described as 'the Sorrowful Mysteries', a section following Jesus's painful passion from the agony in the Garden of Gethsemane to his crucifixion and death. The choice of this isolated section is possibly referring to a necessary painful passage, a transitory period of darkness and hopelessness culminating in death which must be experienced in order to heal a separation (originating in the Fall, again deriving from female's deceit). It is through Christ's passion, death and resurrection that Mary becomes part of the design of redemption: at the end of the Sorrowful Mysteries she is called to extend her mothering love to humankind, a call which seals her function of making the Divine accessible, of allowing for the passage of Heaven into Earth not only through the acceptance of virginal motherhood but also through an ongoing mediation between man and God/Spirit/Divinity.

The train's final destination, as pointed out earlier, is a journey towards the maternal, embodied by the Madonna of Loreto. This choice might be of symbolic relevance as Loreto is believed to have been the elected destination for the miraculous transferring by angels of the Holy House from Nazareth: the Holy House was supposedly transported first to Yugoslavia in 1291, as the crusaders were finally expelled from Palestine, and later in 1294 to Loreto. The event is brought to the foreground by De Sica by superimposing the opening credits on a relief sculpture representing the miraculous transfer.[4]

Moreover, in *The Collected Works* Jung mentions the 'symbolic attributes of the Virgin' as they are listed in an ancient prayer called 'the Litany of Loreto' where amongst the expected description of Mary as 'Mater amabilis' (Lovable Mother) and 'Mater admirabilis' (Wonderful Mother) that of 'Janua Coeli' (Gate of Heaven) stands out as the possible origin of the film's title (*C.W.*, Vol. 6:

4 www.santuarioloreto.lt

para. 379). The 'gate of heaven' is then the Virgin herself, confirmed as physical point of passage, as an opening towards an integration with a higher Self, but at the same time the very point of closure, exclusion and containment. The safety of her embrace, also materialized as the concrete enclosure of the Holy House of Loreto, offers definition within the walls of a familial setting, a definition which is psychologically sought for by a broken nation as a containment of the only identity remaining, that of the chosen heir of the Catholic tradition. Loreto, as the elected site for the preservation of the house of the Holy Family, is also De Sica's elected site for a journey of hope, a choice possibly reminiscent of a fascist reliance on the family unit as representative of the nation.

Once inside the basilica the emphasis is on collective prayer, on repetition, in a candlelit, vast and still rather dark environment, of litanies and songs. The opening prayer is directly descriptive of the condition of a collective exemplified within the individual: 'Lord, son of David, Shepherd. . . . The one you love is ill.' Rather than a request this is a reminder and an acceptance of the status of recipient but is also a statement which emphasizes the centrality of the Father as warrant of worthy identity while offering the Virgin a lateral interceding function. The request of healing is directed to 'the Lord': 'Lord, lay your hand and I shall be healed', while Mary is asked merely to serve as a communicating bridge between man and her divine son. Notwithstanding the obviously maternal nature of the basilica both in its dedication (to the Madonna of Loreto) and in its atmosphere (dark, cavernous and enclosing) the longing remains clearly one for the evidence of a paternal presence and power. The feminine, rather than a destination, remains a place of departure for a new level of integration with a higher consciousness, again mediating between polarities and providing at last (or rather, eventually, with the confirmation of the dogma of the Assumption only proclaimed in 1950) a balancing 'feminine factor within the precincts of the masculine Trinity' (*C.W.*, Vol. 18: para. 1606).

Miracles happen as direct consequences of the specific demands. A woman regains the use of her legs soon after the crowd implores 'Lord allow me to walk' and it is the only visible and most direct of the miraculous events. Other miracles are symbolic healings of physical disability: as the blind man wants to see again it is his friend who gains vision of his unworthiness and with it an awareness of responsibility which will serve as guidance; the wheelchair-bound little boy finds in the old man an opportunity to explore his untapped potentials; and the pianist finds relief in his despair as the crowd seems to incite him to believe, leading him to abandon his suicidal plan.

De Sica redirects spectatorial attention to the one effective miracle as the crowd recites 'Thank you, Lord, one of us is healed . . . one like us', reaffirming the importance of the individual as microcosm and as representative of the collective which becomes healed as a consequence of his or her transformation. Opposed to a fascist doctrine which affirmed that 'the individual has no existence except insofar as he is part of the state and subordinate to its requirements' (from *Opera Omnia di Benito Mussolini*, Vol. 24: 145, cited by Mack Smith 1981: 173), De Sica then tries to deliver a Christian perspective as one which considers the individual as agent of the otherwise impossible transformation needed for the community. The quiet, subordinate acceptance of a status quo imposed by the egocentric wants of a dictator can be swept away by the simple belief in the possibility of change, even if or rather because that change has already taken place within a minority. The minority is possibly one formed by revolutionary intellectuals and by a Resistance movement which at the time of the film's production had just become organized under the CNL. Although counting on a significantly smaller number of armed forces than the invading Nazis, the efforts of the Resistance were turning the fate of many provinces in the north of Italy and indicating the possibility of a 'miracle', which like the ones performed at the end of the film might not result in the longed for end of suffering (war) but in a change in state of consciousness leading to trust, hope and, most importantly, solidarity.

Roma Città Aperta (Rome Open City, 1945)

The gospel of the Resistance

Rossellini started the shooting of *Roma Città Aperta* in January 1945, about seven months after the liberation of Rome by the American Allies on 4 June of the previous year. It is a film about heroism, or rather a search for much needed heroism amongst the ruins of a nation that, having lost its political – Mussolini – and symbolic – the king – leadership, now had to quickly find new unifying points of reference. *Roma Città Aperta* seems to carefully avoid the singling out of an individual narrative leader and allows instead for the emergence of innocent and trustworthy, if effectively powerless, means of identification from both the social (Pina), religious (Don Pietro) and political (Francesco and Manfredi) landscape. The fragmented plot reconstructs the action of the Roman Resistance during the Nazi occupation of the city begun in September 1943. Manfredi is a Resistance leader who, actively searched for by the Gestapo, needs the support of his friend Francesco and of a priest, Don Pietro, close to Francesco's wife-to-be Pina, known for having embraced the Partisans' cause. Pina is brutally killed during a round-up which ends with Francesco's capture. Francesco is immediately freed by the Partisans but Manfredi is eventually arrested, beaten and tortured to death. Don Pietro is also taken prisoner and, accused of supporting the Resistance, summarily executed. The heroism of the protagonists is not necessarily to be found in their courageous actions but rather in their defiance, and in the almost passive yet dignified resistance to the persecuting evil embodied by the German Gestapo officers.

At first the film follows Manfredi as he escapes from the Gestapo's search of his house. The escape route is through the window and across the roofs, possibly as a metaphor, if associated with Manfredi's education which offers him a position of 'higher' knowledge and control, for the inexpugnability of intellectual freedom and, as will become evident later, an exclusively masculine prerogative.

Having briefly introduced the spectrum of torture and the cruel and sadistic intentions of the Gestapo officer Bergmann who works with the complicity of the chief of the Roman police, the narrative shifts to the streets where Pina (Anna Magnani) has just led other women to the raiding of a bakery in a desperate search for a food that is obviously present but held back by those who produce it. Her aggressive language, unmitigated by Magnani's captivating Roman accent, and the violence implicit in the past action are immediately softened by the admission of her delicate pregnant state. Pina is a mother-to-be, expecting the child of her new, politically involved lover Francesco, militant of the Roman Resistance and friend of Manfredi. She is also mother to a young boy, the son of a deceased husband and member of a gang of children with supposedly political agendas, whose actions parallel those of their adult models.

Pina, as well as a point of intersection between the Resistance and the Church, represents the desire for an unsentimental, generous participation of the working class in the reconstruction of the social fabric of the country. It is clear, however, that her relationship with the Resistance is one of ideal rather than practical participation while that with the Church takes the form of a devoted compromise. Her confession to Don Pietro is a questioning of God's unwillingness to end the misery she sees around and suggests an ability to reject masculine authority, a rebellion which remains, however, effective only verbally.

Nevertheless, Pina's ability to exercise authority through language is considered a threat which, according to Rocchio, calls for containment. As evidence of such a threat Rocchio suggests a closer reading of the scene where Pina admits to Manfredi that she would rather be married by a priest who is 'one of them' (effectively working for the Resistance) than by a fascist official in the city hall. After Manfredi necessarily yet reluctantly agrees with her, she adds that she actually believes in God. The power of her speech has had the effect of obtaining the consent to the marriage from her lover, the 'working class Socialist' Francesco, and of silencing the objections of Manfredi, 'an educated, bourgeois Communist' (Rocchio 1999: 44). Rocchio points out:

> The ease with which she appropriates the moral authority of the Resistance and uses it to overcome male prohibitions further constitutes a threat to the operations of patriarchy. Pina thus functions to represent an ideological peril that the film contains: future subversive collective action against patriarchal capitalism's attempt to represent a new Italian state. In this respect, Pina, and the threat she embodies, must be killed off.
>
> (Rocchio 1999: 44)

At first, Pina's exclusion from the world of politics and therefore of action is portrayed as a voluntary exit, as she humbly steps out of her lover's house where Don Pietro and Manfredi meet to organize the delivery of funds to the Partisans. Her little son's emphatic and rhetorical words, 'We must form a united block', are not only dissonant with the boy's tender age but immediately disavowed by Pina's willing retreat into the family unit where her authority and role are unchallenged but participation is contained and politically negligible. Moreover, it will be the little boy who later suggests that unlike men who can become 'heroes' women are nothing but 'trouble', a prophecy which will become manifest as Manfredi's rejected, drug addict, bisexual lover betrays him in exchange for drugs and expensive gifts.

The woman's death, which in *Ossessione* had been the direct consequence of a consummated Oedipal narrative (Gino's inability to see), becomes in *Roma Città Aperta* the execution of a voice abusive of the power of language (the symbolic realm controlled by the Law-of-the-Father). Rossellini frames this power, visually, in the only scene in the film which allows a moment of intimacy between Francesco and Pina on the night preceding their wedding. Pina is describing her first meeting with Francesco: she furiously knocked on his door after his hammering of a nail into a common wall had caused her mirror to fall but not break. His forceful, masculine, penetrating activity might have affected her self-image but has had no lasting consequences. Her ability to 'reflect', threatened by his attitude, which she describes as that of one 'who believes to be the king of the universe' had been easily restored and reframed thanks to her aggressive verbal intrusion. The reference to Pina's own mirror confirms her resemblance to the Anima as 'the unconscious, feminine aspect of man' (E. Jung 1985: 64). Emma Jung points out that 'one function of the anima is to be a looking glass for a man, to reflect his thoughts, desires, and emotions'; it is through her 'either as an inner figure or projected to an actual, outer woman' that he 'becomes aware of things about which he is still unconscious' (p. 65). While self-knowledge is the desired outcome, the power conceded to the anima (and consequentially to the woman invested with the representation) is experienced as danger. Francesco's initial action had temporarily disavowed this power which Pina then reclaims verbally.

Nevertheless, the scene's visual composition redirects the aggression towards Pina who, sitting on the stairs one step down from Francesco, looks up at him from the right in an act of finally resigned submission. His words of comfort further create a distance which almost denies the sexual nature of their connection in favour of an authority Pina is more willing to submit to, that of the Catholic Church. He explains to Pina how he knows that the war will end and there will be a better future for the children to see but, most importantly, he emphatically exhorts her to 'not be afraid', as they are fighting for something that 'has to come, and can only come' echoing the words of Moses in the book of Exodus and those of Jesus to his disciples the night before his death.[5] Francesco, however, will be spared from the sacrifice his messianic words would imply and Pina will die instead.

---

5 Moses answered the people, 'Do not be afraid. Stand firm and you will see the deliverance the Lord will bring you today' (Exodus 14: 13).

   'So do not be afraid of them. There is nothing concealed that will not be disclosed, or hidden that will not be made known' (Matthew 10: 25–27).

   'You will hear of wars and rumours of wars, but see to it that you are not alarmed. Such things must happen, but the end is still to come' (Matthew 24: 5–7).

In the morning, before the wedding, the Germans raid the building. Pina manages to respond with controlled violence to the German soldier's unwelcome effusions but when Francesco is captured Pina's desperate chase of the vehicle carrying him away is halted by the gunfire which kills her. She dies in Don Pietro's arms. Her first instinctual desire to protect the man who has fathered her unborn child drives her out of a fearful, subdued crowd of women. Her arm raised as she runs calling his name, her full maternal body thrown towards a hope which is quickly slipping away can, in this very scene, be superimposed on to an image of liberty borrowed from the artist Eugene Delacroix in his celebration of the July Revolution in France, *July 28: Liberty Leading the People*, (1830) (see Figures 5.3 and 5.4). Here the hopes inspired by the French Revolution are expressed through the shameless leadership of a bare-breasted woman holding the tricolour flag in her raised right hand and an infantry musket in the other. Representing the power of the will to freedom as the leading spirit of popular revolution, the woman's body is, in the painting, exposed as if to acknowledge the positive energy of the maternal. Moreover, in the painting, the working class and the bourgeois are fighting side by side and a child imitates the woman's movement but holding, instead of the flag, a pistol in each hand describing a commitment to freedom involving the population as a whole, notwithstanding class, gender or age differences. In Pina's almost identical movement is, however, the last act of rebellion of a revolution where people have been and are, as they watch her die, just powerless spectators.

Figure 5.3 Pina's rebellion is an isolated gesture. *Roma Città Aperta*. Roberto Rossellini (1945). (Thanks to Roberto Rossellini's Estate).

Figure 5.4 A people's revolution. *July 28: Liberty Leading the People 1830* (oil on canvas) (for detail see 95120) by Delacroix, Ferdinand Victor Eugene (1798–1863). Louvre, Paris, France/The Bridgeman Art Library. Nationality/copyright status: French/out of copyright.

As mentioned earlier, the revolutionary action of volunteers of a nation 'abstractly conceived' (Gramsci, in Hoare and Nowell-Smith, 1971: n203) does not, in fact, succeed in awakening a united national spirit which could have translated the actions of the Resistance into political choices at the time of the 1948 general elections. Pina's death, and its mode, might then be read as comment on the limitations of the Resistance as well as a resolution of the anxieties derived from the perceived danger implicit in giving women the vote (a voice, well represented by Magnani's loquacity), an inevitable outcome of the now envisaged 'democracy'.

As she willingly takes on the fate she believes has befallen her lover, Pina also becomes the sacrificial lamb, the offering whose death is functionally worthless yet essential in its symbolic effectiveness. Rossellini's framing of her death in the arms of Don Pietro transmutes an episode of social history (the true story of Teresa Gullace, a woman killed in Rome by the SS in 1944; Katz 2003: 183) into one of spiritual significance. Don Pietro holding Pina's lifeless body is a cinematic reproduction of Michelangelo's sculpture *La Pietà* (1499), depicting a timelessly young Mary holding the lifeless body of Jesus. The genders are inverted but the meaning distilled: a powerless Mother Church can do nothing but 'hold' a sinful yet loving and courageous humanity and transmit, through this gesture, a hope granted by a tradition of suffering as a vehicle to immortality (see Figures 5.5 and 5.6)

Figure 5.5 Pina dies in Don Pietro's arms. *Roma Città Aperta*. Roberto Rossellini (1945). (Thanks to Roberto Rossellini's Estate).

Figure 5.6 *La Pietà* (marble) by Buonarroti, Michelangelo (1475–1564). St. Peter's, Vatican, Rome, Italy/The Bridgeman Art Library. Nationality/copyright status: Italian/out of copyright.

The religious iconography throughout the film forms a parallel subplot which is an attempt at mythologizing the Resistance by suggesting a resemblance with a religious tradition of martyrs, rituals, sacrifices and beliefs. The sharp distinction between good and evil, traditionally drawn and held, in Italy, by the Church's authority, is discussed throughout the film through the actions of highly polarized characters. The good 'Italians' depicted by the film (and on reflection the film itself) become invested with the duty of providing the country with a sort of political spiritualism, with a socially written 'Gospel' which vindicates a past of compromise and inaugurates, with sacrificial deaths, a future of renewable hope and goodness.

Soon after Pina's death Francesco, Manfredi and his spy/girlfriend Marina witness the killing of two lambs by German soldiers. This scene has again the function of catalyst of religious meaning and its positioning between Pina's and Manfredi's killing proposes an understanding of the suffering endured during the Resistance as a point of intersection between a working-class and a bourgeois Italy from which a future of hope can be developed. The scene also reintroduces Marina to the narrative as a substitute for the maternal protection offered so far by Pina. Pina's ultimate inability to protect her beloved and her narrative exclusion offer Marina the opportunity to emerge as the other aspect of an archetypal feminine. Her dancing and her light-hearted attitude, as well as her ability to provide the interface, if with negative consequences, between Manfredi (consciousness) and Ingrid (a Shadow figure), constantly accompanied by a pure personification of evil (Bergmann, the German officer) defines her as an anima figure. The anima has, in fact, been described as a bridge between ego and Self. More specifically both anima (in man) and animus (in women) function as connections to the 'other's' world, an 'other' which is gendered as a representation of opposites. Anne Belford Ulanov describes them as 'border figures, taking us from one to another sexual departure point, from the personal to the collective, the conscious to the archetypal, the ego to the Self' (Ulanov 1992: 26–27).

Consistent with Jung's description of the anima as bipolar, appearing 'positive one moment and negative the next; now young, now old; now mother, now maiden; now a good fairy, now a witch; now a saint, now a whore' (*C.W.*, Vol. 9i: para. 356), Marina is depicted and discussed (through dialogue) as a negative version of Pina. Moreover she offers Francesco and Manfredi food, music, drinks and shelter while later she will betray them. She has religious icons hanging on her bedroom wall (the Virgin Mary holding an infant Jesus) while she talks about her survival strategy which is a form of sophisticated prostitution and, most importantly, she accuses Manfredi of her downfall, suggesting that had he really loved her she would have been redeemed ('if you had loved me you would have saved me') necessarily implying a departure from a point of potential goodness.

The encounter with the anima is, indeed, often described in fairy tales and myths as the rescuing of the captive or the awakening of the sleeping princess. This is considered, in analytical psychology, as a representation of the natural movement from puberty to adulthood: once the 'mother archetype wanes', the 'anima, a sequentially linked nucleus of the archetypal feminine, waxes' (Stevens 2002: 159). Neumann found consistent mythological representations of this stage in development which demands that after the fight with the dragon (unconscious/ Terrible Mother) the hero rescues the captive (anima). This passage from the dependency from the Mother to the ability to relate (both in a heterosexual relationship and to the unconscious) is not exclusively tied to a particular moment in physiological maturation. In fact, the 'integration of the anima, the feminine element, into a man's conscious personality is part of the individuation process' (E. Jung 1981: 87), a process that will continue to search for its own fulfilment throughout life.

Notwithstanding Marina's charm, Manfredi seems impermeable to her seduction. As anima she represents the opposite to his conscious self, an unknown of which he is now weary and suspicious. It is when she senses his distance and his distaste for a financial independence she has obtained through prostitution that she reminds him of his failure to protect her virtue. Manfredi agrees and apologizes before leaving the room. This point in the film contains in itself a forecasting, in psychological terms, of a damaged relationship to the feminine which, if not restored, might have dramatic consequences. Manfredi now experiences what once was attractive as corrupted and untrustworthy. His turning away from Marina apologetically is an admission of a failure in relatedness and the last glance toward a feminine which the new Italy, like Manfredi, honest and uncompromising, will want to do without.

Significantly, throughout the film the protection provided by women as either mothers or lovers has been at first deficient, then hysterically fruitless and finally treacherous while, at the same time, a masculine world capable of taking over the traditionally maternal functions comes to the foreground. After Pina's death Don Pietro looks after her little boy, Marcello, with the help of the deacon who cooks and shops while remaining financially dependent from Don Pietro, and Manfredi looks after Francesco while he grieves for Pina. At the end of the film the only available model for identification, the remaining figure representative of a 'nation to be' is that of Francesco – a working class socialist with an innocent, spiritualistic view of the future which is closer, at least in his verbal expressions, to a Christian belief than it is to Marxism.

The involvement of the Church in the Resistance is discussed through the development of the character of Don Pietro, based on the real lives of both Don Giuseppe Morosini executed in Rome on 3 April 1944 by the SS[6] and Don Pietro Pappagallo killed in the massacre of the Fosse Ardeatine in March 1944. Don Pietro's positive, active and courageous contribution is both narrativized as an open condemnation of a past of 'sin' (in the acceptance of fascist dictatorship) which, in his words to Pina, had inevitably to lead to war as a price to pay for a much needed forgiveness, as well as a willingness to use his supposed immunity

---

6 http://www.comune.ferentino.fr.it/morosini.php

as priest in support of the Partisans. While Don Pietro is depicted as a paternal (at times 'maternal'), caring and ultimately heroic figure, Rossellini does not shy away from commenting, through him, on the overall role of the Church during the war years. He points to two lines of conduct that search for a positive point of intersection throughout his films (*Paisà, Francesco Giullare di Dio*): one sees the Church as an active presence embedded within the social, while the other describes it as a contemplative force, relegated to the safe isolation of the monasteries.

Both at the beginning and the end of the film Don Pietro is associated with the care of children. He is first seen playing football with youngsters and refereeing at the same time, emphasizing his double role as social participant and guardian of rules/law/order. Called to the meeting with Manfredi he invests an older child with the controlling role, forecasting the dramatic void he will leave at his death, a death which will in fact be witnessed by the children.

In order to pick up the money he will deliver to Resistance groups, Don Pietro is sent to a shop selling antiques and religious artefacts. When he asks for a statue of Saint Antonio Abate (Saint Anthony Abbot or the Great) he is told that it is a saint not in fashion and offered a 'San Rocco' (Saint Rocco) as a more attractive purchase. Saint Antonio Abate is considered the father of monasticism, a spiritual practice involving exclusion from the world in pursuit of solitary prayer.[7] The reference to monastic life and its questioning becomes more explicit when Don Pietro meets the men responsible for the Resistance's propagandistic leaflets who, at his suggestion of a possible hiding of some men in a monastery, argue that the limited number of Partisans demands that they all remain active. Moreover Saint Antonio is also the protector of farmers and agrarian life and of all those who are looking for something lost. It would then seem consistent with an anti-fascist ideology to temporarily reject a past where the agrarian Italy glorified by Mussolini had become associated with backwardness and poverty.

The offering of San Rocco as more popular saint is also worthy of consideration. During the fourteenth century San Rocco, originally from France, travelled to Italy and devoted himself to the care of those suffering with the plague. Returning to France after surviving the disease himself, he was not recognized and, considered a criminal, imprisoned until his death. The saint is then possibly associated with an active participation in the struggle against 'the plague' of German invasion and his death as misjudged innocent is suggestive of the inevitable fate of those involved in such struggle.

The saints are often represented together on either side of the Virgin Mary,[8] maybe to outline the double (contemplative and active) legacy given to the 'maternal' institution of the church. The absence or rejection of the contemplative

---

7 http://www.newadvent.org/cathen/13100c.htm
8 *Crocifissione con la Vergine, San Giovanni, San Rocco e Sant'Antonio Abate* by Vincenzo de Ligozzi, 1605. *Pala dell'altare dei SS. Rocco, Antonio, Sebastiano* by Angelo Ceroni, 1862. *Sant'Antonio Abate, San Sebastiano e San Rocco*, Maestro di Tavarnelle, San Casciano, Museo di Arte Sacra, Italy. *Three Saints: Roch, Anthony Abbot, and Lucy* by Giovanni Battista (c. 1513).

side leaves the other exposed to the temptation of the external world, temptations embodied by the feminine body and expressed cinematically through the unlikely closeness of the San Rocco statue to that of a naked nymph. Such dangerous exposure is reorganized by Don Pietro who moves the two statues to face in opposite directions. It is later reorganized, narratively, with Pina's death.

At the end it is indeed the movement of Don Pietro and his protegés towards the safety of the monastery that leads to the arrest. Francesco is saved by indulging in a long goodbye with Marcello. The scene is a negative parallel to the one which, in De Sica's film *I Bambini ci Guardano*, sees the father leaving the child in the hands of the Church and then committing suicide after the discovery of the mother's adulterous relationship. Francesco is now the one in the hands of the Church that is protective of the father as well as the children. At the end of the encounter he becomes a 'consecrated' father both verbally, through Marcello's calling, and visually through the almost ceremonial gift of a scarf which belonged to Pina. It is the same scarf she held when she was shot and it becomes, retrospectively, a symbol of her desire for recognition in marriage.[9] The child's offering of the scarf continues and completes her desperate trajectory and demands a loyalty which will be expected in fatherhood as it cannot be consummated in marriage.

The absence of fathers in the film is indicative of a lack, a void which becomes the site of contention between a ruthless military and a Church complacent to revolutionary Communist activities. Neither will succeed. With Don Pietro's execution the Church remains an empty superstructure supported by tradition towards which a hopeful youth walks in search of shelter, an outcome beautifully suggested visually in the film's last shot.

The theme of the loss of practical 'paternal' leadership continues with Manfredi's death. He dies of torture in a scene constructed as to make of his death a re-enactment of the death of Christ on the cross. Marina receives a fur coat in payment for betraying him, completing the analogy with the Gospel. His death seems to suggest that a chance of a 'fathering' the young country coming from the intellectuals is not an option either unless it is understood as 'spiritual' legacy rather than political leadership. Significantly there is no development of the relationship between the sparing of Francesco from capture and the possibility of a political consequence of the Resistance's actions. In fact even if Francesco, thanks to his narrow escape, is the only positive figure left who can be invested with the role, his last words to Marcello – 'For a while we won't see each other but I will come back and we will always be together' – resemble again the words of Jesus

---

9 In the seventeenth century Croatian fiancées gave their fiancés a scarf as a sign of mutual faith, especially before they went to war (from http://academia-cravatica.hr/interesting-facts/potential/). Also in Shakespeare's play *Othello*, Othello asks his wife Desdemona to produce the scarf he gave her as a gift as it is now lost. He tells her that as long as she kept the scarf she would retain her husband's love, but if she ever lost it, her husband's love would turn to hatred and infidelity (*The Tragedy of Othello, the Moor of Venice* by William Shakespeare, A Précis www.hermes-press.com/othello.htm).

to his disciples ('My children, I will be with you only a little longer. You will look for me, and just as I told the Jews, so I tell you now: Where I am going, you cannot come', John 13) and emphasize the expected outcome of the Resistance as an opportunity for spiritual renewal through a necessary cathartic sacrifice rather than as politically significant presence.

But the insistent references to the figure of the Christ, both in images (Manfredi), words (Francesco) and behaviour (Don Pietro) might also have an archetypal significance. Jung dedicated an entire essay to the discussion of Christ as a symbol of the Self where he suggests that 'the spontaneous symbols of the self, or of wholeness, cannot in practice be distinguished from a God-image' (*C.W.*, Vol. 9ii: para. 73). Through his acceptance of manhood and through his death Christ provides an opportunity for the restoration of a wholeness damaged by the Fall, but it also becomes, symbolically, the representation of the fulfilment of a psychological process which Jung has described as individuation. Bringing together the opposites, divine and human, and providing through death and resurrection a point of passage from sin to goodness, a mediation between creator and creature and a 'cross' standing between that of two thieves as a site of reconciliation, the figure of Christ appears, archetypally, as an anticipation by the psyche of a necessary movement towards wholeness (*C.W.*, Vol. 9ii: para. 73).

The emergence of an archetypal image of such significance would seem fitting within the historical moment which sees Italy as a divided country not only through its traditional regional diversity but also thanks to a class structure only exacerbated by the policies of Fascism. During the last years of the war, following the flight to the south by the king and Marshall Badoglio and the founding by Mussolini, rescued by the Germans, of the Republic of Salò, the problem of divided loyalties also added to the confusion and weakened the efforts of the Resistance. The need for a 'passion' (in the sense of a suffering) and a sacrifice which would unite the opposites and bring, through resurrection, the much desired spiritual rebirth of the country is then represented through the central male characters of the film. Yet the sacrifice of Manfredi, a sacrifice of silence, only achieves a temporary disarmament of a temporary evil. Francesco's words remain unfulfilled through his sudden narrative departure and only Don Pietro's death offers the possibility of a legacy implying rebirth.

Don Pietro's execution, a scene which ends the film, is treated cinematically as an opportunity for both 'forgiveness' and renewal. Rocchio, in his analysis of the scene, suggests that the fascist squad's refusal to fire at the priest, which forces the German officer to shoot Don Pietro with his own pistol, is an attempt at 'constructing a fascist identity free from guilt and condemnation' in order to exonerate 'those Italian subjects who, through either complacency or direct approval and participation, made up the consensus of the fascist state' (Rocchio 1999: 47). In juxtaposing Don Pietro's death to the children's walk toward a city dominated by the dome of St Peter's, Rossellini gives purpose to his 'passion' (Don Pietro's last words are those of Jesus 26: 'Father forgive them, for they do not know what they are doing', Luke 23: 34) by suggesting a possibility of

Resurrection (Rocchio 1999: 48). Yet the option for rebirth is contained within a discourse of forgiveness that later became the political strategy of the Christian Democratic Party 'which sought to contain the effects of the fascist past in order to reorganize patriarchal culture and gain ascendancy over the Communist Party, by co-opting the hegemony of the former fascist consensus' (Rocchio 1999: 50).

In this scene Rossellini is also 'directing spectatorial identification toward the Resistance youth' (Rocchio 1999: 49). But if the children, a consistent presence throughout the film, are given a legacy of renewal they are also deprived, and so is the audience through identification, of the opportunity for leadership. Their walk towards the city is in fact 'directed' towards an authority, that of the Church, depersonalized and unassumingly imposing (the dome of St Peter's) Moreover, little Marcello, who becomes significantly representative of the nation, now orphan of both mother and father and lacking the guidance of his self-appointed guardian (Don Pietro) had already 'anointed' Francesco as leader when, at the time of their already discussed farewell, he offers him Pina's scarf while verbally asking for a renewal of a paternal bondage. The abundance of Christian references in the film allows for another reading of this gesture as an investiture which parallels that of a priest who receives the stole during the ordaining celebration. Francesco, however, quietly disappears from the narrative leaving an uncertain leadership vacuum, mirroring the lack of guidance experienced in the summer of 1943, which calls for the selection of a reliable substitute. The solidity of the Church is the only suggested option.

In a speech given shortly before the end of the war Pope Pius XII emphasized how the work of reconstruction which was to follow 'would only be fully realized within the context of a *civiltà cristiana* (Christian civilization) in the construction of which the Eternal City of Rome ... had a special mission' (Bedani and Haddock 2000: 219). This suggestion was preparing the way for a more direct participation of the Church in political life, which was to come into effect with the support given by Giovanni Battista Montini (future Pope Paul VI in 1963) to De Gasperi's Christian Democrat Party (DC). Born out of De Gasperi's perception that in 1943 the immediate 'need was to prepare Catholics to become future leaders of the nation' (Bedani and Haddock 2000: 217) the DC, thanks to the Church's support, was likely to appeal to a wider range of social groups, including those who had benefited from Fascism. Rossellini's film seems to support and foresee a future where a party of a more 'ecclesiastical' (p. 217) orientation (such as the DC), thanks to such a widespread appeal, would be able 'to realize the objectives of Montini to place a Catholic leadership at the head of the country, and De Gasperi's objective of enabling Catholics, for the first time since unification, to participate in the political life of the country through a mass party' (Bedani and Haddock 2000: 222).

Conclusion

Erich Neumann suggests that during times of social and political unsettlement a perceived crumbling of values allows for the emergence into consciousness of the manifestation, through art, of two great archetypal figures, that of the Devil and of the Terrible Mother (Neumann, 1959: 113). While the presence of 'evil' and demonic characters in neo-realist films becomes more significant towards the end of the war, embodied by Nazi officer Bergmann in Rossellini's *Roma Città Aperta* and in some of the films of the post-war period (the paedophile teacher Ennings in Rossellini's *Germania Anno Zero, Germany Year Zero*, 1947; or the tycoon Mobbi in De Sica's *Miracolo a Milano, Miracle in Milan*, 1951), the negative pole of the archetype of the Mother has certainly found either manifestation or manifest suppression in the films produced during the war. De Sica's *I Bambini ci Guardano* and *La Porta del Cielo* clearly suggest a patriarchal alternative to the dangerous emergence of a 'wanting' (in Jungian language, devouring) maternal while Visconti's *Ossessione* does not shy from visual representations which clearly associate conception and sexuality with death, inexorably pointing to the woman's fertile body as the obstacle to innocence, growth and renewal.

In *Roma Città Aperta*, as in *Ossessione*, the woman who dies a senseless, rather than a sacrificial death is pregnant and while neither Giovanna nor Pina seem to possess the typical attributes of the Terrible Mother they both demonstrate an ability, respectively in action and in loquacity, to overthrow male authority. A pregnant Giovanna in particular, with her direct involvement with her husband's murder, fits Neumann's description of the Great Mother's ambivalence: 'this woman who generates life and all living things on earth is the same who takes them back into herself, who pursues her victims and captures them with snare and net' (Neumann 1963: 149). In the dialectical relation of consciousness to the unconscious, symbolically and mythologically portrayed as 'the struggle between the Maternal-Feminine and the male child', the 'growing strength of the male corresponds to the increasing power of consciousness in human development' (Neumann 1963: 148). Eliminating the threat that would correspond to a later, necessary struggle cannot produce the same advancement in development. It points possibly to a power acknowledged and feared and to the desire to postpone its confrontation.

The social significance of the killing cannot, however, be reduced by or find a substitute in the archetypal reading. The way women are excluded, isolated, punished, condemned and murdered in the films of this period is symptomatic of a fear of losing, together with the war, an authority that to women had been granted by the fascist regime by associating women's biological function with politics. The same regime, associating masculinity with belligerency and physical prowess, risked damaging both men's personal pride and their confidence in the validity of their political participation as the negative unfolding of the war exposed their military inadequacy. The return to the domestic could not happen on the basis of a shared responsibility in an act of conception that was understood as giving women the implicit power of participation. It had to involve first the active partaking in another process of conception, one from which women could be more easily excluded: the conception of a new nation, both in its political and economic form

In *La Porta del Cielo* this exclusion, or more accurately women's marginalization, is constructed through the clear association of the male characters' ailments with the actions, neglects or misunderstanding of seductresses, adulteresses and insensitive mothers; actions which are unevenly counterbalanced by the positive intervention of virginal nurses, abnegating old maids and interceding godmothers. The 'delivery' conceded to the Feminine consists of mediation, in providing the gate, as the title implies, both emotionally – through the women's supporting role – and physically – as the dark, cavernous Basilica – through which the miraculous agency of the Heavenly Father can have effects. The single miracle that by offering independence of movement to the individual becomes the sufficient means to healing through hope and solidarity for all is, in 1944, at the time of the film's production, the miracle brought by the liberating action of the Allies' democratic powers. By 1945 the practicality of such a miracle had become a complex diplomatic affair and the importance of redefining, after the trauma of the armistice, the idea of nation through effective Resistance action became an absolute priority.

Roma Città Aperta responds to such urgency by isolating forms of heroism in clear contrast to those proposed by the fascist ideal of manhood, and by eliminating modes of rebellion that, gendered through their association with female characters, again dispensed with women's active participation in the process of liberation. With the exception of the attack aimed at freeing Francesco and other prisoners, the actions of Resistance members throughout the film are demonstrations of high moral stature rather than physical endurance while Pina, leading the attack at the bakery and slapping the German who tries to befriend her, represents the negative outcome of reactive instinctual violence. When Pina dies it is in order to protect the father of her unborn child with the naked tool of a voice which however loudly it proclaims its wanting cannot restore by words alone what violent events have and will continue to destroy. According to Della Loggia, the 'patria' (homeland) also died on the announcement of the armistice with the Allies as a consequence of beliefs sustained by words alone, those of Mussolini's empty rhetoric first and of Badoglio's double and deleterious negotiations which led to the tightening of the terms of a surrender which as 'unconditional' left nothing to negotiation.

Pina's death, Manfredi's girlfriend's prostitution and the German spy's lesbian dealings confirm women's sterile participation, which in leaving no constructive trace is in stark contrast to the men's ability to deliver a legacy of spiritual guidance after their elimination (which significantly happens as executions rather than in battle). The longstanding value of such a legacy is sealed by narratives clearly reminiscent of contents from biblical texts (Old and New Testament), a reference which has certainly the function of validating Resistance activities as acts of spiritual salvation as well as suggesting the compatibility of Communist ideals with those proposed by Catholic tradition. This reference, however, also naturally amplifies the singular, individual narrative by tying its interpretation, through amplification, to the history of a collective as described by images of archetypal value.

As pointed out in the film's detailed analysis, Francesco, Manfredi and later, Don Pietro in Rossellini's film are associated through dialogue, actions or mise-en-scène with the figure of the Christ which Jung considers as symbol of the Self. Representing as such the realization of the process of individuation, Christ is the point of paradoxical union of historically defined temporality and humanly expressed uniqueness with divinely derived universal and eternal qualities (*C.W.*, Vol. 9ii: para. 115). The felt need for a rebirth of a national identity fatally damaged by Fascism and war is drawn, throughout the film, as the equivalent of the dawning of an ego-consciousness which should find, in the Christ-like figures of Manfredi, Francesco and Don Pietro (respectively portraying the Passion, the Ministry and the possibility for Resurrection) the image of its own development, the projection of the future fulfilment of the process of individuation, the visible expression of the achievement of wholeness.

Understood as a relatively conscious production of a Resistance gospel and as a way to escape, with the creation of martyrs whose sacrifice is presented as witnessed rather than constructed, the responsibility for past passive consensus and humiliating subservience, Rossellini's film would be susceptible to the negative scrutiny of historians and cultural analysts who could dismiss it as partial and pretentious. Rather, the universality of the film's enduring appeal and the unanimously positive critical responses it continues to elicit support the hypothesis that the 'history' it presents us with is that of an unconscious desire for rebirth, of a process envisaged rather than completed, of a consciousness recognizing a potential that, in the universality of its unfolding, remains also universally appealing.

Despite the positive legacy implicit in the sacrificial deaths of Manfredi and Don Pietro and the attempt, whether conscious or not, to point to the solid foundations offered by the Resistance to future reconstruction, the film imagery also unwittingly exposes the weakness already presented in the films preceding the armistice. Neither Manfredi nor Francesco have a place of their own and their shelter is provided at first by women who consistently fail to protect them and later is offered by the Church but it never materializes as a safe destination. In a manner similar to Gino in *Ossessione*, the two men's lack of commitment, Francesco to Pina as wife and Manfredi to Marina as the soul to redeem, and both to the Church as religious rather than just humanitarian organization, destines them to a wandering without focus. Their development, expected as the mythologically described psychological unfolding of an heroic journey as well as an accomplishment of positive historical value, is somewhat frozen, immobilized – as the many references to the inability to move suggest in De Sica's film and any attempt at movement remains hindered by the dependency this immobility implies – as the unsafe shelters to be used 'in waiting' point to in Rossellini's piece.

The war and the Allies' landing made the renewal a necessity of survival, rather than of transformative growth. The rebellion against the father (Mussolini) and against the old order (Fascism) is an action pursued by an external agent (Allies) and joined out of the realization of the possible annihilation by the new, namely democratic (maternal) saviour of the newly delivered national consciousness. The fear left behind by the fascist 'paternal castration' which the pre-armistice films describe so clearly is replaced by the fear of a castration effected, this time, by the Mother (Anglo-American control). The action taken against her overruling of the nascent ego is only anticipated, in Rossellini's *Roma Città Aperta*: the elimination of Pina, carrier of a life conceived out of matrimony (unrecoverable dignity) is carried out by the Germans, and the declared unworthiness of Marina, whose desire for wealth ends in prostitution, is a downfall Manfredi has no interest in halting.

A similar inhibition and passive expectation of freedom is also present in De Sica's *La Porta del Cielo*. De Sica's train seems an obvious metaphor for national unity. Travelling across diverse regions and traditions, it presents faith as a viable alternative to politics as a powerful unifying force. It also represents a journey towards healing that materialized as the newly acquired ability for movement as well as the capacity to 'see' and face responsibilities. The immobility so many characters in the film suffer from can be likened to the consequence of the petrifying gaze of the Medusa, an aspect of the Terrible Mother, an effect overcome only through reflection, through a 'seeing' in a mirror which necessarily makes one's presence visible to oneself, claiming the birth of the subject from the overruling of the devouring maternal which is now object of a conscious gaze. This consciousness seems to be missing and the ability to move is a miracle obtained through motherly intercession and offered as a gift which does not require payment except through faith. Faith somewhat circumscribes the field of movement to that which happens within its confines, within the litany of prayers, within the walls of the Church, inside the 'house of Nazareth' as the representation of the supremacy of traditional Christian values. Yet this is considered enough, at this point in the development of Italy as new nation, to inspire a solidarity that has been for too long missing from the field of politics and has to be borrowed from the more consistently unifying capacity of the traditional institution of the Church. Whether this solidarity would be maintained throughout the process of reconstruction of a significantly damaged national ego only the future could tell.

Chapter 6

1947-1949

Clearing the debt to the maternal between war and reconstruction

Introduction

The journey of hope, endured as an allegorical parallel by De Sica's train in *La Porta del Cielo*, reached its destination for Italy with the end of the war: the accomplished sacrifice of the innocents who died in the ranks of the Resistance, mythologized in Rossellini's *Roma Città Aperta*, was now a legacy to be delivered as committed political action.

Rossellini and De Sica both directed more than one film in the years between 1945 and 1949, but this chapter focuses on the films closer in production time to the 1948 first general elections. Rossellini's *Germania Anno Zero* (*Germany Year Zero*, 1947) Visconti's *La Terra Trema* (*The Earth Trembles*, 1948) and De Sica's *Ladri di Biciclette* (*Bicycle Thieves*, 1949) are analysed within the context of a period in the history of Italy defined by an unprecedented potential for radical social and political renewal.

The expected enthusiasm and positive attitude towards a future that promised to bring the realization of that dream of unity, democracy and mass participation which had fuelled the final rebellion against Fascism and against the murderous ideology of Nazi Germany, did not leave, however, visible traces in the films here considered. Rather, the narratives are driven by a movement that only briefly overlaps with conscious direction but is otherwise contained within the frustrating ellipsis of apparent lack of resolution. Moreover, the claustrophobic entrapment and utter desolation of the landscapes are only amplified by the corresponding moral disintegration and fatal lack of solidarity consistently represented in the three films.

The summary of the historical events that were to determine the future political and economic development of the country and which unfolded while the films were made offer an only partially satisfactory justification for the hopelessness, loneliness and dramatic helplessness described through the protagonists' ordeals. The analysis of the individual films and the amplification of their symbolic content provide the material for a comparative review and for a reflection of the significance of the recurrent themes and images, not only as conscious elaboration of the directors on the disappointing outcome of the much awaited political revival, but also as descriptive of an unconscious striving towards the independence of the ego, understood as a newly emergent national consciousness, from the implicitly demanding generosity of the maternal.

There is certainly great political and historical value in associating this 'maternal' with the specific forces that manipulated events in favour of the exclusion from positions of leadership of the parties more substantially and directly involved, both ideologically and practically, with the Resistance. The adoption of the Jungian perspective, however, will also reveal the existence in the films of a positive trajectory, descriptive of a psychological process of affirmation of ego-consciousness which because of the specific historical context of its unfolding, can be confidently recognized as the effort of a collective unconscious to compensate for otherwise dangerously alienating events.

The discussion of the absence, marginalization and exclusion of mother figures from the films naturally attracts a feminist reading that is not weakened by an understanding of a process of psychological development described by images which are necessarily gendered. Undeniably, the paradoxically positive outcome of the unconscious process is the birth of an awareness that, in line with psychological traditions as well as with the prevalently masculine gendering of the Italian body politic, is decidedly male. This chapter aims to convey both the importance of the film text understood as the site of exposure of patriarchal anxieties which demand and effect the suppression, disempowerment and weakening of women's active contribution to the social and political life of the country, as well as the relevance of the images as indispensably gendered sites of departure for the unfolding of a psychological birth which, as such, demands the distancing from a necessarily feminine maternal body.

Historical background

The years between the armistice of 1943 and the end of the war were, as we have discussed, not only years of uncertainty and confusion but also a time for the development of rich expectations which saw the end of the conflict become the receptacle for hopes and dreams, the point where all desires for renewal converged and ideals of freedom clustered in the form of ambitious prospects.

After the diplomatic anticlimax that dampened the enthusiasms and the memory of the nineteenth-century Risorgimento, the efforts of the Resistance and its role in the liberation of northern Italy seemed to offer Italian people a second chance. The freedom they had fought for directly now demanded the responsible extension of that effort into the construction of a structure capable of maintaining the benefits that freedom implied. The revolutionary spirit of the Resistance had proven to be the propelling force of an ideology that could lead the country to radical social and political change, and the affiliation of most partisans with the parties of the left seemed a good basis on which to build both the challenge to old systems – Fascism as well as weak liberalism – and the identity of a new nation. However, the early enthusiasms were soon frustrated and the years between 1945 and 1948 were to 'mark the triumph of continuity' (Duggan 1994: 245), an outcome partially attributable, according to historian Mack Smith, to a supposedly 'conservative instinct' (Mack Smith 1997: 421) and certainly conditioned by the presence of a relationship of dependency with the 'liberating' Anglo-American allies.

It seems fair to comment that although the popularity of the Resistance would suggest the presence of an instinct which can be described as anything but conservative, the forces at work to repress any revolutionary tendency certainly contributed to the frustrating results. Dependency on the liberating US was measurable as significant financial support to the Christian Democracy (DC) during the 1948 electoral campaign and as substantial contributions to the cost of reconstruction and economic recovery coming with the Marshall Plan – contributions which were not offered without conditions.

Moreover, the sense of a unified identity as nation, if temporarily galvanized by the patriotic fervour of the partisan activities, had been jeopardized by the splitting of the war of liberation into two episodes each relating to areas already divided by profoundly different economies, the North and the South. From the time of unification, industrialization and capital investments had been a northern affair both because the interests of the new government often coincided with the private interests of its northerner ministers and because of the stronghold of the southern *latifondisti* (landowners) who used their financial influence to maintain a semi-feudal system of agriculture, supported during the fascist dictatorship by Mussolini's insensitive policies. His attempts at stopping the haemorrhagic flow from the countryside into the cities by prohibiting such movement, the emphasis on agriculture as the centre of Italian economy and the limitations imposed by autarchy did not coincide with reforms aimed at improving living and working conditions in the regions most exploited by such changes. Overpopulation, lack of or inadequacy of infrastructure, low wages and unemployment were problems that Mussolini had preferred to ignore, hoping that it would be sufficient to censor any public reference to the 'problem of the south' for it to be contained (Mack Smith 1997: 432).

The war only exacerbated the developmental distance and although it was the civilians' revolt in Naples, at the end of September 1943, that pushed the Germans to abandon the city, the Allies' landing in Calabria and later in Salerno brought freedom to the rest of the South and King Vittorio Emanuele III and Badoglio considered it safe enough to establish the newly formed Kingdom of the South's headquarters at Brindisi in Puglia. Strong in a tradition of organized class struggle associated with the development of industry, the population of the centre-north could count on a political awareness, which facilitated the structuring of a partisan revolt, and on a complicity between workers and intellectuals which proved powerful in inflaming patriotic spirit. While people south of Rome were enjoying the benefits of a re-established monarchy that met the approval of the British government as well as the peace brought by the now cobelligerent Americans, in the north people were fighting and dying for the ideal of a freedom which could not be reconciled with that of a government tied in any way to a ruling aristocracy.

The referendum held in 1946, which offered people the choice between monarchy and republic, marked the end of a reign stained by acts dictated by cowardice, self-interest and lack of vision, but it also materialized the differences in perspective, political awareness and confidence in popular initiative: the votes for the republic were only marginally greater in number than those supportive of a return of the monarchy and the majority of the latter were collected in the South. Unity, sanctioned by the elections for a Constituent Assembly held at the same time as the referendum, was to be built on an acknowledged difference.

Visconti's *La Terra Trema* (*The Earth Trembles*, 1948) was the result of the conscious realization of such profound differences. The film originated in 1947 as a project for a short documentary commissioned by the Communist Party. Once in Sicily, Visconti felt compelled to transform the documentary project into one comprising a trilogy of films each presenting the story of the oppression and exploitation of workers from different trades and of their effort to break free and acquire political and economical independence. Only the first episode was ever filmed and it is the one known as *La Terra Trema*, telling the misadventures of a family of fishermen who invest everything they own in the setting up of an independent business, realizing a dream of freedom from the exploiting wholesalers. Both lack of planning and unfortunate circumstances lead to financial disaster, family disintegration and the furthering of their misery.

As well as presenting the seemingly unchangeable predicament of poverty, backwardness and abuse as endemic to the South, the film also points to the pressing power that a tradition of oppression exerts on the masses to the point of hindering solidarity and fomenting mistrust in the possibility of revolutionary changes. Indeed, the events leading to the 1948 elections seemed to confirm the applicability of the film's message to the situation of Italian politics.

The 1946 elections for the Constituent Assembly had certainly brought to the foreground the Communist and Socialist presence in the country. Despite the fact that the majority of the votes went to the Christian Democrats, thanks to the support from the Vatican in the form of unashamed propagandistic sermons and campaigns against the Communist 'danger', Communists and Socialists obtained between them equal representation in the coalition which produced a Constitution to be put into effect from January 1948. Trying to make of his party a worthy partner in the sharing of parliamentary power, Togliatti, the leader of the Communist Party, demonstrated unexpected tolerance and a willingness to work side by side with the Christian Democrats even if it meant forfeiting the party's traditional anticlericalism in order to support the inclusion of the 1929 Lateran Pacts into the new Constitution.

Togliatti's careful participation was, however, short-lived. While the Vatican viewed the Communists' contribution with increasing suspicion, with the onset of the Cold War in 1946 America's unease about their participation in government grew stronger. On his visit to the US, De Gasperi, the Christian Democrat Prime Minister, was made aware of the possibility of substantial financial aid on the condition of the Communists' ejection (De Blasio Wilhelm 1988: 260; Duggan

1994: 254). In April 1947 De Gasperi declared the existence of a crisis in government deriving from dissentions amongst members of the coalition and in May the Communists were excluded from government and 'effectively consigned to permanent opposition' (Duggan 1994: 255).

Strong from an electoral campaign supported financially by the US and ideologically by the ever-present Church, the Christian Democrats enjoyed an overwhelming victory in the 1948 elections. Aware of the fragility of a majority obtained through the backing of the Church, De Gasperi set out to secure a broader electoral base by gaining mass support independent from the Vatican. The South became then his prime target and the establishment of the Cassa Per il Mezzogiorno, a fund in aid of the development of the South, became a means to exchange votes for subsidies, contracts and jobs, indeed a 'remarkable efficient system of "state clientelism"' (Duggan 1994: 260).

Poverty and unemployment seemed to claim their victory over ideology and fear and conservatism prevailed over the spirit of renewal and transformation. The dream dreamt by the Resistance disappeared even from the screens of the neorealist directors here considered and with the return of American films to the Italian screen from 1946 (Torriglia 2002: 152) another dream was to take its place.

Germania Anno Zero (Germany Year Zero, 1947)

The responsibility of awareness

> It is therefore crucial to recognize when we have lost touch with our archetypal ground. When that happens we dream of crumbling foundations and flooded basements, collapsing underground parking lots, disintegrating retaining walls, cellars that have caved in. It is then our task to go down and do something about the chaos below.
>
> (Woodman 1982: 126)

With *Germania Anno Zero* (*Germany Year Zero*), dedicated to his son Romano, who died in 1946 at the age of nine, Rossellini completes what is considered his 'war trilogy', begun with *Roma Città Aperta* (*Rome Open City*, 1945) and inclusive of *Paisà* (*Paisan*, 1946). In the words of the director delivered through the voiceover which accompanies the film's opening sequence, the film wants to be a 'document', a 'serene' and 'objective' portrayal of the effect of the war on the morality and attitude of people for whom tragedy has become a 'natural element'. As the film closely follows a 12-year-old boy and his efforts to sustain his family amongst the rubble of a desperately poor post-war Berlin, the intention of producing a 'document' is overshadowed by the direct spectatorial interaction with the single, fictional narrative backbone provided by the boy's wanderings, encounters and actions. Moreover, the voiceover explicitly offers a directly pedagogical intention with the suggestion that the film might serve as an incentive for the realization of the need to 'teach German children how to love life again', an intent which certainly positions the film beyond the 'objectivity' it has just claimed.

Set in the Berlin of 1947, the plot develops around Edmund Koeler, a 12-year-old boy who lives with his bedridden father, his brother and his sister in an apartment shared by five other families. The flat's owner, Mr Redemeker, has reluctantly given up his space and openly despises his forced guests. Edmund's sister, looking after her father during the day, goes out with Allied soldiers at night in the hope of bringing home some cigarettes she can exchange for food. His brother, Karl Heinz, a former Wermacht soldier, will not present himself to the police, an action which would guarantee a much needed extra food token, for fear of being sent to a concentration camp. Edmund is the sole breadwinner in the household and spends his days wandering around the rubble, hoping to fill his bag with anything exchangeable for food on the black market.

When he meets his old schoolteacher, Ennings, the boy believes he has found a glimmer of hope. However, it is obvious from the outset that the man has dubious intentions: he insistently touches the child and keeps him uncomfortably close, demanding an intimacy extending clearly beyond the boundaries of their previous teacher–pupil relationship. Ennings is a survivor of a Nazi ideology he openly discusses with the little boy who asks for advice about his now hospitalized father. The teacher's words are direct: the weak must be eliminated by the strong, they must be sacrificed because 'in a defeat like this the important thing is survival'. Edmund reads these words as an order and proceeds to poison his father once he is sent back home from the hospital. The little boy, tormented by guilt, searches for comfort in his teacher who sends him away afraid of being accused of instigating murder. Edmund, alone with his tragic secret, commits suicide by throwing himself from the top of a skeletal building while his father's funeral takes place.

The film opens with images of a desolate and dilapidated post-war Berlin accompanied by the voiceover which anticipates the film's documentary and pedagogical intentions. After dedicating ample footage to the shooting in wide angle of the physical damage endured by the city, the camera finally pans to the cemetery where Edmund, the child protagonist, is working, digging graves with a group of women workers who soon ask him to leave. The women's concern is not, however, with the child's own welfare, but with his taking up a place which should be given to another woman, supposedly more in need and more capable than Edmund.

Anna Maria Torriglia, in her discussion of the film as descriptive of a loss experienced by humanity as a whole, considers that 'nothing could be more effective than post-war Berlin as a setting for the representation of ethical annihilation' (Torriglia 2002: 33). The collapsed buildings, the empty, skeletal structures which form the desolate backdrop to the story, are a visual indicator of a parallel emotional emptiness and desolation that seems to have taken hold of the people who inhabit the city. Indeed, in this first encounter with Edmund and his reality, the most dramatic symptom of the profound trauma suffered by the child and his contemporaries is evident in the women's response to him: the maternal instinct, protective of the future as a potential alive in the child, has been overshadowed by that which safeguards personal survival. Edmund is too young to be digging graves yet his journey leads to death and the graves the women are digging, obsessively measured by the male attendant, become a forecasting of his destiny.

Jung actually lists the grave as one of the symbols representative of the negative aspect of the Mother Archetype. Both Jung's own and Neumann's study of this particular archetype are in fact consistent with a definition of archetypes as bipolar, possessing both a positive and a negative side (*C.W.*, Vol. 10: para. 461, Vol. 9i: para. 415; Neumann 1963: 64–83). While the positive qualities associated with the Mother Archetype are 'maternal solicitude and sympathy; the magic authority of the female; the wisdom and spiritual exaltation that transcend reason . . . all that is benign, all that . . . fosters growth and fertility', the negative side of it 'may connote anything secret, hidden, dark; the abyss, the world of the dead, anything that devours, seduces, and poisons, that is terrifying and inescapable like fate' (*C.W.*, Vol. 9i: para. 158).

The two aspects seem to frame the film in opposition to Edmund's presence: at the beginning of the film are the grave diggers who by sending him away deprive him of a possibility for survival and, metaphorically, prepare his deathbed, and at the end is the woman who kneels by his dead body in a gesture of universal maternal compassion. Between these two images Edmund's longing for an absent maternal protection becomes evident as the plot develops and it escalates together with the increasing loneliness the boy experiences.

Expelled from the cemetery Edmund continues with his search: he finds a few chunks of charcoal and shares meat cut from a horse found dead in the street (see Figure 6.1). The image of the horse surrounded by people desperate to grab a piece is placed at the uncomfortable border between a surreal and a documented reality, yet associated with Edmund it acquires another layer of meaning. Jung suggests that 'the mother-imago is a libido-symbol and so is the horse . . . the factor common to both is the libido' (*C.W.*, Vol. 5: para. 421). Also, according to Jung, in Helios' quadriga (the four horses of the sun god) the horses represent the four elements and Jung specifies that their meaning is an 'astronomical symbol of Time' (pp. 422–423). Contained within the city landscape and fully bridled, the horse becomes symbol of the submission and 'domestication' of natural, libidinal instincts (Neumann 1954: 218) and its butchering in the name of survival a marker of a group regression to the wilderness preceding culture. So in Edmund's story both the mother-imago, the positive and effective channelling of libidinal energy and the possibilities for continuity which a symbol of time would suggest are eliminated at the outset. Indeed, the negative symbolism creates an unnatural downward pull, an intense opposition to the potentially positive image of the child-hero who begins his journey with the abandonment and rejections typical of his mythological, religious and fairy tale counterparts, but is deprived of the divine 'sonship', as well as of any spiritual guidance which would sustain him in his ordeals.

148 Secondo tempo

Figure 6.1 Violation of the sacred. *Germania Anno Zero*. Roberto Rossellini (1947). (Thanks to Roberto Rossellini's Estate).

At home Edmund is welcomed by his family and questioned about his findings. Here identities and roles have been reshuffled: the father, from provider has become dependant, the sister has taken the role of mother and Karl, Edmund's brother, from active fighter has become 'invisible' to the authorities and only existing as another mouth to feed within a desperately needy household. Projecting their own discomfort about a situation which alienates them from their previous identities, they discuss Edmund's function as breadwinner as 'impossible'. The use of the word seems inappropriate because the adults are all aware of and benefit from the fact that Edmund actually is working to feed those who should provide for him. His work is not just a possibility (to be discussed as 'impossible') but a reality, notwithstanding his tender age and his rather fragile and delicate look. The fact that what he does should be described as 'impossible' implies a wish to deny a condition which has reversed the course of natural development and altered the structure of relations between family members. Anna Maria Torriglia sees this behaviour as symptomatic of a dissociation 'so deep that it resembles a mental pathology because, in the same person, ideology and praxis run against each other as two opposite and irreconcilable drives' (Torriglia 2002: 36).

Moreover, as the plot develops, the situation in the house becomes just another example of a crisis of masculinity which the film insistently presents as endemic. In fact, the men in Edmund's family and most of the men the child encounters in his wanderings are weak, or fearful, cruel or perverse. Edmund's natural searching for a model of manhood leads him to blindly trust the man who used to be his teacher, but this new 'father' also uses him as a mediator for his black market sales. Ennings in fact asks the boy to sell one of the Führer's speeches recorded on a disk: the 'voice of the Father', resonating within the empty corridors of the dilapidated building where Edmund's plays the disk to amused American soldiers, is the empty sound of an authority whose power turned into self-destruction, a beheaded power which, held without ethics, left nothing but empty rhetoric as legacy. The selling of his 'father's' voice together with his shameless display of paedophilic intentions makes Ennings a symptomatic example of a failure to relate positively to either past or future, but it also describes his position as parallel to that of a doomed mythological hero who, choosing to side with evil rather than engage in the 'heroic' battle against it, has forfeited the chance of emerging from the ordeal as a victorious ego now capable of relatedness.

Ennings's, portrayal is consistent with Rossellini's association of sexual perversion with evil and moral decay already explicit in *Roma Città Aperta* (*Rome Open City*) where the German woman working with the unscrupulous officer Bergmann seduces an Italian girl into a lesbian relationship. This emphasis works as both a reinforcing of the opposite association of virility (a characteristic 'Italianized' by the fascist ideology) and heterosexuality with positive ethical values as well as an unconscious safeguard against the 'reproduction' of evil, only possible as a consequence of heterosexual intercourse.

Nevertheless both Edmund's meetings with Ennings end with metaphorically reproductive attempts. At the end of the initial meeting the teacher sends Edmund off to his first sale of goods under the care of two older teenagers creating a temporary familial nucleus which allows for the unfolding of Oedipal dynamics. Edmund insistently follows the older boy, eager to learn from him but then, when the boy leaves with his peers after stealing Edmund's money, the little boy finds comfort from his fear of loneliness and abandonment in the girl's maternal arms. At the end of the second meeting the teacher's words work as a legacy, as a hypnotic order and metaphorical impregnation which matures into Edmund's murderous action.

Marion Woodman interprets dreams of 'crumbling foundations and flooded basements, collapsing underground parking lots, disintegrating retaining walls, cellars that have caved in' as symptoms of a loss of 'archetypal ground' and as an unconscious suggestion of the need to take urgent action (Woodman 1982: 126). Despite the desolation and severe structural damage visible throughout, Rossellini's film alternates moments of striking symbolic significance, such as the image of the horse, the grave digging, a stealing of scales, Edmund's ritual undressing at the end, with others which seem intentionally severed from their archetypal origin. Edmund's killing of his father is an example of the latter. The struggle of the mythological hero with the tyrannical father ends with the hero's victory and allows for the construction of a new kingdom. The hero as 'bringer of the new' responds to the voice of the internal archetypal father, to the voice of a higher consciousness which needs to become integrated, i.e. 'I am in the Father and the Father is in me' (John 14: 10). In this tale of distortion, the emptiness left by the traumatic loss of a higher figure of authority (Hitler) is filled by the perverse command of a man who functions as the empty medium of the transmission of the still resonating voice of evil. Moreover, Edmund's father repeatedly expresses the desire to die in order to relieve his children of the burden of his presence, further deflating the conflictual nature of the murder and transforming the heroic battle into the senseless killing of a surrendering enemy.

Invested with a responsibility greater than his understanding, Edmund is not driven by Oedipal jealousy, envy or anger. Weakened by poverty and despair he chooses what seems the best solution to the imminent problem of survival: he sacrifices his father, his weak and burdensome past, in the name of the future which he, as child, stands for. His sacrifice, however, is disavowed by his brother's final resolution to present himself to the authority, relieving the family of the responsibility to cater for an invisible, 'tokenless' dependant. The positive change which will derive from Karl Heinz's decision reconfirms the father's death as a familial tragedy rather than as a dramatic necessity, recalling Edmund's humanity and, with it, the awareness of his horrifying crime.

When the support Edmund expects from the mentor whose spoken ideology he put into practice does not materialize, the child faces the profound loneliness of his new condition as orphan. This forced birth, an untimely self-delivery into independence, finds his embryonic ego defeated by the chaos he has no means to master. Awareness, the unforgiving 'sword of distinction', finally separates good from evil, morality from perversion, but only to reveal the abyss of guilt and offer no alternative but to face the void it has opened. Edmund's death is the final act of a consciousness too fragile to develop its spark into consistent light. Performed by Edmund as a consciously enacted ritual, the suicide becomes a willing submission to the power of the maternal, a yielding to the now materialized darkness and a closing of the circle of destiny opened by the women who prepared the graves (maybe Edmund's and his father's) at the beginning of the film. The circle closes with the image of a woman kneeling by the lifeless little body, ambiguously reminiscent of the mother of Christ kneeling by her child both at his birth and after his death.

The shockingly crude ending completes a narrative that challenges traditional ideals of childhood and points to the war (possibly to 'war') as responsible for the upturning of the most fundamental rules of nature. To reveal and to warn was indeed Rossellini's intention, explicitly declared in the voiceover, but more than in a few words spoken outside of the film's own diegetic, the director seems to rely here on an implicit definition of his film as neo-realist notwithstanding the 'non-canonical choice' of situating the action outside of Italy, contravening the principle which tends to consider neo-realist film as devoted to presenting more than just 'representing' Italy (Torriglia 2002: 33).

Through Edmund's story, however, Rossellini does present Italy and, whilst revisiting the past from within an Axis perspective, he also forecasts an imminent future. His choice of location, rather then a change of cinematic subject, represents a shift of perspective, a wide-angled view which not only allows for a retrospective study of the ideological ties between Nazism and Italian Fascism but also facilitates a deeper psychological understanding of the traumatic effects of the war on those who shared the defeat. While both Italy and Germany 'looked to their leaders, respectively the Duce and the Führer, as fathers of the nation (Torriglia 2002: 32) it is Germany that is traditionally known as the 'Fatherland', a detail which transforms the loss of the Führer into a questioning of national identity, damaging the very pillars upon which that identity is constructed. The devastated Berlin, the flattened landscape of ruins is not simply representative of a people orphaned of a paternal leadership. The loss of the father, of the Führer as spiritual leader, has indeed left the people barren and confused but his demise has also destroyed the kingdom he inhabited, both the material and the ideological: the Father has died and with it the Fatherland. Significantly, the voice capable of erecting an empire of darkness now resonates across the empty remains of the once monumental buildings and is sold as souvenir to the victorious enemies.

Susceptible to the hypnotic power and authority of that voice, Mussolini (a teacher before entering politics thus maybe suggested in the character of Ennings) modelled himself on Hitler's figure. Rather than assuming the role of protector of the purity of the race or herald of a distorted ideology which would be criminally put into practice, Mussolini assumed the role of provider and made of random practice (the implementation of incoherent policies) his ideology. Indeed, the process that led to the end of liberalism and the establishment of a dictatorship ran alongside the implementation of policies aimed at offering (or seemingly doing so) leisure and education to working class children and at sustaining large families and prolific mothers. Anna Maria Torriglia's suggestion that 'the fascist ideological attempt to make coincide [sic] public and private sphere, provide the elements for identifying the head of the nation with the head of the household' (Torriglia 2002: 38) supports then the identification of Edmund's father with a Mussolini approaching the end of his life as both political and spiritual leader. Edmund's father, aware of his child's vulnerability, sends him out into the open searching for means of survival. However weak and dependent he is, he still scolds Edmund for returning home late and, finally, he is eliminated in the name of a future which he seems to prevent from developing. In 1940 Mussolini sent his 'children' to war in order to placate his own hunger for power, aware of their military unpreparedness and the abysmal lack of resources of his army. In 1943 he continued to exercise his authoritative power when, weak, ill and defeated he was rescued by the Nazis from his prison and taken to Salò, on Lake Garda, to form the puppet Repubblica Sociale Italiana (Italian Social Republic). Finally he was murdered by the Resistance at a time when his death, seen as ideologically necessary, was, in its overstepping of justice, morally and possibly politically damaging.

Edmund's murder of his father can indeed be interpreted as 'the metaphorical killing of that archetypal *padre della madrepatria* (father of the motherland) who is Mussolini and, figuratively, the historical past' (Torriglia 2002: 38) and the child's suicide as a surrendering of the hope for a future. Yet between the two dramatic gestures is the one important spark of awareness which transforms Edmund into a hero whose rediscovered humanity does not belong in a landscape of untamed instinctual drives but raises him higher, high enough for a fall to be a fatal new beginning in the arms of the ever-present, soothing, dark mother.

Rossellini's Germany is an Italy that, on the eve of the first general elections (1948), needs to take responsibility for its own immaturity, to become humanized by guilt and to take the spark of awareness, represented by the ideals of a young, impulsive and yet courageous and resourceful Resistance, higher into the sphere of a realizable political programme. The fall might be a necessary end but the understanding that motivates it contains in itself hope in the undefeated goodness of humanity and with it the possibility for the beginning of a new journey of redemption. The film's inescapable closure excludes the protagonist from such a journey, positioning that beginning outside the narrative, as a visible legacy for the spectator. Edmund's death becomes in fact a beginning only if his hopeless story works as a document: it then acquires the desired function of catalyst for change. It calls for the awakening of a dormant consciousness and mobilizes into action.

La Terra Trema (The Earth Trembles, 1948)

A bitter sea

Based on Giovanni Verga's novel *I Malavoglia* (1881), *La Terra Trema* was released in 1948 and originally intended as a response to the Communist Party's request to produce a documentary on the condition of fishermen, to be used as propaganda in the upcoming election campaign. When Visconti visited the Sicilian village where Verga's *I Malavoglia* (*The House by the Medlar Tree*) was set, he decided to shoot on location using the people of Aci Trezza as actors.

Much of the critical discussions that followed the film's release focused on the questionability of *La Terra Trema* as a masterful example of neo-realism. The choice of ancient Sicilian as the language spoken by the fishermen is only apparently a realist trait as it was in fact a dialect unfamiliar to the younger generations and incomprehensible even to Sicilians coming from other districts. The images, although capturing spontaneous enough movements and expressions, are carefully constructed within 'tightly framed shots' (Liehm 1984: 81). Indeed, the film's 'realism' is to be found in its being the product of a 'continuous interaction with the subject matter at hand' (Bacon 1998: 39) and in Visconti's ability to reflect the changed political circumstances in Italy with the aid of subtle symbolism and uncompromising narrative solutions.

The *Malavoglia* of Verga's novel become the Valastro family in Visconti's *La Terra Trema*, a family of fishermen whose lives are governed by the cyclical, entrapping routine of hard work which gives in return barely enough to sustain a miserable survival. The claustrophobic isolation configured by the extreme poverty and enclosed environment prevents the fishermen from acquiring the awareness of their exploited condition, an ignorance enforced by the cruel opportunism of the fish wholesalers who, explicitly supported by equally mean political forces, continue to underpay for the product of the fishermen's hard work. 'Ntoni, the eldest of the Valastro children, having experienced the possibilities of the world outside the confines of Aci Trezza during his army training, is prepared to risk his pride and his family capital to demonstrate how courage, clear vision and solidarity can break the chains of social exploitation. Unfortunately, the initial excitement fuelled by 'Ntoni's symbolic throwing of the wholesaler's scales into the sea is soon replaced by indifference as the Valastros lose the boat and subsequently the family house they mortgaged, and with them any hope of social and economic improvement.

Mira Liehm argues that in *The Earth Trembles* 'the downfall of the male character is not brought about by a woman but by his own action' (Liehm 1984: 82). 'Ntoni's motivations are, nevertheless, still subject to the distorted demands of class structure on the natural rules of desire. His love for Nedda blossoms at the prospect of the success of his enterprise and quickly fades away as failure looms. While 'Ntoni's destiny, however negative the outcome, is in the freedom of his own choices, Nedda's fate is determined by a rooted patriarchal capitalism. The difference is described visually through a careful positioning of the lovers as they walk back to the village: Nedda in and out of the shadow cast on the road by the ancient wall and 'Ntoni, cheerfully maintaining his distance which keeps him steadily in full sunlight (see Figure 6.2).

Figure 6.2 'Ntoni walks in full sun and Nedda in and out of shade. *La Terra Trema*. Luchino Visconti (1948). © MARZI Srl. All rights reserved. Courtesy RIPLEY'S FILM Srl.

Women do not possess a political voice; their movements as well as their life-giving activities are frozen by the absence of men. If they represent 'the poetic component of the film' they do so by providing the emotional pillars to a narrative that leaves them powerless and 'condemned to eternal sadness' (Liehm 1984: 82). They stand silent on the rocks and sit in the barren house waiting, renounce their aspirations and desires to preserve intact the core of dignity that economic disaster threatens to erode.

If women are to represent the nation it is either as promoters of what Gramsci has described as 'social passivity' or as embracing, if old and powerless, mothers, only figurative but still needed at the delicate time of reconstruction. 'Ntoni's sister, Lucia, becomes the mistress of a police officer. Her blind trust in the unconditional friendship of a figure of authority who will abuse her desire for wealth is an acknowledgement of the political immaturity of a nation still unable to distinguish between rhetoric and honesty in the imminent elections and it receives violent punishment within the narrative and then narrative exclusion within the film economy.

In a manner strikingly similar to the already discussed episode in *Ossessione*, towards the end of the film 'Ntoni opens his heart to a little girl: 'One day they'll realize I was right. Then it will be a blessing for everybody to lose everything as I did. We have to learn to stand up for each other . . . only then we can move forward.' Unfortunately, after the elections of 1948 the hoped for 'move forward' proved to be an illusion as the Christian Democrats were brought to power after the short-lived coalition with the Communists and Socialists as part of the Constituent Assembly.

Psychologically, 'Ntoni's return to the sea after having lost everything can be understood as a forceful regression, a 'naked' return to the arms of a maternal, which again is the only choice left for an unprepared hero whose weakness is possibly spelt out in this brief encounter with the emerging wisdom of the feminine; the hope in the victory of romanticised Marxist ideals which are unlikely to be popular in a society distressed by endemic poverty and ready to enjoy the benefits of financial help even at the price of its own dignity.

Visconti's choice to eliminate the father in his adaptation of Verga's novel transforms the Valastro family into a nominally matriarchal unit with a widowed mother whose age, in contrast with the tender youth of her last children, points to her archetypal significance. It also seems plausible that there might be a resemblance between the Valastros' mother and the political 'Mother Nation' who, in the late seventies of her unification, watches her children leave for a promised land where wealth is represented by the immaterial smoke of a packet of American cigarettes. She sees them exchange their honour and their innocence for the apparent safety of a friendly and bribing authority and invest their energy fighting to realize dreams of economic freedom soon crushed by indifference and lack of solidarity. These actions respectively forecast the politically damaging effects of the Marshall Plan, the almost inevitable return to an old system of bribery and corruption under the new name of democracy and the failure of the Resistance to germinate into a solid political reality.

The Valastros' mother is a mother powerless to hold her children together once the containing structure she provided them with (the house) is exchanged for the acquisition of the means of production (the boat); a sacrificial action which we will see is also described by De Sica in *Ladri di Biciclette* (*Bicycle Thieves*) and which lends itself to a Jungian reading.

In his description of the mythological stages in the evolution of consciousness Neumann uses, as an illustrative example of the main features of the Archetype of the Great and Terrible Mother, the great Egyptian myth of Osiris and Isis. In the myth, Isis, Nephthys, Set and Osiris form a quaternity of two brothers and two sisters. 'When Osiris is done to death and dismembered by his enemy and brother Set, it is his sister-wife, Isis, who brings about his rebirth, thus proving herself to be . . . the mother of her brother-husband.' Neumann sees 'Isis later struggle to get the legitimacy of her son Horus recognized by the gods' as the surrender of matriarchy to the patriarchal system, and the willing act of giving up her matriarchal dominance as 'an essential function of the "good" Isis' (Neumann 1954: 63–64).

In *La Terra Trema* the function of 'putting together a dismembered Osiris' is probably the one the Mother, as representative of the Mother Nation, is asked to perform simply by remaining a symbolic point of reference now safely emptied of any economic power of exchange. If the necessity for the 'surrender of matriarchy to the patriarchal system' is only hinted at in an apparently accidental and rather dormant subplot to the main narrative in *La Terra Trema*, it forms the propelling narrative agent in De Sica's *Ladri di Biciclette*.

Ladri di Biciclette (Bicycle Thieves, 1949)

A father, a son and a redundant mother

The minimalist narrative of *Ladri di Biciclette* (*Bicycle Thieves*) centres around a father's and son's search for a stolen bicycle, the essential means necessary for the maintenance of a long-awaited job. Although never found, the bicycle has the positive function of creating an opportunity for the development of a new relationship between father and son and, possibly, to their social environment.

Most critical readings of *Ladri di Biciclette* focus on the two parallel journeys that form the minimalist narrative backbone of the film. One, following the psychological restoration of the father–son relationship, focuses on the emotional importance of the walking 'with'. The other, suggesting a critical evaluation of post-war social institutions, develops an analysis centred on the walking 'through' (Marcus 1986: 64). Both critical approaches seem to unjustly disregard the relevance of the narrative leading to the search for the stolen bicycle which actually shifts the attention to the reason for the 'walking without' as it points to the exclusion of the mother from the journey. In reintegrating the early domestic scenes into the critical analysis it becomes possible to isolate a sequence of images rich in archetypal significance.

At the beginning of the film Antonio, after years of hopeless waiting, is offered a job as bill poster, but in order to accept it he needs the bicycle which has been given up to the pawnbrokers. He does not have the money and goes home to complain to his wife who is carrying water back to the house. In his anger at the social injustice that paradoxically demands 'a foot in the door of capitalism in order to enter that privileged domain' (Marcus 1986: 67), Antonio walks ahead of Maria. His exasperated monologue as he supposedly shares his despair consists of a loud regret that he was ever born and a wishing for the courage to end it all by jumping into the river. Verbally he is giving Maria, as embodiment of the archetypal Mother, the giver and taker of life, the full responsibility for his misery. Once in the house his abdication of responsibility is also delivered visually. Antonio will not take the bucket of water he has helped to carry to the kitchen and Maria has to walk back to him to collect it. He refuses to enter a space traditionally organized by women and in so doing he admits his inability to participate in creative production and to act as an agent of change.

His inconclusive attitude and his reluctance to carry the full responsibility for his family's well-being are the manifest symptoms of the weaknesses and faults of the patriarchal system. In exposing them truthfully De Sica reveals his awareness that only by proving uncompromising identifiability with the real can he later justify the inevitability of the restoration of patriarchy despite its faults. In juxtaposition to his immobility Maria acts resolutely and prepares the ritual which will restore Antonio's individuality and authority with the repossession of his bike. The new sheets that Maria retrieves from the bottom drawer to be pawned instead of the bicycle are what is left of her dowry, the last tangible object representative of a feminine ritual of extension of the matriarchal line otherwise truncated in the passage from daughter to wife. She also strips the conjugal bed, calling for a fresh start, one which wants capital rather than love and traditions as the root of the new society.

At the pawnbrokers Maria's sacrifice is completed. She gives in the white sheets, spells out her name and receives in exchange the sum necessary for the retrieval of Antonio's bike. In the next, much discussed, scene he gives the accurate details of his vehicle metaphorically anticipating the reacquisition of the individuality tested by years of unemployment which anonymously listed him as 'unskilled labourer'. While one employee searches for his bike, another walks across the frame carrying Maria's sheets, and as he walks out of frame the next medium shot sees Antonio through the opening at the counter, his eyes following the employee's movement. The attention then shifts from 'the activity of obtaining the bicycle' and with it the right to individuality and identity to the massive set of shelves packed with myriad white undifferentiated, indistinguishable sheets, providing a truthful picture of the extent of post-war poverty. The employee drops Maria's sheets among the others, metaphorically 'dropping' her character into insignificance forecasting the imminence of her narrative exclusion.

Like 'Ntoni in La *Terra Trema*, Maria has lost everything for the good of others but together with her material possession she has also lost the right to 'look', a loss that the elderly professor in De Sica's *Umberto D.* (1951) recovers through awareness, a possibility that for Maria remains unexplored. When Antonio picks her up in order for her to peek through the window of his locker room, the shutters close on her face as she is about to look in, thus claiming the privacy and separateness of male from female space (see Figure 6.3).

Vincent Rocchio points out that as Antonio 'becomes the site for the restoration of patriarchy . . . Maria, as the maternal, must be dismissed (as she is in the narrative) lest patriarchy "owe" anything to the maternal for its restoration or, even more threatening, become an option for reorganising Italian culture after the fall of Fascism' (Rocchio 1999: 76).

Before the trip to the pawnbrokers Maria had washed the sheets coming from the stripped bed. Washing away from them is the residue of sexual closeness experienced in marriage. Returning to their original white they testify to Maria's need to be reinvested with virginity, associated with chastity by a Christian reading but also, mythologically, a reminder of both the feminine surrender to the divine and again of the disposability of 'fathers'. The possibility of the matriarchal reclaiming of the independence from any man in the true meaning of Virginity is exorcized by the superimposition of the meaning of anonymity, and even more significantly with the erasure of the sacrificial object which becomes indistinguishable. The sacrifice, the debt to the maternal, is paid off and forgotten when the bicycle is stolen. It is then just a handing over of the son to the father, a gesture in support of the re-establishing of paternal authority and with it patriarchal superiority.

Figure 6.3 Maria is denied participation as the shutters close on her gaze. *Ladri di Biciclette*. Vittorio De Sica (1949). (Image courtesy of Arrow Films).

As if compensating for the exclusion Maria admits to her past interactions with a clairvoyant and to her belief that Antonio's new job is, indeed, a direct consequence of her saintly intercession. Although Antonio vehemently despises her naive behaviour he will himself return to the clairvoyant for advice when he is about to lose hope of finding the stolen bicycle. The clairvoyant and her audience are but caricatures of a static, fatalistic yet opportunist society, where stupidity and gullibility find no mitigation in innocence and again, as in *I Bambini ci Guardano*, such an ineffective, corruptible society is, in De Sica's interpretation, predominantly female.

The clairvoyant episode belongs to a subplot initiated by Maria's confession at a crucial point, preceding her exclusion. It can be considered psychologically as an admission of dependency and a justification for rebellion. Neumann, in his analysis of the Great Mother archetype, discusses in particular the transformative power of the Feminine and the presence of 'magical-mantic' figures in the life of primitive mankind. If this presence, expressed mythologically through figures such as Medea and Circe and later symbolically through the legendary healing powers of containing vessels (Holy Grail), is supposedly testimony to a surpassed matriarchal epoch, it is also an archetypal marker of a specific psychological situation. In fact, Neumann suggests:

> When consciousness cannot . . . be drawn upon to decide a situation, the male falls back on the wisdom of the unconscious, by which the female is inspired; and thus the unconscious is invoked and set in motion in rite and cult. It is evident that in this phase the woman's pre-eminence – quite aside from her sociological position – is firmly entrenched.
>
> (Neumann 1963: 296)

Antonio's decision to 'have a go' at the clairvoyant's house is a last concession to a Mother which is, as a consequence of this very action, disempowered, stripped of another residue of her dominant attributes. The disarmament of the Mother, which, with subtle superimposition, has a social referent in the bourgeois, continues when Antonio and Bruno, searching for the bicycle thief, enter a church. Here wealthy ladies proceed to shave and clean up the men before they become worthy of a 'necessary' participation in a mass which will then be rewarded with the distribution of soup. The conditional offer of nourishment is an example of a maternal (here represented by the Church) 'withdrawal of love as an instrument of power . . . as a means of . . . preventing her offspring from achieving independence' (Neumann 1963: 68).

The intolerance and rebellion towards the perceived danger represented by the Feminine is taken, by De Sica, to the sphere of politics, when Antonio, returning home after the loss of his vehicle, 'escapes' to an all-male basement where political activities and theatrical rehearsals are taking place. Maria's worried intervention is perceived as unwelcome interference by Antonio. It constitutes the last act of her exclusion from the sphere of social and more specifically political activities which, combined with a refusal to preserve her role of indispensable mother through the portrayal of Bruno's maternal care for his sibling, finally confines her outside the narrative.

When Antonio eventually corners the thief, he finds him to be a negative reproduction of himself, driven to criminal action by poverty and incapable of holding a job. He works as a Shadow figure, a repressed aspect of his own unconscious and a forecaster of what Antonio must, and eventually will, face. Moreover the young man, in his unwillingness to conform to the law (the Father), is supported and protected by a possessive mother as well as by an illness, epilepsy, historically associated with hysteria. He actually manages to get away from questioning thanks to a well-timed fit.

Neumann, interestingly, suggests that 'in hysterical reactions, the failure of the ego and its suffering are frequently accompanied by a "smile of pleasure" – the triumphant grin of the unconscious having taken possession of the ego' (Neumann 1954: 347). Within this perspective the theft of the means of individuation and individuality (the bicycle), and therefore ego development, is at the hand of the Feminine (hysterical thief, his covering mother), capable of incorporating, dissolving, devouring the emergent ego, and it therefore requires vindication.

In his analysis of the threats to paternal authority and, consequentially, to ego development, De Sica also de-emphasizes the natural interdependence of the feminine with the maternal by isolating Maria from the care of her children without suggesting the possibility for reconciliation offered instead to Antonio and Bruno. If neo-realism was 'dedicated to exploring and exposing the rhetorical lies of the fascist period and confronting the social reality of the present' (Overbey 1978: 10), *Ladri di Biciclette* fits the task by denouncing the irrationality of the fascist demographic policy, which, in addressing the natural as political, left women's roles vulnerable to the subconscious rejection and exclusion from the positive wave of reconstruction. In condemning their positive response to the exaggerated demands of the regime, neo-realism comments on women's fragility in a society shaken by the tragic consequences of a complex war, where the children of the prolific mothers of the fascist era grow up without childhood and, metaphorically mirroring the state of the nation, without a parental point of reference.

In order to re-establish a patriarchal superiority weakened by a war won without heroes, the role of women needs a forceful reframing. The unconscious recognition of the powers associated with the archetypal image of the Great Terrible Mother, emerging unaltered from the rubble of war, calls for her disarmament, or maybe just the safe distancing that isolation affords. But if this reactive need for containment and distancing becomes manifest, on a social level, as an attitude of refusal and as a desire to confine women back to a domestic sphere now stripped (both here and in *La Terra Trema*) of its function as solid point of reference, the weakening of the collective 'ego', a result of both the dictatorial and the war trauma, has more complex consequences. The following dramatic turn of events leading to the film's final scene describes the situation of a collective struggling to come to terms with its own fragility.

Antonio, having lost all hope of finding his bicycle, arrives still accompanied by Bruno in the area of the football stadium where a game is about to finish. The area is crammed with parked bicycles and Antonio is visibly distressed by the temptation to reverse his situation of victim to that of perpetrator. Having instructed Bruno to go back home ahead of him on a tram, he resolves to run off with a bicycle left leaning by a door. Antonio soon finds himself chased by the bicycle's owner joined by an increasingly large and angry crowd, under the horrified gaze of Bruno who, unwilling to abandon his defeated father, had returned to join him. When caught, Antonio seems unresponsive to the accusations and contempt of the men who now proudly hold him captive and intend to present him to the authorities. Bruno, in tears, pulls on his father's jacket, desperately calling him back to reality. It is a crucial moment in the film as Antonio's temporary isolation from the present describes a state of unconsciousness he now, thanks to Bruno, has the opportunity to overcome. Having seen Bruno, the men decide to let Antonio go, pointing to his irresponsibility as father and to the negative modelling he provides for his child. Antonio, still in shock, begins to walk, joining the crowd of football fans who now fill the streets. Bruno looks up at him and holds his father's hand in a gesture of both forgiveness and recognition as he joins his father in a walking which finds its purpose within their relationship rather than in the search for an absent, external object.

On 27 December 1947 the first Constitution of the newly found Italian Republic was promulgated and became official on 1 January 1948. Drafted by the Constituent Assembly, formed (mostly) by a coalition of Christian Democrats, Socialists and Communists elected in 1946, the fundamental values of the Constitution seem to be put into question by the film. The first of the 'fundamental principles' listed in the Constitution in fact reads: 'Italy is a democratic republic founded on work'. Article three further underlines the social and political importance of the position of workers as it states:

> It is the duty of the Republic to remove those obstacles of an economic or social nature which constrain the freedom and equality of citizens, thereby impeding the full development of the human person and the effective participation of *all workers* in the political, economic and social organization of the country.[1]
> (www.senato.it/documenti/repository/istituzione/constituzione_inglese)

Antonio's participation in 'the political, economic and social organization of the Country' is hindered by the inaccessibility of the means which would restore his identity as 'worker'. The overstepping of basic moral values becomes a necessity in the light of an embryonic political morality which seems to justify its existence through the pursuit of economic stability. Without work Antonio is not a citizen, or at least not one entitled to participation and his failure to 'deliver' himself as such

---

1 Translation and italics mine.

is symbolically described by the film in two images: the first sees him putting up his first poster close to a tunnel and through that tunnel chasing the thief who takes his bicycle, the second is his own unsuccessful stealing of another bike. The tunnel is the Traforo Umberto I which joins Via Nazionale with the historical centre of Rome creating a passage under the structure of the Palazzo del Quirinale, the official residence of the president and a symbol of the new republican state. Emerging from the tunnel Antonio is, like 'Ntoni in *La Terra Trema*, deprived of an identity he held only briefly thanks to his temporary entrance into the world of social and economic participation that a job signified. He is born again and his journey in search of the bicycle is really a movement away from the external structures that represent the new Italian state, both physically by running through a tunnel cutting through them and symbolically as a necessary journey towards a new definition of citizenship not necessarily dependent on employment status. However, Antonio's journey is consciously a search for an old identity in a desperate longing to re-enter, once recovered, the new life of which he caught a glimpse. Significantly that glimpse was to fall on the poster portraying Rita Hayworth in her role in *Gilda* that Antonio was pasting onto the wall while his bicycle was taken.

The association between the future of the newly founded republic and the penetration of the American dream into Italian culture through the Hollywood medium is paralleled at the end by the association of a typically Italian form of entertainment – the football match – with a loss of moral integrity justified by the desperate need for economic recuperation. The financial support coming from America had its cost and at the time of the film's release in 1949 the cost was already quantifiable as a significant support of the Christian Democrats' electoral campaign which had resulted, in the 1948 general elections, in their unexpected victory over the Popular Democratic Front formed by a coalition of Communists and Socialists. De Sica is here justifying the 'stealing' of a bicycle, a metaphor for a possibility for change obtained through someone else's means, as a desperate last resort and, at the same time, offering an alternative which, understood archetypally, becomes consistent with that offered in Rossellini's and Visconti's films of the same period. Bruno's forgiveness, the forgiveness coming from the new generations, the new Italy the child represents, restores Antonio to the community, not a community of workers or politicians or revolutionaries but a community of men. Holding his son's hand Antonio walks with the crowd, defeated and humiliated, undifferentiated and undistinguished, yet he is no more the hopeless 'unemployed' but a human being returning, with the acquired wisdom of the child, to the archetypal maternal (as the uncertainty and darkness of an unimaginable future where the death of the old and the gestation of the new coincide) which will, hopefully, deliver him again.

Conclusion

At the end of the war Italy found itself on the side of the victorious having narrowly managed to change its destiny of occupied and therefore conquered territory into that of liberated nation, a status strengthened by the undeniable contribution of the Resistance to the success of the Allies' advance. The American 'occupation', however, continued, long after US troops left (or at least 'most' US troops),[2] in the form of an invasion realized through channels clearly exposed by the films analysed in this chapter.

In *Germania Anno Zero* the American soldiers are the only presence with which direct trade remains possible, as fellow citizens are either the victims or the perpetrators of theft. The traded object is a document of a past which the defeated country wants to erase and to which the winners wish to bear witness. With it the Americans are buying the right to write the history of the conflict in exchange for an economic support which the flattened landscape of a bombarded Berlin renders indispensable. The reference to the Marshall Plan is relatively faint, yet the presence of Allied soldiers in the clubs visited by the women at night points, in the form of the exchanges that happen between them, to a dependency consistent with that expected by the Plan's implementation: the girls accept the cigarettes, offered in exchange for their company, but rather than consumed the cigarettes are stored with the intention of using them as currency on the black market. The help offered is a marker of a consumerism which is already of value on the black market but which, once the economies benefiting from the American aid recover, will become a common currency providing greater returns to the investing benefactors. Survival is guaranteed by the desirability of an object which has both the effect of providing elementary sustenance and of preserving the desire through its very circulation.

Cigarettes are also exchanged for loyalty and traditional family ties in *La Terra Trema*. For 'Ntoni's younger brother, Cola, a packet of Lucky Strike (incidentally the brand name contradicts the unlucky turn of events which befell the family) becomes in fact the attractor that, associated with the freedom to travel and see only known through his brother's postcards, leads him to a fortuitous flight. While the cigarettes are not themselves the dream of freedom from the claustrophobic entrapment of the tiny village, their possession confirms the availability of such a dream. The 'strange' man who gifts the packet is believed to be English or American and in exchange for the pleasure he has offered he demands that the hope for independence is forfeited in the name of envisaged progress. Cola's escape is a betrayal that leaves 'Ntoni weakened and more vulnerable to the pressure of the old system which asks for and obtains his humiliating submission. Here the reference is direct and offers a comment on the destiny of the Communist ideals of class struggle and participation which, crushed between the power of an old system reliant on endemic passivity and that of the dream of immediate prosperity as proposed by American propaganda, has little chance of survival.

In *Ladri di Biciclette* Antonio's bicycle is stolen while he puts up his first poster which happens to be for Charles Vidor's *Gilda* (1946). As pointed out

---

2 Details of 'operation stay-behind', consisting of undercover agents and troops left in the country in order to control and if necessary contain Communist takeover, are discussed in the next chapter.

before, from 1946, after an almost complete absence from Italian projection rooms during the war, American films literally invaded the screens proposing standards of living that, to the majority of the population, seemed more desirable and certainly suggested a more clearly positive practical goal than the one associated with an alternative Communist ideology, which attached to traditional means of mass communication failed to bridge the gap 'between high-level cultural action and the real level of comprehension of many of the party followers' (Gundle 2000: 40).

In the film, while the presence of the Hollywood product guarantees Antonio's first job after a painful gap, it also functions as the sensually distracting image of a change which leads to a loss. The loss is not only significant as that of a traditional means of transport which will be soon replaced by the modern status symbols of the economic boom (the Lambretta is an example which becomes part of the cinematic tradition of the 1950s), but because of the process of retrieval it demanded and of the permanence of its disappearance it also leads to a reading which connects the three films through a reflection on its symbolic meaning.

The three films are centred, not temporarily but dramatically, on a temporary hope obtained at the price of a sacrifice. Edmund's sacrifice is that of his father's life, and of his own innocence, in the name of survival; 'Ntoni can buy the fishing boat thanks to the mortgaging of his mother's house; Antonio's bicycle is reclaimed from the pawnbrokers because of Maria's offering of the remnant of her 'bottom drawer' wedding dowry. Each of the offerings is systematically disavowed by a loss of the object obtained in exchange, a loss that again in all three cases finds no resolution except in a return which, according to traditional narrative standards, seems unfruitful.

Because of the actual absence of a physical mother from the narrative, Edmund's trajectory only seems to join the ones described by the other films towards the end. Nevertheless, the child's function of provider of nourishment, his identity almost defined by his continuous carrying of the large leather bag which holds and carries and is emptied and refilled in the child's incessant, tireless, abnegating searches, associates him closely to the elementary character of the feminine as described by Neumann (1963: 24–28) Neumann in fact maintains that 'the basic symbolic equation woman = body = vessel corresponds to what is perhaps mankind's most elementary experience of the Feminine', but he also adds that the Archetypal Feminine 'is not only a giver and protector of life but, as container, also holds fast' and 'takes back the dead into the vessel of death, the cave or coffin, the tomb or urn' (Neumann 1963: 39, 45). Edmund's murder of his father, consistent with this symbolic reading, becomes an appropriation of the supremacy over life and death archetypally claimed by the maternal. It is also an act of freedom as it liberates from a depriving dependency and has the effect of releasing the energy (libido) necessary for the emergence of consciousness (Neumann 1954: 280). Karl Heinz's sudden decision to re-enter society borrows from this energy and it threatens Edmund's own newborn ego, his newly conquered identity as child which the now changed circumstances allow him to reclaim.

The little boy becomes a 'hero' for the brief moment between the murder and the suicide when isolation literally raises him higher (his climbing the steps inside the building) and the ability to distinguish between good and evil, right and wrong invests him with the responsibility of choice characteristic of the acquired state of consciousness. The suicide is a return dictated by the weakness of the newborn: 'the weaker the consciousness and the ego, the stronger becomes the psychic gravitation tending to restore the unconscious state' (Neumann 1963: 26). This 'regression' is described by Neumann as 'uroboric incest', 'a longing for death [which] is a symbolical expression for the tendency of the ego and consciousness to self-disintegration' (Neumann 1954: 278). Understood symbolically the film's end also offers a new meaning to the title: 'so long as an apperceptive ego consciousness is lacking, there can be no history; for history requires a "reflecting" consciousness, which by reflecting constitutes it' (Neumann 1954: 281). The idea of a 'year zero' works then as a marker of beginning if the film is considered as a document with pedagogical and political value, and it becomes an end within a psycho/historical perspective.

Unlike the other narratives that, as will be discussed, psychologically compensate for the negative external circumstances, *Germania Anno Zero* describes, when understood analytically, the state of a collective national consciousness filtered through the director's own unconscious, revealing at the same time the unfolding of processes evolving along archetypal patterns of development.

The same pattern, synthetically definable as the precarious birth of an ego-consciousness followed by the return to the maternal/unconscious, is traceable in both *La Terra Trema* and *Ladri di Biciclette*. The first rebellion, the first expression of unease with the safe anonymity of the unconscious condition represented respectively by the unquestioning, mindless offering of one's workforce to the discerning exploitation of another and the demoralizing listing as 'unskilled labourer', is the first dawning of consciousness. It is marked by the desire to obtain independence and with it identity, an identity which in its meeting with society demands for its recognition the visibility of an object, a mask as an interface: for 'Ntoni a boat and for Antonio a bicycle.

The acquiring of the object at the expense of the maternal invites a social, a psychological and a political reading. The first, considering the nature of the mothers' offerings – the family house to be mortgaged and the wedding sheets for the pawnbrokers – sees the women's willingness to release possessions which signal a matriarchal hold over continuity and time, as a renunciation of their right to be included in the cycle of history. Antonio's refusal to carry the water to the kitchen, the closing of the shutters on Maria's curious gaze and her repetitive exclusions from participation in the narrative progression would support an interpretation that considers these actions as symptomatic of an anxiety which calls for the necessity of the re-establishment of traditional patriarchal superiority.

The debt to the maternal needs to be repaid only if the identity purchased with her capital is maintained long enough to be productive. The debt must be written off if the acquired object is lost or damaged. The loss of what is given deletes the contribution except for its functional disempowering: an outcome negative from a social standpoint but necessary from that of the symbolic description of the process of ego development. 'Ntoni and Antonio in losing the fictitious identities of employer and of bill poster have freed themselves from the dependency of gratitude and have matured as individuals and as fathers ('Ntoni's new role as both the grandfather and Cola have gone).

The returns to the Mother as death (*Germania Anno Zero*), as the sea (*La Terra Trema*) and as the undifferentiated crowd (*Ladri di Biciclette*) are preceded by loneliness and by the understanding which in itself distinguishes. Compensating for the political solution which, with the exclusion of the Communists and Socialists from the government's coalition, denied the possibility for a unity tolerant and respectful of differences, the films offer the incentive to preserve an ego/sense-of-nationhood strong in its ability to untie itself from the false definition offered by imported capital.

This compensating is, however, supposed to work at the level of the unconscious. As Cesare Zavattini (the movement's most prolific screenwriter) emphasized, neo-realism did not consciously offer solutions. Yet it remains debatable whether this was a well conceived stylistic choice or a necessity derived from the very reality the films were mediating. If neo-realist films were to give the Resistance a historically visible point of departure for the construction of a new country, if they were to provide a tangible site of protest, a receptacle for the convergence of revolutionary ideals, the failure to fulfil these unspoken goals probably has its roots in the very reflective nature of the texts. Out of focus, yet visible, behind the futile heroism or the profound humanity of the protagonists, is, in fact, the hopeless, immobilizing containment of an ideological surrounding represented through either suffocating landscape or as narrative dispersion. The inconsistency of solidarity and of social commitment is 'visible' in the films of Rossellini, Visconti and even of De Sica, suggesting that maybe a 'revolution' as such was not a realistic expectation to be laid out over a country 'founded' on an almost traditional passivity of the masses.

The Resistance itself was yet another example of that voluntary action that Gramsci himself had described, when analysing both the advent of Fascism and the nature of the Risorgimento, as 'a surrogate for popular intervention, and in this sense a solution of compromise with the passivity of the masses of the nation' (Gramsci 1971: n.203). This passivity, which might be one of the elements conducive of a failure to translate the impetus of the Resistance into an eligible (or elected, as it were) political option, is possibly founded on an impossibility for the masses to grasp an abstract idea of nation which found little referent in the hopeless reality of post-war desolation, confusion and poverty. Again, Gramsci's analysis of the Risorgimento, obliquely of Fascism, is applicable to the post-war period and helps in partially explaining the unexpected victory of the Christian Democracy (DC) over the Italian Communist Party (PCI), ideologically at the heart of the Resistance, in the 1948 elections. He suggests that 'an organic adhesion of the national-popular masses to the State is replaced by a selection of "volunteers" of the "nation" abstractly conceived' and that this 'voluntarism is an intermediate, equivocal solution, as dangerous as the phenomenon of mercenaries' (Gramsci 1971: n.203). Still, the Resistance had provided a glimpse of what was possible and that 'moment of awareness' can be kept for the future, as Rossellini suggests with his *Germania Anno Zero*, for a time when conditions will allow it to germinate into a more positive political reality.

Chapter 7

1949–1952

Redeemers, tricksters and the wisdom of the unconscious

> The starting point of critical elaboration is the consciousness of what one really is.
>
> (Gramsci 1971: 323)

Introduction

The films chosen for analysis in this chapter are each considered as departures from both the aesthetic and the thematic purity of neo-realism. Rossellini's concessions to bourgeois interiors in *Europa '51* (1952), Visconti's melodramatic interludes in the star-centred *Bellissima* (1951) and De Sica's abandonment of reality for the magical atmosphere of a fable in *Miracolo a Milano* (*Miracle in Milan*, 1951) have each been criticized as acts of betrayal of the ever imperfect stylistic and thematic parameters the directors had themselves established.[1]

The continuous revision of neo-realism's defining criteria has helped reclaim the films' 'realist' value which rather than in the absence of stars or in unstaged exterior settings has to be found in the emphasis on the process more than on the resolution, on movement rather than on its destination, on the unity between protagonists and landscape rather than on the analysis of character, characteristics which definitely describe the films selected for a close analysis in this chapter.

The sense of disillusion, hopelessness and defeat that formed the common thread of the films produced immediately before and after the elections of 1948 becomes, in the films of these first years of reconstruction, an open criticism of the colonization of Italian culture by a corrupting American dream of wealth and consumerism and a questioning of the little resistance offered by those whose ideals of unity and independence had given the country the opportunity to emerge from a humiliating war with some dignity.

The films' protagonists embark on journeys that move them across timelines drawn between dreams of stability, fame and idyllic social harmony and the

---

1 See, for example, Aristarco's negative review of *Europa '51* in 1952 (Forgacs *et al.* 2000: 156–157).

realization of the fragility of such dreams when confronted by the void, the cruelty and indifference of the environment which fostered their emergence. The representation of the seducing and blinding effect of a wealth severed from social and political awareness reflects the contrasting attitudes of the Christian Democrats who, in agreement with the United States, believed in the primary importance of economic rehabilitation as the prerequisite of political stability, and that of the Communists whose faith rested in the possibility of awakening a social consciousness through the exposure to high culture and in the intellectuals' ability to empower the working classes through education.

The historical background to the three films is necessarily that of a significant cultural transformation which certainly had its roots in the effect of Marshall aid on the economy but was also supported by the new dynamics in effect between political forces, dynamics which had been transformed by the election results and now included the Church as an important fulcrum of influence and as a major catalyst of consent. In the years following the elections the ideal of a national unity based on inclusion, integration and dialogue – characteristics of a successful psychological process of individuation organized by the archetype of the Self – was compromised by a closing of communications and by a polarization of politics which the crusades of both the Church and the US against Communism as 'evil' had helped crystallize.

This chapter, after considering the films' individual archetypal material and relationship to historical events and cultural shifts, attempts to determine through comparative analysis the common trajectory descriptive of a psychological process of development which, notwithstanding the seemingly negative resolutions of seclusion, surrender and flight, is ultimately aimed at safeguarding the survival of an ego identity endangered by its own immaturity. The hypothesis that describes this development as relating to a collective search for an identity representative of the national self will be explored throughout the chapter.

History and cultural transformation

The years that form the historical background to the films considered in this chapter were years of transition, characterized by the need to adjust to a new speed of industrialization and economic growth, to a new form of government and to an opening to international influences and exchanges certainly not contemplated by the imposed provincialism and autarchic pretences of the fascist regime.

It was also a time conditioned by the realization of the extent of poverty, destruction and backwardness that, only thinly masked by Mussolini's rhetorical pomposity, had been exacerbated by a war fought on both sides but on one soil. After the Peace Treaty of 1947 this realization was accompanied by that of the mistrust, on the part of the greater economic powers signing the treaty, in the ability of the antifascist forces which now appointed themselves as guardian of the national interests to act as such (Galli della Loggia 1996: 99). The debate over responsibilities, possible alternatives and lack of appropriate reaction to the unfolding of events which were to make Italian politics ideologically subservient to the demands of economics must be left to the historians and the social and economic analysts. The films of this period, however, are clear comments on a situation that, considered dangerously annihilating, demanded a response, affected through cultural means, aimed at preserving the will to active political participation and the pride of an identity not yet solidly established.

Indeed, during these years the relationship between cinema and Italian political history became particularly direct. As mentioned in the previous chapter, after 1946 Hollywood literally invaded the Italian screens with a backlog of unreleased films. In line with the intents of the Psychological Warfare Board set by the Allied military regime in 1944, the objective of Hollywood producers was that of putting over 'in as short a time as possible, a mental picture of America and its values which was entirely and exclusively positive' (Brunetta 1994: 149). Nevertheless, the films imported were a combination of the ones recently produced with the older stock which the 1938 laws on film import had forced the distributors to withdraw from the Italian market. The simultaneous presence of films produced across seven years, rather than deliver an homogeneous message, highlighted the inconsistencies and reflected the American policy of increasing containment of Communist ideals which culminated with the declaration of the Truman doctrine in 1947, often considered as the marker of the definitive start of the Cold War. Such inconsistencies and contradictions made it 'even more difficult to define coherently what the American myth included, or what the "all American" qualities truly were' (Brunetta 1994: 150). While not necessarily disturbing or reducing the enjoyment of the majority of filmgoers, the ideological contamination and effect on politics of the American 'colonization' of Italian culture was finally acknowledged by Italian Communists in 1948 as corrupting and weakening (Gundle 2000: 49).

The realization, however, had come too late and the corruption and weakening manifesting as both a cultural invasion and the financial support offered by the US to the Christian Democrats' electoral efforts contributed to the Communists' defeat at the 1948 elections. The PCI leader, Togliatti, considering the 'realm of culture as a vital sphere in the construction and maintenance of a social order', had isolated the role of the intellectuals as central in 'legitimating social and economic relations' (Gundle 2000: 12). Believing in the eventual victory of superior models of culture over the frivolous and superficial 'capitalist culture' of which cinema was a tool, the Communist Party invested resources in the persuasion and education of the working classes to the appreciation of art, literature and philosophy (Gundle 2000: 39). Such attempts at bridging the gap between intellectuals and workers, between high and low culture, were pursued through traditional, outdated modes of mass communication with a conscious rejection of new media, a rejection which left the field open to those more readily prepared to make use of the effective instruments of the new culture to exert their influence on the masses. The Catholic Church and the Christian Democrats certainly took advantage of both the gap left by the Communists' indifference and the appeal and wide-reaching influence of cinema.

Aware of the importance of cinema as a social phenomenon, the Church managed to use it to reinforce its influence by significantly expanding, in the immediate post-war years, the network of parish cinemas where American films that 'contained no subversive impulses and functioned to blot out the memory of the recent past' were shown (Gundle 2000: 45). The battle against those subversive and revolutionary ideologies that had found new validation in the liberation struggle was intensified after the elections and the suspicion which surrounded the works of neo-realist directors, considered unsuitable and opposed to Christian morality, became outright rejection. The Vatican announcement in 1949 of the excommunication of all Communists and their supporters combined with electoral victory of the Christian Democrats in 1948, which signified greater government control over every sector of film production, contributed to drastically contain the possibilities for social criticism explored by neo-realist films (Gundle 2000: 45).

In 1949 the Undersecretary of Public Entertainment, Giulio Andreotti, with a law named after him (the Andreotti Law), offered financial backing to Italian film productions on the condition of state approval which, it was made clear, would not be granted to films projecting a 'non-edifying' image of Italy (Shiel 2006: 86). Notwithstanding the neo-realist directors' protests against a censorship which echoed the interfering attitude of the fascist regime, the ostracism continued and culminated with Andreotti's open attack in 1952 on De Sica and his film *Umberto D.* (1951), an attack in which the director was asked to 'accept his social responsibilities' and cinema was called to relay a 'healthy and constructive optimism' (Shiel 2006: 86). So if action was taken, and the Andreotti Law can be considered an example, to protect the Italian film industry from Hollywood's extensive competition, Italy's dependence on American aid tied political resistance to economic necessity and brought the 'country more and more firmly within an American sphere of influence' (Shiel 2006: 85).

Between the loans and aids offered by the United States between 1943 and 1948 and the support coming from the Marshall Plan between 1948 and 1952 the recovery and transformation of the Italian economy proceeded at a steady pace and went parallel to the assimilation into popular culture of a 'new model of society that had the consumption of goods as its primary rule of social conduct' (Gundle 2000: 33). The potential corruption of Christian values that the assimilation of such a model implied was not underestimated by the Church which was quick to perceive the dangerously emancipating nature of an economic progress originating from the desire to emulate a country where liberal ideals were in stark contrast to Catholic teachings. Women were to bear the burden of the Church's ambiguous attitude towards progress: the reasserted value of the family as 'basic social unit on which both society and the state were founded' demanded that women's role within it be that of submissive helpmate 'with its attendant virtues of modesty, submission and sacrifice' (Allum 1990: 83). The Virgin Mary was presented more emphatically as the model of abnegation and humble submission to a greater will, a model which was free from the vanity and sensual wants of the sinful heroines proposed by the screen. The proclamation of the dogma of the

Assumption in 1950 was to offer definitive guidance and an ideological response to the dangers of materialism and to the despiritualization of culture.

All three films discussed in this chapter deal with the envisaged consequences of consumerism on the family (*Bellissima* and *Europa '51*), on the individual (*Europa '51*), and on the assumed innocence of the working classes (*Miracolo a Milano*). The films' protagonists embark on journeys of transformation which follow unexpectedly closed trajectories leading (at least seemingly) to surrender, imprisonment or flight from realities which offer no chance for dialogue. Indeed, the dream of unity held by the Resistance had been shattered by the rejection of Communist and Socialist participation in government coalitions and instead a party backed by an intransigent Church and a manipulative economic ally was to provide Italy with a new, glossy image of a national self built on a model of unity which did not contemplate tolerance and integration. The inclusion of Italy in the international picture (NATO in 1949 and European Coal and Steel Community, ESCS, in 1951) became a token of reassurance against the fear of a Communist takeover, a possibility that the Cold War had transformed into a threat requiring the active distancing of the Communist enemy, its clear definition as 'other', its demonization as evil and, as far as Italy was concerned, its hopeless relegation into opposition.

Moreover, NATO and the Central Intelligence Agency (CIA) as early as 1951 sponsored a 'stay-behind' programme aimed at preventing the accession to power of the Communist party and suppressing any rebellion which might be seen as leading to a subversive takeover. Although details of this operation, which in Italy later became 'operation GLADIO', were only made public by Giulio Andreotti himself in August 1990, the efficacy of the operation, amounting to a defeat without a battle, contributed to the establishment of an atmosphere of frustrating entrapment and hopeless resistance that the films of this period convey (Ganser 2005: 1).

Bellissima *(1951)*

Mary Magdalene's tears

> Purity of the soul depends on her being clarified by a life that is divided, and on her entering into a life of unity.
>
> (*Meister Eckhart*, c.1260–c.1327)[2]

After *La Terra Trema* and its rather poor immediate reception Visconti was ready for a change of direction. He wanted 'to take some distance from realism' as he believed that its role 'should not be reduced to [that of] a confinement, a law' but

---

2 Eckhart von Hochheim, commonly known as Meister Eckhart, On Death. Cited in http://www.jungcircle.com/muse/negcap.htm, last accessed 23 February 2010.

rather should be understood as an 'approach' and, as such, allow for individual artistic freedom (Bacon 1998: 51–52). In 1951 Visconti's next film, *Bellissima*, was the application of such a principle and, as Nowell-Smith points out, can be considered 'at its highest level ... a denial of all stereotypes, about Visconti, about Italian films in general, about neo-realism, and even about the sacred monster, Anna Magnani, who is the star of the film' (2003: 45).

The subject for *Bellissima* was written by Zavattini and portrays the vicissitudes of a mother and her daughter who, like their male counterparts in the similarly hopeless journey in *Ladri di Biciclette* (also a Zavattini subject), will fall victim to their social circumstances (Liehm 1984: 55). Anna Magnani is Maddalena Cecconi, a mother who sees in her little daughter Maria the potential for success in the glittering world of the movies, specifically that of Cinecittà. It is a world treated by Visconti with irony and self-deprecation and with a compassionate understanding of the illusions it creates in the people it both depicts and entertains.

The plot develops around the selection process leading to the choice of the prettiest little girl in Rome for a supporting role in the next film by director Alessandro Blasetti. Maddalena's ambition and her motherly devotion to the future of her child carry the narrative forward and her powerful presence prevails even in the instances of physical violence and prevarication at the hand of her otherwise peaceful, reassuring and quietly understanding husband, Spartaco. Maddalena, who earns her money travelling across Rome to give injections, invests all of her savings in ballet lessons, photo sessions, clothes, hairdresser and acting tuition for her little daughter Maria and pays an exorbitant sum, equivalent to most of a month's mortgage, to a con man who promises to push Maria forward in the selection process. When Maddalena is allowed to watch, unseen, the projection of her daughter's audition tape to an audience consisting of the director and his assistants, she hears them unashamedly voice humiliating comments on the helplessly crying and excessively small child. Her anger and despair prompt the director to review the audition tape and to select Maria for the film. However, having regained a sense of pride, Maddalena will refuse the contract she is finally offered for her daughter.

The film opens with a choir singing an aria from the opera *L'Elisir D'Amore* (*The Elixir of Love*) by Gaetano Donizetti. The narrative justification for the music is its use as an introduction to the radio announcement of an audition for the selection of 'a pretty *Italian*' little girl for a part in a film directed by real life director Alessandro Blasetti, who plays himself in the film. Visconti's love of opera and his understanding of the melodramatic atmosphere it evokes might explain his predilection for operatic arias as musical background to many of his cinematic successes: notes from Verdi's *La Traviata* accompany the introduction of Gino to the narrative in *Ossessione*, a flute plays an aria from *La Sonnanbula* by Bellini in *La Terra Trema* and in 1954 Verdi's *Il Trovatore* will provide a strong melodramatic parallel to the narrative development in *Senso*. The choice of operas is, however, never coincidental and in *Bellissima* it encapsulates the film's message both visually and dramatically: *L'Elisir d'Amore* is the story of young peasant who falls in love with a wealthier woman and, having heard of the effect of a love potion on Tristan and Isolde, seeks the help of a bogus doctor who diligently provides him with the prodigious elixir. The potion he buys with all his savings is nothing but wine yet it seems to be effective. The beloved girl was, however, already in love with him and the miracle, which had already happened, was attributed to the magic potion. In a similar way, through tricks and deception Maddalena will obtain confirmation of her daughter's beauty, something which is always there but she cannot fully acknowledge until she accepts the image of Maria as independent from her own.

Providing a visual contrast to the idealized grace and innocent beauty associated with the words of the announcement is a pan of the women singing in the choir, 'middle-aged dowdy maidens and matrons' as Geoffrey Nowell-Smith calls them (2003: 46), who seem to represent one of the sides of a metaphorical space that contains the gap between the idealized (the little girls and their innocence) and the unpleasant (the affectation, arrogance and blind ambition of their mothers). The gap is a reality that Maddalena and Maria explore together, moving at times with the herds (mostly of women) which constantly cross the screen aspiring to reach, through their precious little daughters, the sublimated reality of the celluloid strip, the place where the validating dream will erase the drama of the present. Like the protagonist of Donizetti's opera, they wish to drink of the elixir that will make of their daughter the 'chosen one', performing, at a price, the magic transformation which will make her stand out from the crowd.

The music joins the cut to the Cinecittà site where the first selection is taking place. The gates have just been opened and the women run in, pulling their daughters along towards the audition studio. As the operatic aria finally fades away, Maddalena emerges from the crowd searching for Maria whom she finds quietly playing by an ornamental pool blissfully unaware of the tension and excitement driving her mother. Maddalena scolds her and Maria begins to cry. The scene is watched by scoundrel Alberto Annovazzi who immediately befriends Maddalena by allowing her into the now filled studio through a side door.

This scene anticipates more directly the themes that the film will examine. Maddalena 'has lost' Maria at a time when her whole attention should have been on her. It is the first symptom of the narcissism which often blinds Maddalena and distracts her from her true role of nurturing and protecting mother. The loss is disavowed when Maria is made responsible for her mother's distraction and scolded for spoiling the preparation of her image, now dirty and untidy. Maria's cry is a reaffirmation of her right to a childhood, a right she insistently and often unsuccessfully claims with tears throughout the film. Annovazzi's intrusion is technically an appropriation of a gaze which had been, so far, anonymously spectatorial. He has been watching unnoticed and now 'reviews' Maria and provides the first of a series of approvals which seem to forcefully push the narrative forward.

Maddalena's trust in Annovazzi's ability to influence the selection process lasts long enough for him to extort the money he needs to buy himself a scooter. The young man seems to serve the psychological function of marker of the changes in Maddalena's perspective on the value of the pursued success. With a symmetry typical of Visconti's film structure, Maddalena trusts Annovazzi while she is also firmly convinced that Maria's talent will be recognized, and it is the realization of his dishonesty that marks the beginning of sequential moments of disillusionment which lead to the dramatic viewing of the audition tape. Annovazzi's behaviour, his lifestyle, his shameless abuse of trust, his stealing and his overtly uninhibited sexual proposals describe in him the characteristics of a mythological figure who has, in relation to those around him, the function of catalyst for change: the figure of Hermes.

Hermes is in fact an aspect of the trickster who, as a representation of the archetype of the Shadow, can perform the positive function of mediating a passage. Bernie Neville describes Hermes as 'the divine entrepreneur, a con man without ethics and without malice. He has no values of his own, no concern for substance. He enjoys doing deals, being clever, playing the game. He is the herald of the gods, the connector, the carrier of information' (Neville: 1992: 344). For John Izod in his analysis of *2001: A Space Odyssey* he is 'the messenger of the gods at large, one of his tasks was to bear the souls of the dead to Hades. . . . Because of this he was given the name Psychopompus, "accompanier of souls"' (Izod 2001b: 142). Just as Hermes mediates the passage of the souls to the underworld, so the Shadow provides 'the door into the unconscious' and the 'gateway' to dreams (*C.W.*, Vol. 9i: para. 222). Annovazzi does indeed allow Maddalena and Maria, through a back door, into a world of dreams which the little girl, with her wandering and natural childlike curiosity, had almost managed to avoid. Later he guides Maddalena through such a world, 'mediating' so that the woman will gain access to the 'dark' rooms: that of the photographer first and later indirectly to the projection room. Moreover, the young man also works as a 'herald' for a god-like Blasetti even when his attempts at saving himself from ridicule (a situation typical of the trickster)[3] cost him a humiliating, if temporary, exit from the world he so boldly claims to be part of; an attitude which is also characteristic of Hermes, illegitimate son of Zeus, who has to steal what he feels has been denied to him as a birthright. Annovazzi's association with 'the god of commerce' speed and swift travel is confirmed by his purchase of a Lambretta scooter, both index of progress and a modern means of swift travelling. Finally, like Hermes, Annovazzi performs 'at the edges': he is indeed a manipulator and a tricky dealer whose influencing power within Cinecittà is that of a ruthless and opportunist mediator (Gray 1996: 116).

The characteristic shadow function of hiding 'meaningful contents under an unprepossessing exterior' (*C.W.*, Vol. 9i: para. 485) is certainly performed by Annovazzi who, consistent with trickster's traits, is presented as 'a minatory and ridiculous figure', an unpleasant yet pivotal scoundrel who for Maddalena and what she represents stands 'at the very beginning of the way of individuation' (*C.W.*, Vol. 9i: para. 486) and carries, as potential, the seed for transformation. Annovazzi, with his boldness, arrogance and corruptness, with his Don Juan attitude and an

---

3 Jung. *On the Psychology of the Trickster-Figure* (*C.W.*, Vol. 9i: para.456–488).

insatiable desire for the possessions which were to become representative of the economic boom (the scooter is one example), is an aspect of the 'new' Italy, imprisoned and blinded by the imported American dream and in need of being confronted with the reality of a political and economical compromise which has broken the hopes of many. Only an awareness of the Shadow's darkness can lead to an interaction with the unconscious which has in itself the possibility for lasting change. Annovazzi embodies such darkness: the corrupt and embarrassingly opportunist attitude which was to become, if it was not already, internationally associated with Italian politics.

Maddalena is attracted, as most Italians were in the immediate post-war years, by the possibilities Annovazzi represents but her passive journey into a world she hoped would allow her to widen her field of vision becomes increasingly uncomfortable. Watching the images of *Red River* (Hawks, 1948) on the screen in her courtyard she longs for the movement they describe, for the experience of another place, for anything but the dark reality of her now despised basement home. Her husband's warning of the futility of what he calls 'fables', of the distance between the real and the projected, is the first beacon to guide her out of a still unperceived darkness.

Spartaco's comment is consistent with his function as stable focal point of continuous return across the film, a function confirmed in the film's conclusion which, with its emphasis on the inward ending, has often sealed *Bellissima*'s belonging to the strain of comic or 'pink neo-realism'. However, only a superficial or incomplete reading would see the film's message as one in tune with that of the light comedies of the fascist era in reiterating that 'everyone should stick to his or her place in society' (Bacon 1998: 54). On the contrary, the message, or rather one of the consciously delivered messages, indeed in line with the one delivered on the archetypal plane, is one of hope for a new awareness, one which redefines class as an empty carcass precariously held together by the outdated belief in artistic education as a means to higher status, and cheaply sold, in the black market of Cinecittà, in exchange for new forms of more immediately obtainable popularity and wealth. Maddalena's own journey towards such a realization becomes then the journey Visconti wishes for the Italy she represents: powerful, beautiful, hopeful for the future of her child, born, like Maria who is now six years old, at the end of a distressing and confusing struggle for ideological freedom, and now vulnerable to the longing for a recognition she has long been waiting for.

Naturally, Annovazzi plays a significant part in the process. Seduced himself by the possibility of immediate gains and pleasures to be obtained by dwelling within a world which is modelling itself on the one described by the Hollywood images, he has become the seducer. Having robbed Maddalena of the material means (money) which would have aided her move away from the social stagnation that her basement accommodation represents, he is now intent on possessing her body, a possibility that Visconti transforms into a dangerously incestual moment of verbal intimacy. Lying next to her on the sand by the river he describes his own mother's efforts to improve his chances of success in life and the extent of her sacrifice, which seems to have produced in him a cynical, although superficial disillusionment and a desire to live the moment without consideration of the consequences. As Annovazzi sits up and comes closer, sensually caressing her naked arm, Maddalena's face displays an array of expressions ranging from confusion to despair through to the resolution of the dramatic tension in a burst of laughter filled with the sad bitterness of unshed tears that only an artist of Magnani's stature could make audible.

As he insists on the lasting effects of his mother's sacrifices, Annovazzi presents a situation of being trapped by a maternal which, in maintaining his dependency through incessant giving, has captured his emerging ego now unable to stand for himself and in continuous need of 'taking' someone else's worth. The mother's sacrifice becomes then, in its endless repetition, the vacuum which the son becomes incapable of refilling. His offerings, his successes, become unsatisfactory tokens of gratitude for an all-devouring Terrible Mother to whom he must return a never measurable gift. His dependency allows him a 'freedom' from adult responsibility which is, in reality, an imprisoning curse. When he invites Maddalena to join him in such freedom by suggesting the sharing of a moment of sexual bliss and abandonment away from the duties of everyday life and a breaking of that 'obedience' which she believes characterizes her, she has already undergone a transformation. Facing the camera and looking away from Annovazzi, her expression becomes that of a woman whose fragility is in her desire, a desire which is now becoming split from the recognition she longs for through public acknowledgment of Maria's beauty.

Maddalena's weakness has been, so far, evident as an unfulfilled sensuality deliberately exposed as she habitually unbuttons or removes her blouse within the confines of her home, a space safely desexualized by the overwhelming presence of herds of fat women in dressing gowns who regularly invade the screen. Away from the safety of structured sexual roles she now senses the power of her own sensuality, a power which she almost relinquishes in the young man's arms. However, his mentioning of the changing colour of her eyes according to the reflection of the water helps her return to the present but also marks her growing realization of the distance between internal and external realities, between herself as perceived from within and her image as reflected by a masculine 'other'. In rejecting her function as holder of the projection of a man's own anima, Maddalena is taking another step towards a more responsible motherhood and a new independence from the approval of the male gaze.

In an early scene, after scaring off the children who peek through her basement window as she dresses up, she turns to brushing her dark hair, her face reflected by two mirrors, and whispers: 'I could have been an actress ... what does it take after all, one just needs to pretend to be someone else.' If this scene can be considered 'crucial because it clarifies the process by which Maddalena projects her own personal aspirations onto Maria' (Torriglia 2002: 71), it also works as an early affirmation of Maddalena's awareness of the inherent power and autonomy of the object of the gaze. Maddalena's preparation of Maria for the various encounters with the camera lens had been an acceptance of the patriarchal rules of female passivity within gaze economy but the film follows the process which leads to her final rebellion.

Men's activities in the film do indeed seem to rotate around the preparation of the object of their own gaze: the director Blasetti, who searches for the prettiest child, the photographer who carefully constructs his images in order to improve the appearance of his models in the static reproduction of the photograph and the hairdresser constantly working within the triangular structure of gazes provided by the reflecting presence of the mirror. The narrative seems to suggest the interdependence between the objects of the gaze – Maria and Maddalena – and the subjects – Blasetti, Annovazzi, Spartaco and the photographer – but it must surrender, at the end, to the passionate reclamation of dignified independence of the object from the authoritative call to availability by the subject. Maddalena's viewing of Maria's audition tape is in fact an uninvited intrusion. She questions male standards of assessment and ultimately refuses to sell her daughter's image and reclaims her daughter's beauty as a source of private as opposed to public pleasure.

It was Visconti who decided to change the film's ending with Maddalena's refusal of the contract. She returns, penniless and humiliated, from her journey through a once tempting 'underworld', to her house where her husband awaits with Annovazzi and the producer, certain that she will sign the contract. She holds her sleeping daughter with renewed maternal protectiveness, like the Mater Dolorosa holding the body of her Saviour child, and she questions the terms of the sacrifice: she asks whether they want Maria to have her hair curly or straight and should she stutter in order to make them all laugh again (see Figures 7.1 and 7.2). What she is actually describing is a sacrifice already consummated and through it she, as Mother, has found salvation. Maddalena has in fact found a connection with Maria which was lost at the very beginning when the little girl, ignoring her mother's intentions, had gone 'fishing' by the Cinecittà pool. Now that connection is emphasized by Maddalena's careful wording: 'The little girl is *mine* and *we* will keep her'; the familial environment is the keeping enclosure of a now restored and whole feminine consciousness, extended both upwards and downwards by the representation of mother and daughter together (*C.W.*, Vol. 9i: para. 316). Maddalena's choice to refuse to sign Maria's contract and her retreat back 'into the domestic sphere', as she walks into the bedroom with the child in her arms, could not possibly be seen as an 'abdication of her feminine power' (Wood 2000: 156). On the contrary, it is a reaffirmation of female autonomy, only paradoxically confirmed by her request for a cathartic beating, a request which her husband, deprived of agency, can only refuse to pursue.

As in the Donizetti opera, the miracle has happened but it is not the expected one. Maddalena's search for validation through her daughter's entrance into the movie world has become unnecessary as it happens, as soon as that entrance is granted. The journey through which Maddalena has prepared Maria for her encounter with the realm of projected reality has ended with a temporary loss, reflective of the episode at the beginning of the film. Maria, during the audition, is alone and lacking her mother's support and becomes vulnerable to abuse. Maddalena and Maria seem to follow the trajectory of Demeter and Persephone in the much discussed myth: Demeter, goddess of the earth and traditionally

178 Secondo tempo

Figure 7.1 Holding her sleeping child, Maddalena questions the terms of her sacrifice. Bellissima. Luchino Visconti (1951).

Figure 7.2 Pietà, 1876 (oil on canvas) by Bouguereau, William-Adolphe (1825–1905). Private Collection/Photo © Christie's Images/The Bridgeman Art Library. Nationality/copyright status: French/out of copyright.

associated with the Earth Mother, loses her daughter Persephone who, while playing with other nymphs, is abducted by Hades, god of the underworld. While searching for Persephone, Demeter abandons the earth to itself causing the unfolding of the first winter. Zeus did then come to an agreement with Hades, who, having ravished Persephone, lets her go back to her mother, to Earth, for a certain period every year allowing for spring to come again.

The violation to which Maria is subjected is, however, neither a union nor a penetration by a darkness, or by an unconscious capable of leaving seeds and generating life. It is a humiliation and an attempt at abusing her image by forcing her to become something to be manipulated for the obtainment of visual pleasure. She is supposed to function as an empty site for anima projections and her cry seems to function as a signal of submission. Maria's crying is unstoppable and it continues as she watches herself, hiding with her mother in the projection booth, and later she will cry herself to sleep on her mother's lap. Maria's tears, a connective continuum throughout the film, are rather than a signal of submission an affirmation of the feeling function, described by Jung as a 'function of subjective valuation' (*C.W.*, Vol. 6: para. 899), an ability to interpret reality according to subjective values determined by affect, to establish a relationship with objects mediated through feeling (*C.W.*, Vol. 9ii: para. 61). By the end of the film Maddalena shares this function with her daughter.

Julia Kristeva in her article 'Stabat Mater' describes tears (and milk) as 'metaphors of non-language, of a "semiotic" that does not coincide with linguistic communication' (Kristeva 1985: 143). Through her crying, Maria expresses a consistent rebellion against a systematic abuse of her innocence and childhood. Tears flow whenever she is asked to comply with others' idea of beauty and perfection: from the early scolding by the pool, when she had made a mess of her mother's preparations, to the humiliating dance lesson when it is hinted that she is neither physically nor mentally suited for ballet; from the photographer's studio where the technology drains her smile, to the solitary cry in her bed while her mother and father watch the 'beauty' of herds (this time of cattle) crossing the temporary cinema screen erected in the common courtyard.

Maria's tears as examples of 'semiotic that does not coincide with linguistic communication' are reinforced by her discomfort with language itself, audible as a stutter, in stark contrast to Maddalena's articulate and powerful use of language as protection against male prevarication. Where Maddalena is the aggressive, larger-than-life, all-pervasive, strong and providing Earth Mother, Maria is the delicate, minute, fragile and sensitive Maiden asking for the encounter with a judgemental masculine to be postponed. Maria's 'symptoms' point to her desire to remain contained within her mother's protective wholeness, to preserve an innocence that she is not prepared to compromise either by entering the aggressive differentiation of language or by performing for men's pleasure. Maria can speak clearly and she does when she accuses her ostentatious middle-aged acting tutor of having helped herself to the eggs her mother kept in the cupboard and again when she directly asks whether she needs to go to school again. The stutter then situates Maria at the threshold between the need to affirm herself by separating from her mother and the desire to return to a state of pre-language and of undifferentiated unity with her. In a trajectory similar to the one at work in *Europa '51*, the mother is ready to deliver the child and remains deaf to her or his desire to prolong the safe symbiotic closeness and to postpone that separation (which, at least in *Europa '51* because of the child's age, is a necessary split), which might transform him or her into the 'visible' object of the mother's desires or rage.

At the end of the film Maddalena takes Maria home and cries with her. It is surely not coincidental that the two crying on a bench holding on to each other are Maria and Maddalena, the two aspects of a feminine embodied in the gospels by one woman, Mary Magdalene (Maria Maddalena), whose tears are openly shed twice, first to deliver herself in a rebirth obtained through forgiveness, and later to mourn the loss of the Beloved. Maria and Maddalena's tears are, indeed, tears of despair and Maddalena actually utters the word 'help' as she cries, but the loss becomes a victory and a new beginning which is marked by Maddalena's ability to say 'no' to compromise, to corruption and to a wealth earned through the humiliation and degradation of what is most precious.

The lyrics of the aria sung at the beginning talked of a wealth the protagonist has inherited which makes him a desirable bachelor and the women's interest he now attracts is not derived from the elixir, as he believes, but from his money. Having become aware of the abuse and depersonalization inherent in becoming a 'public image' Maddalena does not want her daughter to pay with her dignity for something she already has. Her refusal to expose her daughter to abusive looks comes with an understanding which was forecast at the beginning through the operatic aria: she tells the men who monetarily price Maria's involvement with the film that for her father and for her Maria 'is very beautiful'. That beauty, derived from innocence and inner wisdom, can not only do without the validation coming from an exposure which involves objectification, but also cannot be maintained within a world of corruption and manipulation.

Bellissima works both as a consciously delivered criticism of the role cinema plays in the corruption of traditional values and as an admission of responsibility on the part of Visconti as director who, as a herald of a movement devoted to representing reality, had tempted into the world of cinema the innocent, unsophisticated faces of those who longed to be transported to a place where that reality could be forgotten. But the film is also a vivid warning, delivered through the archetypal content, of the effect of the American dream on a collective consciousness still lacking the very function Maria stands for; the feeling function which supports the capacity for 'subjective valuation' and instinctually refuses objectification. The ability to see and evaluate is an endangered function but, Visconti's images suggest, one that, despite the contagious degradation of values, is still preserved and because of its immaturity and fragility needs to be protected and nurtured.

Maria's struggle with the external pressures urging her to 'become' an image and with a separation from her mother which she both needs and loathes, force the film's return to a pre-Oedipal enclosure. Something went irremediably wrong with the involvement of Maddalena and Maria with the producers of dreams. Something went irremediably wrong with Italy's involvement with those in a position to offer the means to the realization of the dream of swift reconstruction. Visconti's solution, however, is not retreat but awareness, a newly achieved social consciousness, and with it the responsibility of nurturing it while it undergoes a necessary gestation, supported by the renewed value of the familial structure. Visconti's cinematic family is one which has undergone a significant transformation from the only nominally matriarchal unit of *La Terra Trema* where the maternal was easily disempowered with the mortgaging of a house which produced a 'sinking' boat. In *Bellissima* Maddalena actively participates in the organization and administration of the family finances, she has a job and relative independence and her submission to her husband's violence is a contradiction she resolves verbally by using passivity as a yielding which disarms him. Even her apparent economic defeat becomes an opportunity for a revindication of her financial independence as she half jokingly reminds Spartaco that she 'will take care of the house even if it means that all of Rome will have to get diabetes', an event which would signify surplus of work for her as a nurse.

Visconti's much questioned narrative solution is a resistance to the 'impulse towards the just "happy ending"' which in melodrama 'usually places the woman hero in a final position of subordination'. Maddalena's rejection of a fate which demands the sacrifice of her dignity and independence reconciles, within the narrative, the division which the maternal melodrama would ask the spectator to resolve. Linda Williams suggests in fact that in the maternal melodrama the divided female spectator identifies with the woman whose very triumph is often in her own victimization, but she also criticizes the price of a transcendent 'eradication' which the victim-hero must pay (Williams 1987: 320). Maddalena's triumph is in the actual refusal to pay such a price, and the rejection of the monetary offer is a rebellion against a 'victimization' which requires the signing of a contract binding her into passivity. She has obtained the contract but will not sign it: her victory is her awareness of her own agency. She is the one to make the choice.

If it is now clear that 'in *Bellissima* Magnani both denounces and refuses women's objectification under patriarchy and claims full, exclusive agency towards her daughter' (Torriglia 2002: 68). The gaze and subsequent objectification from which Maddalena is now protecting Maria is not just that of a patriarchy intended as 'male' but also, and maybe more importantly, that of an infiltrating capitalism which is necessarily patriarchal in attitude rather than in the gender of its agents. It is an attitude which imposes rules and structure and aims at manipulating the 'other' (environment, women and circumstances) in order to maintain control over it.

Miracolo a Milano (Miracle in Milan, 1950)

The good, the bad and the mother

> The children follow,
> Not knowing the taste of wine, or how
> His drunkenness feels. All people on this planet
> Are children, except for a very few.
> No one is grown up except those free of desire.
>   Rumi, 1207–1273, *A Children's Game*

Based on Zavattini's novel *Totò il Buono* (*Totò the Good*), *Miracolo a Milano* (*Miracle in Milan*, 1950) is often considered the beginning of De Sica's departure from neo-realism. Nevertheless, despite its surreal atmosphere and a marked narrative dependence on supernatural events the film, depicting the lives and vicissitudes of a community of poor and homeless people, remains ideologically close to the post-war cinematic movement.

The fairy tale atmosphere is conjured up by the juxtaposition of images of an idyllic village setting near calm reflective waters and the unequivocal superimposed words 'C'era una volta' (Once upon a time). An old lady, while watering her vegetables, finds a crying baby under a cabbage and raises him as her own. The boy's childhood is consumed within an extremely condensed temporal ellipsis which sees the little boy, now of school age, staring at boiling milk as it overflows and spills onto the floor. His adoptive mother transforms a potentially upsetting incident into a learning opportunity by arranging the boy's toys around the spilt milk. She creates an imaginary city around a foaming white road and exclaims, 'How vast is the world!', thus producing an 'historical' precedent to what will be the thematic template of the film. Following her death the little boy, Totò, spends the rest of his childhood in an orphanage but when, as a young man, he enters the world again, he fulfils his destiny by helping a group of homeless people create a structured and organized community. The finding of petrol on the land the community has settled on attracts the attention of developers and business tycoons who insist on evacuating the poor from the now profitable site. When all seems lost, Totò's adoptive mother appears from heaven and gifts him with a magic dove which Totò uses to satisfy anybody's wishes. The desire to prevail over injustice and to preserve a simple yet dignified community life are soon forgotten in the name of the endless possibilities of ownership of status-defining goods the dove can help materialize. The dove is then taken back to heaven and the people carried away in trucks. The bird is returned to Totò just in time for a final miracle which consists of a literal flight for freedom aboard the brooms of the cleaners of Milan's Piazza del Duomo. Singing the song that has become their anthem, the poor fly towards a 'kingdom where good morning really means good morning'.

Totò's anonymous fathering and his discovery under a cabbage are not synonymous with abandonment, but rather from the very beginning place the little boy on the path of the mythological hero whose birth remains either partially (when one earthly parent is known) or completely mysterious (Neumann 1954: 133). The traditional involvement of a virgin as heavenly or earthly mother is here substituted with a temporary fostering by the harmless, mild-tempered and older Lolotta. Lolotta's age and her single-handed upbringing of Totò not only remove the essential criteria necessary to the unfolding of conflictual Oedipal triangulations but also disempower the feminine by mitigating her potentially destructive sensuality and by justifying her autonomy from the masculine with an age which places her beyond the possibility of sexual desirability. Moreover, the frightening aspect of the Terrible Mother is diluted to non-existence when Lolotta, rather than reacting with rage to the milk-spilling incident, manages to produce an image of creation: Totò will enact the fantasy and transform it into reality.

The incident of the spilling of milk establishes Totò's first characteristic as witness to the effects of powers he does not wish to change. However, it is his inaction that provides a possibility for a transformation which Lolotta can only represent, making the most out of loss within a miniature model of a reality she never enters. In fact, she actually remains the fairy tale character of a world which, temporarily, dies with her. Totò's removal from that same idyllic fantasy of symbiotic union with a positive mother is enacted by male authority represented by a succession of men dressed in black and always working as a partnership of two; two are the doctors who, emotionless, hold Lolotta's wrists and read her pulse; two are the carabinieri[4] searching for a thief; two the men who accompany Totò to the orphanage; and two again the ones who bid him farewell from it. This splitting, together with a lack of positive or significant action (the doctors fail to heal Totò's mother), points to a weakness in the institutions which have become automated providers of services, but most significantly it is an indicator of a divided masculine consciousness that, unable (or unwilling) to stand alone and offer fathering, substitutes it with faceless institutionalized care. The absence of a father, which within the fairy tale is indicator of 'higher fathering', becomes in reality a lack both of guidance and protection, reflective of the recent experience of loss of leadership after the fall of Fascism and the establishment of a government unfit to stand as a trustworthy authority in its place.

As Totò follows Lolotta's funeral carriage he enters the dull reality of the city with grey skies and a damp fog which renders the landscape of tall, anonymous buildings bleak and uninviting. It is the loneliness of separation which Totò experiences as a second loss of familial identity: the first transformed him into a fairy tale hero, the second deprives him of a connective link to the social fabric by reinstating his original condition as orphan. The fairy tale begins to intersect with reality, as in reality orphans are 'mothered' by institutions, so the little boy has to enter the orphanage. Nevertheless, the orphanage, which is only visible as a door that closes behind the child and reopens to allow him out as a young man,

---

4 Military police force.

represents a place of latency, a time for a second gestation which will lead to a second entrance, once an adult, into a world where his 'ministry', his work as bringer of new, as forecasted by his miraculous birth, can finally begin.

A grown up Totò wanders around the streets of Milan in search first of connection, with his insistent offering of greetings ('Buon giorno') which eventually irritate an unfriendly passerby, later of work and finally of entertainment, offered by the sight of richly dressed upper class ladies who leave the theatre after a performance. Within the briefly condensed space of a day, Totò has encountered representatives of bourgeois, working and upper class and has not been able to claim a belonging to any of them.

In his discussion of the psychology of the child archetype, Jung refers to the conditions of abandonment and neglect which accompany the birth of the archetypal child. Although Totò is now an adult the transition from childhood to maturity has not been validated externally, it has not become manifest to the outside world. This transition is his birth to society, represented as an exit from the orphanage door into the cold of a snowy winter day. It is punctuated by rejections, similar to the ones endured by the Holy Family looking for shelter in Bethlehem, which lead to his meeting with the old beggar who welcomes him into his corrugated tin shelter on the outskirts of the city. When, the next morning, Totò crawls out of the tin tubular shape he is again delivered and the process of self-realization can begin (see Figure 7.3).

Figure 7.3 A new birth. *Miracolo a Milano*. Vittorio De Sica (1950). (Image courtesy of Arrow Films).

Marion Woodman suggests that 'the discovery of the creative masculine involves dream sequences that swing from encounters with intense light or swift winds to equally powerful encounters with chthonic passion' (Woodman 1990: 204). After joining the homeless as they follow the rare rays of sunshine in search of warmth, Totò finds himself in the mist of a windstorm which threatens to destroy the hazardous shelters. As the vulnerability of the disjointed community and symbolically that of his emerging ego are exposed, the young man's creative energy is activated and the building of structure becomes a positive compulsion. Totò's work, his ability to transform the desolate homeless camp into an organized city of more dignified huts and shelters, is indeed the manifestation of a discerning ego and of a growing masculine awareness, but as a materialization of his mother's early design it does not represent, from a psychological point of view, the 'will of the Father', the response to the call from a 'higher consciousness' – or at least not directly. As his counterpart heroes of mythology and fairy tales, Totò's transformative actions should be a response to 'the "inner voice", to the command of the transpersonal father or father archetype who wants the world to change' (Neumann 1954: 174). The hero, called by the powerful voice of the archetype to 'awaken the sleeping images of the future' (Barlach 1912, cited in Neumann 1954: 174), necessarily comes into conflict with the personal father, representative of the 'old law'. Totò's shelter city, his 'missionary' organization where huts are moved so as not to disturb the linearity of the street and where people are grouped according to marital instead of class status, rather than provide an 'image of the future' seems to obey rules based on traditional 'pre-capitalist' values. Between the hero's option of conflict with an absent father and the more ordinary handing down of a heritage which in his case is maternal, Totò chooses the latter.

Nevertheless, because of her singular insistence on Totò's memorization of the timetables, even on her deathbed Lolotta can be considered the vessel, the guardian and carrier of a traditionally 'masculine' organizing principle. For Jung:

> Number helps more than anything else to bring order into the chaos of appearances. It is the predestined instrument for creating order, or for apprehending an already existing, but still unknown, regular arrangement or 'orderedness'.
> (*C.W.*, Vol. 8: para. 870)

By offering Totò an exclusively mathematical education Lolotta has provided him with a link to a patriarchal culture he would otherwise have missed as an orphan and, now a young man, he willingly and dutifully transmits his knowledge to the children of the community in an attempt to establish a continuity synonymous with cultural stability. That the children actually refuse to learn is a detail which links more clearly Totò's educational effort to that of the Communists in the immediate post-war years, not necessarily because of the form it takes but in view of its destiny of failure.

Judging from his decisions and action as community leader it soon becomes obvious that Totò's ideas and values, although conceptually sound and rooted in uncompromising visions of equality and peace, lead to actions of dubious efficacy and to unsatisfactory solutions. Mirroring the physical defects of those who feel excluded and frustrated by their handicap implies distrust in the actualization of equality understood as integration rather than negation of difference. Settling a dispute by asking one of the parties to blow a whistle is substituting the traditionally articulate unfolding of courtroom justice with a distracting strategy normally successful with infants. Teaching reluctant children the timetables by adopting them as street names equates the process of education to a mass delivered, minimalist, informal and impersonal transmission of memorized, meaningless results of ordered multiplication. Finally, rescuing a 'bored' young man from the 'thrill' of suicide with the promise of a life becoming fulfilling and beautiful to the sound of one's song is a poor sample of a 'sustainable' salvation. Indeed, from the beginning of the film to this point in the story Totò has experienced emergence into several layers of reality, each time fulfilling the criteria of a metaphorical birth fit for a hero, yet so far he has consistently failed to become one.

His failing, however, can only be understood as such if the story is interpreted psychologically. Hart Wegner (2000: 189–219) draws a convincing parallel between Totò, as founder of a 'humanistic City of God' and the hero of the *Aeneid* (Aeneas), legendary founder of the city which was to become Rome. Aeneas' city was, however, an example of a community where 'the supremacy of the State was proclaimed in an earthly city' (Wegner 2000: 191) and by a hero 'prepared to sacrifice his happiness or the happiness of any other person' for the sake of Rome (Wegner, citing Muller 1957: 221). Totò's city is, in contrast, 'founded under the ideal of unselfishness' and it is a place where 'man and his needs are central' (Wegner 2000: 192). According to Wegner, Totò's role is 'to cleanse men from prejudice, to diffuse principle in harmony with the spirit of the times, and to undertake the education of the young' and, within this view, *Miracolo a Milano* 'appears as an original, even revolutionary neorealist film, offering a militant alternative to what had become traditional "acceptance of fate" in modern films' (Wegner 2000: 193).

If the parallel with Aeneas provides ample material for an 'amplification' of the film's symbolic content, the positive heroic role of 'revolutionary' implicated by Wegner's parallel is not consistent with the development of the story from this point onwards. Totò's city is built at the margins of another, larger, more solid one. His energy is spent reproducing, in self seclusion from an older, richer and more complex centre, a small scale model of the same but free from both political and religious institutions. It is an ideal (Communist?) community where everyone is given nothing in excess of basic provision and seems satisfied with sharing simple forms of art and basic modes of entertainment. However, the movement towards consciousness and the conflict it entails can be postponed and rejected but will not be suppressed. Totò has improved the state of the homeless and given them purpose and structure but that in itself did not involve a heroic encounter with a terrifying dragon, nor an heroic journey into a swallowing underworld or the creative undertaking of complex tasks. Totò has built something new but at the margins, without transforming the 'old', without enforcing a change which by overturning the 'oppressor' becomes meaningful to humanity as a whole. The 'revolution' that leads to a movement to a higher state of consciousness requires a courageous 'turning away from home', the abandonment of childish role play in search of an identity which defines itself in relation to another. In a sense Totò needs another entry, another 'birth', to allow this time for a point of departure and arrival, for a reason to move away from the idealized, forcefully equal, unaware but happy society he has constructed – a fragile pre-pubertal ego – and a reason to return, after a threatening victorious encounter with the dragon/father, to rescue what Neumann has called 'the treasure hard to obtain': 'i.e. the throne of a kingdom and a beautiful princess for his bride' (Stevens 2002: 158). Stevens describes how 'failure to overcome the monster signifies failure to get free of the mother'. Indeed, in order to enter in relationship with the feminine, with the 'princess', or maiden in distress, the hero must 'undergo a second birth from his mother' (Stevens 2002: 158). Totò's meeting with the representing 'Fathers' of the city existing beyond the borders of his is indeed anticipated by a symbolic 'baptismal' rebirth.

The one to provide the 'baptismal' water is, not coincidentally, a young woman, Edvige, who works as maid for a family which has come to benefit from the free offering of accommodation in Totò's city. As she accidentally empties a glass of water on Totò's face she ignites her mistress's rage and risks losing her job. Totò, in order to protect her, emphatically claims that he actually loves water and, grasping a full bucket, proceeds to soak himself. Neither the accidental nor the self-imposed 'cleansing' can be considered the enacting of a symbolic ritual but the girl, trusting in Totò's words, completes the task by searching for another full bucket she dutifully empties on his head. Her inability to read beyond the literal meaning of words, also interpretable as a projection on the external world of her own innocence and straightforwardness, makes of Edvige a reflective vessel, a projection of Totò's own vulnerability and surreal 'goodness'. Indeed Totò's vulnerability is in the one-sidedness which needs to be sacrificed to the 'distinction' and duality characteristic of the emergence of consciousness.

That the water works as initiation into a new adventure, 'the' adventure which will take Totò face to face with that which he has worked to keep unconscious, is confirmed by the scene that immediately follows the 'soaking' incident. Two flashy cars arrive and stop at the edge of the city to let out smartly dressed overweight men who begin to haggle over the price of the land where Totò's city has grown. Mobbi, the potential buyer, questions the ease with which he will be able to get rid of the poor and, sensing their hostility, joins them around the fire to give a pacifying equality speech welcomed by the simpletons' excited clapping. When, during a celebration, oil is accidentally found on the land, a dissatisfied, grumpy resident betrays his fellow citizens and takes the news to Mobbi who buys the plot and sends his administrators to proceed with the evacuation. Totò has no choice but to face Mobbi in his own office in town. It is Totò's first attempt at claiming his 'kingdom' by accepting a direct confrontation with a 'tyrannical father' and to do so he has to leave the safety of the place he had constructed to protect himself and others from an unpleasant political awareness and, psychologically, from consciousness. His is the symbolic fight of the hero who, in order to enter adulthood, a stage when 'sexuality has become admissible [and] the beloved takes the place of the mother' (Neumann 1954: 409), must sever his ties with the latter and conquer consciousness.

Totò's meeting with Mobbi is, however, ineffective. Mobbi, in his marble palace of high ceilings, serves Totò and his friends tea while sending out the sinister trucks to the homeless people's city. Totò's attempts at reminding Mobbi of his equality speech are proof again of his inarticulacy and inadequate language skills. Mobbi sends them back with a reassuring and emphatic 'buon giorno' (good morning) which both Totò and the other city representatives, immersed within a single-faced, undistinguished reality of their own, read as a true blessing. Similarly to Maria in *Bellissima*, Totò's immaturity is manifested as a linguistic limitation which not only exposes his weakness as leader but also confirms his inability to perceive a reality beyond the literally enunciated. The ties which still hold him fast to his mother, expressed both by his uncomplicated use of language and a one sidedness he projects on to the world, keep him from the actions which require an opening of his field of vision.

The return to the city of shelters marks the end of Totò's passive and pacifist attitude. As he witnesses the 'deportation' of his friends from this 'promised land' he joins the revolutionaries and attacks the armed guards. The release of smoke candles amongst the citizens works as a deterrent and they retire from the fight notwithstanding Totò's reassurance that the smoke will not kill them. Totò climbs the maypole erected for the celebration in order to wave the white flag, but above the cloud of smoke he meets the ghost of his mother who, obviously disobeying 'higher' orders, gifts him with a magic dove which will make all his wishes come true, including his childhood dream of possessing the moon. This is, without doubt, the most richly symbolic scene in the film. The climbing of the maypole, erected between earth and heaven and symbol of the movement towards higher consciousness, could represent for Totò an initiation ritual. Isolated from his companions he rises above a world that used to be safe and has a chance to be born a 'higher man', one able to 'act independently as a responsible ego' (Neumann 1954: 142), and deliver himself and others by 'overcoming the father' (Neumann 1954: 176). Citing Rank (1941), Neumann points to how, in the hero myth, 'the hero by solving the tasks which the father imposed with intent to destroy him, develops . . . into a socially valuable reformer, a conqueror of man-eating monsters that ravage the countryside, an inventor, a founder of cities, and bringer of culture' (Neumann 1954: 176). Totò, however, notwithstanding the archetypal pull represented by both the 'baptismal' water and the ritual climbing of the maypole, does not seem to be able to shift what is now clearly described as a 'mother complex' and re-enter the world a 'spiritual man'. Instead, he leaves the reality of conflict and retires back into the fairy tale where his mother comes back to him offering the possibility of obtaining that which he wanted as a child: the moon, the blissful abandonment into maternal unconsciousness. All can be done with the mediation of the dove, a magic tool, obedient to the most outrageous desires as long as they come from Totò.

In Creto-Aegean culture the Great Mother was considered a nature goddess and 'the dove especially was her attribute, and she still remained a dove-goddess, both as Aphrodite and as Mary' (Neumann 1954: 76). The magic that Totò becomes able to perform is not identical to the miracle which would prove his oneness with the Father, his integration of the higher Self. It is a power his mother has 'stolen' from heaven in a last hope to protect her son from a conflict he is not, at this particular stage in his life, likely to win. What is at stake is survival, spiritual awareness can wait. Totò has so far followed a hero's trajectory notwithstanding his evident inadequacy. Events have, however, moved faster than his ability to cope with the increasingly demanding tasks and the story allows him to retrace his steps and reunite with his mother and the magical world she surrounds him with. Back in the fairy tale he can open a path across the smoke, provide his friends with means of non-violent self-defence and, finally, offer them the chance to transform any wish into reality. The failure to achieve either a personal or a group consciousness is manifest in the fact that everyone's wish is for a tangible product, for an object which defines a status, and not for the status itself. Mobbi is ridiculed but, although this would have seemed an obvious outcome, he is not eliminated. De Sica's comment on Italy's inability to cope with the dramatic changes brought by the war is clearly a condemnation of the ideological corruption at the heart of economic development. The one without the other amounts to possession without ownership, wealth without status and most importantly economic stability without either independence or agency.

Neumann, summing up the mythological descriptions of the early emergence of ego consciousness, suggests:

> The magical forms by means of which archaic man comes to terms with his surroundings are ... anthropocentric systems of world domination. In his rituals he makes himself the responsible centre of the cosmos; on him depends the rising of the sun, the fertility of crops, and all the doings of the gods.
> (Neumann 1954: 126)

Ritual and magic were then the tools through which man imposed order on the world. Although, as Neumann specifies, this order is different from order as we understand it, the important thing is 'that consciousness as the acting centre precedes consciousness as the cognitive centre' (Neumann 1954: 126). Totò satisfies materialistic desires without consideration of the larger picture. He does indeed ask for the sun to rise to enjoy the spectacle with Edvige but his lack of understanding leads to the loss of the dove.

The film's depiction of a maternal intervention at a time of surrender together with the blinding of awareness brought by the consumerist craze point to a direct discussion of the state of post-war Italy. The figure of Mobbi is an obvious caricature of Mussolini, with his empty rhetoric, his monumental art deco palace, his corruptible police force and his use of gas candles (Mussolini used mustard gas bombs in his infamous 1935–6 Ethiopian war). Rather than Mobbi himself what

Totò as representative of a new Italy fails to overcome is the ideology he represents. The maternal help is likely to parallel the American financial support which allowed for a new beginning after the unconditional surrender that left Italy vulnerable to the will of the conquerors. This is not necessarily portrayed here as negative. Totò is offered a chance, and so was Italy, to 'rise above the smoke' and hold a higher perspective with the institution of a democratic republic, with the writing of a Constitution, and with the suggestion of political freedom. Later, the use of the dove, the possibility to realize the dream of constructing a new society, is poisoned by narcissism, by the contamination of images of a wealth defined by fur coats and cylinder hats, vacuum cleaners, radios and crystal chandeliers. The American help was never detached from the American dream which certainly contributed a powerful 'distracting' agent to the smooth shift of loyalties from the ideals of the Resistance to those of an economic stability to be bought at the price of a flattening of political identity. The 'miracle' the dove is asked to perform is, indeed, the economic miracle. Everyone can obtain the goods which give the illusion of victory but the deportation, the spiritual entrapment, still happens.

When Totò and his friends are carried away in vans by Mobbi's police, Edvige desperately searches for the magic dove. She finds one in the henhouse and runs after the vans trying to reach Totò. De Sica, typically, deprives Edvige of agency. The magic only works if it is Totò who wishes. Moreover, as Edvige frantically runs, Totò's mother appears, also holding a dove, obviously the magic one, which she leaves in her son's hands after taking Edvige's bird away. The competition between the Mother and the Beloved is won by the former, even though she is finally carried away by the dove-searching angels. Totò's final miracle takes the form of a flight on broomsticks towards the sky. Unable to successfully change reality Totò chooses to leave, riding a traditional instrument of feminine, witch-like magic. It is a form of self-exile, an ascension without a redemptive death, a solution without gain, a victory without a battle. Gian Piero Brunetta beautifully and perceptively describes the film's ending as 'the acknowledgment of a social condition effectively unchangeable in the period the film is realised. It is also the denouncement of a defeat, without however being a declaration of surrender' (Brunetta 2001: 434).[5]

Europa '51 *(1952)*

From matter to heaven and back

> And the dragon hastened against the woman who had brought forth the male child, and there were given to her an eagle's wings, and she was carried off into the wilderness, that the dragon might not seize her.
>
> (Acts 12: 13–14)

---

5 Translation mine.

The film, together with *Stromboli Terra di Dio* (*Stromboli*, 1949) and *Viaggio in Italia* (*A Voyage to Italy*, 1953), forms that which is considered the 'Bergman cycle' (Nowell-Smith 2000: 12), having Ingrid Bergman, now sentimentally involved with Rossellini, as leading actress. In contrast with the unwillingness to single out heroes and heroines in the crude objectivity of his unequivocally neo-realist war cycle (*Roma Città Aperta, Paisà* and *Germania Anno Zero*), Rossellini gives preference here to an introspective narrative style which relies on the subjective perspective of the point of view of the Bergman character. As well as providing direct access to the female character's feelings and emotions, this kind of narrative, which also benefits from Rossellini's own 'external' (personal) view of her, 'function[s] . . . to stress her social and psychological isolation and non-communication with her surroundings' (Nowell-Smith 2000: 12).

In *Europe '51* Ingrid Bergman plays Irene, a wealthy lady married to an American businessman and living in Rome. The tragic loss of her only child, who attempts suicide while she hosts a dinner party, and her increasingly significant friendship with a Communist journalist transform her life and lead her to dedicate herself to the care of the poor and needy. Her family's inability to understand and accept her transformation, in sharp contrast to the ordinary people's belief in her sanctity, informs their decision to lock her up in a mental hospital.

Crammed within the first few minutes of the film is the distancing of Irene from a reality she interprets as obstacle and threat to the preservation of her tidily constructed space. A strike involving public transport directly affects the working class represented by a couple who, having to walk home, teasingly but painfully describe the necessity of their discomfort in the name of a 'social conscience'. The strike, however, does not awaken any such conscience in Irene who only perceives it as a negative effect, without an origin or purpose, on the timely preparation for the dinner party she is hosting. Although portrayed as capable of skilfully managing her space Irene has difficulty in making sense of a society outside the range of her homely kingdom populated by maids, cooks and instructors for her child. Irene's inability to relate to a pressing social reality as well as the refractory nature of communication within her family are, at first, presented as a malady of a class. Irene is the careful and exquisitely refined lady whose attention to detail in organizing a dinner party at her house would confirm an established and solidly owned sense of belonging to a distinctly upper class. Irene's busy and focused actions are supposed to preserve a position imposed by her elderly mother, on the one side, and a loving if insensitive husband on the other. Nevertheless, the fragility of such a position is somewhat acknowledged as Irene insists on avoiding the mention of Communism at the dinner table, betraying an anxiety shared with the older generation and the class she is trying to protect.

The indifference to a world beyond the structured borders of her ego, as well as refusal to engage in a maternal role transformed by the young son's imminent puberty, are only to be shattered by the son's attempted suicide, closely connected, in the narrative to Irene's exasperation with his increasingly insistent demand for attention she perceives as unjustified and inconvenient. His act of self-violence, which takes the form of a near fatal leap into the void of a spiral staircase, becomes a metaphor for another necessary fall which, in its apparently downward direction, seems at first to take Irene close to her son in despair. The relationship between the child's presence and Irene's imminent destiny of inner transformation is already forecast as just before the party she arrives to a home where, notwithstanding the active presence of her servants and family, all the lights are off. Irene, followed by her son Michel, switches them on as she enters the hall, the dining-room and finally the bedroom. The 'bringer of light', symbolically embodied by the child both in mythology and in religion is an enlarger of consciousness, capable of overcoming a darkness understood as an 'earlier unconscious state' (*C.W.*, Vol. 9i: para. 288). Jung points to how such a 'higher consciousness, or knowledge going beyond our present-day consciousness, is equivalent to being *all alone in the world*'.[6] This consciousness expresses the conflict between the bearer or symbol of higher consciousness and his surroundings (*C.W.*, Vol. 9i: para. 288).

Irene's inability to understand the changed nature of Michel's needs who refuses her physical effusion but insistently requests her engagement in verbal communication provides a contrast. Irene's refusal to yield to the pull from the unconscious bars, in fact, the emergence of that much needed 'higher consciousness' which remains, at this point, suffocated by her carefully constructed 'persona', or, more consistent with the symbolism, unlistened to and ignored as an inconveniently clingy son. In fact, it is the child who feels alienated from his surroundings and 'all alone in the world' and his needs for closeness remain frustrated. When his mother finally responds to his calling and points out that he 'is not a child anymore' he becomes agitated and pushes her away screaming that 'she is all naked'. Irene's insistent requests for independence are now fulfilled: the union with mother (unconscious state) which allowed for an intimacy without shame is now lost. The Garden of Eden, a place of undifferentiated and unconscious bliss has now become a place where nakedness is acknowledged as difference and as separation; it is now a point of departure for a redemptive suffering.

For Jung 'child' means something evolving towards independence. This evolution cannot happen without the detachment from an originating point: abandonment is therefore a necessary condition' (*C.W.*, Vol. 9i: para. 287). At the dinner table 'isolation' is actually discussed as dangerously spoiling and the suggestion of the healthier social environment of a boarding school is hailed as a wise alternative. It is maybe significant that the new isolation the boy experiences as a consequence of enforced separation from his mother drives him to suicide contemporarily with the adult's suggestion for further physical distancing. With the attempted suicide the child forfeits his symbolic duty as redeemer and opts for a death which in its visual materialization (the falling within the enclosing

---

6 Italics are Jung's own.

circularity of a spiral staircase) is clearly a return to a maternal, or rather, because of its ineffectiveness as agent of death, a demand for the maternal to return to him (see Figure 7.4).

Michel is also a child who has witnessed and suffered the horrors of war. He is described by his mother as extremely sensitive and difficult to understand. This association of the child with the war is re-emphasized when, back at home from the hospital, the child, before dying of a stroke, briefly regains consciousness. Here he finds his mother now willingly lying next to him in bed and reassuring him of her desire to form again a preferential bond, similar to the one experienced during the war, when the father was safely excluded from their relationship. The child's sacrifice has functioned as a reminder of Irene's vocation of motherhood, a vocation which the woman-of-the world 'persona' had temporarily and dangerously obscured. Michel's sensitivity and his disdain of his mother's exposure and embrace of materialism seal, together with his death, a condemnation which translated socially might be read as a condemnation of Italian society's betrayal of the ideals of the Resistance. Yet both the child's symbolic function of redemption and resolution of conflict and that of hopeful social and political renewal would remain unfulfilled with this untimely death. The focus, however, soon shifts from the tragic event to the need to validate his sacrifice through a 'purification' from the contamination of materialism on the one side and a political education on the other which will make Irene worthy of the love she has not been able to recognize and nurture. Through Michel's death Irene is 'delivered' as the one (not quite 'the

Figure 7.4 The spiral staircase is a vehicle of return to the Mother/Womb. *Europa '51*. Roberto Rossellini (1952). (Thanks to Roberto Rossellini's Estate).

One', as will be explained later), the repository and bringer of a love which, described by Irene herself as deriving from her son, remains in its sacrificial and sorrowful attributes, maternal. Nevertheless, the love she feels for humanity as a whole is definitely originating from a masculine source embodied by the idealized dead son. Her practical engagement with the working classes, with the extremely poor and needy and with those rejected by the judgement of society also has its origins in the vision of a man, her Communist friend Andrea, the journalist. Andrea who is quick to suggest the possibility of comfort in active political involvement functions as Irene's animus, mediating her encounter with the unconscious.

After her first meeting with Andrea she returns home to a worried husband who gently yet forcefully points her back in the direction of submissive matrimonial union. This moment of apparent abandonment in the arms of her husband, now representative of past attachment to class and status and of a familial love no more sufficient, is clearly a starting point for Irene's appropriation of what will be considered a dangerous independence. This independence, perceived first through the encounter with Andrea, is increasingly affirmed both verbally and visually and with particular emphasis in the following three sequential scenes.

As Irene arrives home, after spending a day in a factory in order to help a woman keep her newly found employment, she is met by an angry husband who accuses her of adultery. Irene shrugs from his touch, a behaviour which he interprets as a confirmation of her guilt leading to an escalation of rage that does not allow for explanations. Irene's weak attempts at defending herself together with her instinctive avoiding of physical intimacy are testimony to the fragile definition of the newly forming ego as well as to the impossibility of re-entering the previously attained, well-constructed role, the 'persona' as Jung would call it, of socially viable wife. Irene has in fact just begun to distance herself from the physicality of her femininity, in favour of its purer, symbolic manifestations. Untouched by man and holder of knowledge she is transcending the immanence of Irene as a person and closer to obtaining the radiance and numinosity of the archetypal image; at this point in the narrative the image is that of the 'virgin' in the ancient meaning of the word: 'unrelated and not dependent upon any man' (Neumann 1954: 52).

Notwithstanding the previous dramatic encounter with her husband, the next scene sees Irene with Andrea. When he, echoing the episode at the beginning of the film, suggests that the poor need to acquire a social conscience Irene contradicts him with the belief that what is to be delivered to them is hope. In a previous meeting Andrea had offered Irene some books to read, books that her mother found 'dangerous'. This offer describes Andrea as the stereotypical leftist intellectual whose commitment, in line with Gramscian ideals, is that of offering both the means to ideological transformation and the possibility of gaining, through work, the social (socialist) consciousness necessary to sustain a revolution. In Gramsci's own words: 'the mode of being of the new intellectual can no longer consist in eloquence . . . but in active participation in practical life, as constructor, organiser, "permanent persuader" and not just a simple orator' (Gramsci 1971: 10).

Andrea does work to 'construct, organise and persuade' Irene. He insists on the possibility of work which, if not happy, will make people less unhappy, on the vision of a society where labour will be equally shared and of a 'humanity' defined by work. Yet Irene's newly found, independent voice is now inspired by experience and, citing the Bible ('By the sweat of your brow you will eat your food', Genesis 3: 13), she declares work a punishment and an expiatory vehicle as well as a duty, only worthwhile if understood within a narrative of salvation. Throughout this sequence Irene's face is shot in and out of the shadow cast by Andrea who stands in front of her. However, while she describes her idealized paradise as an 'eternal one, for both the living and the dead' her face is lit as to emanate radiance, suggestive, as her eyes look dreamingly upwards, of a mystical, possibly religious inspiration, as well as confirming the newly acquired archetypal significance of Irene's presence in the film.

As the agent of the Fall (literally) Irene retraces the steps of a suffering humanity and believes in the redeeming effect of the acceptance of the shared burden of humiliation. Having experienced, as Eve, the consequences of her desires as a separation from blissful union with the one she did not understand (Michel/bringer of higher consciousness) she has now invested herself with the mission of extending her son's love to the whole of humanity. In so doing she takes on the role of 'mediatrix', a role which is traditionally accredited to the Virgin Mary and that, significantly, Pope Pius XII was to highlight more or less directly in his post-war encyclicals and exhortations (in September 1950 he described Mary as 'the Beloved Mother of God, mediatrix of heavenly graces')[7] culminating in the declaration of the dogma of the Assumption in November 1950.

Almost as a direct visual consequence of Irene's inspired speech, the next scene sees her approaching, in the dark of night, a church in the centre of Rome. She enters almost in search of refuge from the noise and light of her previous life's wealth, and piously covers her head, looking up towards the altar. This is clearly not a moment of ecstatic spiritual union; rather, Irene's body language speaks of renunciation and loneliness as she lowers her face and covers it with her hand before slowly walking away. Outside she will encounter a prostitute who is evidently unwell. Irene will take her home and nurse her for days until her death.

The church chosen by Rossellini for this scene is the Church of the Immaculate Conception also known to Romans as the Church of the Capuchin Monks, a branch of the Franciscan order formed in the sixteenth century with a desire to remain closer to the original intentions of St Francis, practising a stricter life of prayer and poverty. The church is famous for its cemetery which is a crypt hosting the bones of 4,000 monks but, coincidentally, is also decorated with two representations of the Assumption of the Virgin (one by Liborio Coccetti [c.1728] fills the

---

7 *Menti Nostrae*, #143, (Apostolic Exhortation of Pope Pius XII to the clergy of the whole world on the development of holiness in priestly life), 23 September 1950.

vault and the other is the choir's altarpiece by Terenzio Terenzi [c.1621].[8] While such details remain obscure to the viewer they are significant as Rossellini's own choice of location for a scene which marks a decisive shift in Irene's personal development. As Irene lowers her eyes a dissolve shows the altar in front of her but the lens is looking upwards and all that is visible are the candelabras surrounding the vault: visual access to the image which Irene has just contemplated is denied. What become visible are the praying monks and the cut back to a distressed Irene confirms the relationship between the two images and her sadness. This might be Rossellini's hidden comment both on a Church that remains distant in its contemplative attitude from the immediate needs of humanity as well as, possibly, on the newly acknowledged dogma of the Assumption of the Virgin, which while offering new hope for resurrection is, in its emphasis on the separation and need for reunion of body and spirit, in sharp contrast with Irene's idea of an immediately accessible paradise where, as she insisted, there is no distinction between living and dead.

In a discussion of neo-realism with Mario Verdone in 1952 Rossellini openly reveals his intention to describe in *Europa '51* his own anxiety at what he perceives as the dangerous denial of a tendency 'towards fantasy', a danger which might lead to the 'killing [of] every feeling of humanity left in us'. Rossellini continues with a remarkable affirmation of his belief in an attitude, which he describes as 'supremely Latin and Italian', that embraces a vision of man seen in his totality, allowing, having seen both sides 'to look at him charitably'. Having recognized this view of life as 'unmistakably Catholic', Rossellini affirms that 'Christianity ... recognises sin and errors, but it also admits the possibility of Salvation' (Forgacs, Lutton and Nowell-Smith 2000: 155). These direct admissions coupled with the shift in Rossellini's attention as director to the introspective journeys of women in the films of this particular period (beginning in 1948 with *L'Amore* and ending with *La Paura* in 1954) as well as the visual clues to the spiritual nature of their personal development allow for the suggestion of a link between some of the film's themes, understood psychologically, and the immediate context of a deeply religious society.

As previously mentioned, in November 1950 Pope Pius XII established the Dogma of the Assumption of the Virgin Mary. In constituting the Dogma, Pius XII laid emphasis on its importance and necessity at a time of perceived moral decay. His own words are rather explicit:

> And so we may hope that those who meditate upon the glorious example Mary offers us may be more and more convinced of the value of a human life entirely devoted to carrying out the heavenly Father's will and to bringing good to others. Thus, while the illusory teachings of materialism and the corruption of morals that follows from these teachings threaten to extinguish

---

8 Capuchins website: http://www.cappucciniviaveneto.it/cappuccini_ing.html.

the light of virtue and to ruin the lives of men by exciting discord among them, in this magnificent way all may see clearly to what a lofty goal our bodies and souls are destined. Finally it is our hope that belief in Mary's bodily Assumption into heaven will make our belief in our own resurrection stronger and render it more effective.

(From Munificentissimus Deus, Apostolic Constitution of Pope Pius XII defining the Dogma of the Assumption, issued 1 November 1950)[9]

Marie Louise von Franz in a 1959 lecture on alchemy points out how Pius XII, when declaring the dogma, was consciously intending to 'hit Communistic materialism by elevating . . . a symbol of matter in the Catholic Church' (von Franz 1980: 215). Jung himself suggests a close relationship between the declaration of the Dogma and the historical context of a post-war society now aware of the atomic threat and of the possibility of annihilation that it entails (*C.W.*, Vol. 9i: para. 195). The Dogma of the Assumption of the Virgin would then provide a 'counterstroke' in confirming the granting of resurrection to the one who not only shares our earthly origin but also embodies, in her pure maternity, endless possibilities for renewal. Jung further develops this particular aspect of the discussion in *Psychology and Religion: East and West* where he places the declaration of the Dogma within a social context but also gives it a psychological necessity. As well as pointing to the inevitability, at this point in history, of an acknowledgment of women's equality, Jung also suggests that the new Dogma 'expresses a renewed hope . . . for a resolution of the threatening tension between the opposites (*C.W.*, Vol. 11: para. 754), as well as revealing in its meaning of reunion of the 'heavenly bride' with the bridegroom and in its exaltation of the Mother of God a 'desire for the birth of a saviour, a peacemaker' (p. 748).

Such tensions and desires are certainly expressed throughout the film's narrative. Irene's detachment from 'matter', from the materialism which used to entrap her, exacerbates the differences, redefines her past and her husband as the anchors to a real that Michel's leap into the void has tragically revealed as superfluous and meaningless. The trajectory, up to this point, has been towards the two ideologies which offer alternative realities and well-drawn new identities, new masks to wear in order to re-establish the communication with a society Irene now seems to observe as outsider: Communism and Catholicism. Having established her unwillingness to be incorporated and defined by such opposing 'descriptions' of utopian realities, Irene transcends the limitations of their ordered but limited perspectives and does indeed 'ascend' to represent a higher function of the archetypal feminine, one which would allow and realize a re-entering of the soul into matter. Nevertheless, walking out of the church Irene begins her descent into

---

9 http://www.vatican.va/holy_father/pius_xii/apost_constitutions/documents/ht_p-xii_apc_19501101_munificentissimus-deus_en.html, accessed January 2007.

darkness and experiences a rebirth which leads to a Calvary but ends in a salvation which maintains its value only symbolically.

After nursing a prostitute until her death Irene helps a youth involved in a robbery to escape with the belief that he will give himself up. Although the young man does indeed voluntarily confess his crime, Irene is arrested as an accomplice, provoking her family's exasperated reaction which leads to her seclusion in a mental asylum. Here she is interrogated by a priest and by a panel of psychoanalysts and lawyers. While she seems at home as 'Mother of all' amongst the children of her newly found poorer friends who come to visit her, Irene clearly struggles to translate into language the extent of her transformation. Presented with a Rorschach test[10] she soon becomes impatient and admits to her inability to see anything but the crude reality of the marks on paper. She has abandoned the symbolic order represented by the 'Fathers' (psychoanalyst, lawyer and priest) and is refusing, by rejecting self-definition, to enter a place where the masculine will again try to organize her. When directly asked by an inquisitive panel whether she is a Communist or a would-be missionary, she replies 'no' to both questions, confirming with her threatening appropriation of a non-identity not suggested by patriarchy the need for seclusion.

Irene, as the Virgin, has earned, through a Christ-like path of suffering, a metaphorical Assumption. She has in fact seen and comforted the loneliness of a prostitute, she has mediated a thief's encounter with redemption, she gathers the children of the world within her numinous radiance, she yields serenely when interrogated without rejecting her truth and, finally, she embraces those who have clearly betrayed her trust. Like the Virgin Mary, Irene is spared both death (the Virgin Mary ascended without dying) and punishment (without sin) and her passage into timelessness (the seclusion 'for life' in a mental asylum) is seemingly passive as it is decided and effected by men (the Assumption is a passive inclusion, Resurrection is an active transition). Irene's refusal to defend herself is, however, an active protest, the consequence of an understanding which only silence can protect. Like Maddalena in *Bellissima*, Irene exits voluntarily a world where success is measured by the degree of compromise of one's own integrity.

The circle closes as Irene, who at the beginning of the film could not save her son, rescues another patient from suicide, so accepting hers and other women's fate of abandonment into a limbo (the mental asylum) where, for the feminine, neither life nor death can be defined by the parameters of patriarchy. Julia Kristeva in her article 'Stabat Mater' discusses the symbolic construction of motherhood in

---

10 'Popularly known as the "Inkblot" test, the Rorschach technique, or Rorschach Psychodiagnostic Test is the most widely used projective psychological test. The Rorschach is used to help assess personality structure and identify emotional problems. Like other projective techniques, it is based on the principle that subjects viewing neutral, ambiguous stimuli will project their own personalities onto them, thereby revealing a variety of unconscious conflicts and motivations' (from B. R. Strickland (ed.) (2001) *The Gale Encyclopedia of Psychology*, 2nd edn, Farmington Hills, MI: Gale).

Christianity and argues that as 'the "virginal maternal" is a way . . . of coping with female paranoia', it becomes possible to suggest that 'the Virgin assumes the paranoid fantasy of being excluded from time and death, through the very flattering image associated with the Dormition or Assumption' (Kristeva 1985: 148). Not only is Irene, now abandoned by the 'materialists' (mother and husband) of her past life and offered the spiritual superiority of sainthood, immune to the containment of time, but also, in her emphatic reticence goes to occupy like 'the Virgin Mother . . . the vast territory that lies on either side of the parenthesis of language' (Kristeva 1985: 144).

The film in its entirety offers itself to layered interpretations. The psychological significance of Rossellini's personal relationship with Ingrid Bergman seems to become manifest in the films in which he directs her. Bergman's powerful radiance and angelic beauty had already worked as clear archetypal attractor when she had become a collective model of purity, of matrimonial devotion and of womanhood in America before the uncovering of her scandalous relationship with Rossellini, which consistent with the projection inspired angered rejections and condemnations. Across the cycle of the six Rossellini films in which she plays the central character (*Stromboli Terra di Dio*, 1949; *Europa '51*, 1952; *Viaggio in Italia*, 1953; *La Paura*, 1955; *Giovanna d'Arco al Rogo*, 1952, and an episode from *Siamo Donne*, 1953) Bergman is asked to provide visual reference to the process of the director's own personal spiritual transformation and questioning. This process, however, is not experienced in isolation and the insistent, powerful and complex archetypal content emerging throughout the film and, specifically, through the visual impact and numinous presence of Ingrid Bergman, is testimony to the unfolding of a parallel collective process, influenced by and influencing social, cultural and political change.

The Church's response to the inevitability of women's emancipation was peculiarly also a reappropriation of a supremacy over matter which, through the Dogma of the Assumption, was now to be 'assumed' into Heaven, deflating the power of the 'Other' (Communism) by a positive integration of its own defining difference. However, despite functioning as a catalyst of hope for renewal and resurrection, the Dogma might also have awakened patriarchal anxieties over the necessity to shed, through this newly dogmatized equality, a superiority so far granted by religion. Irene as 'bringer of light' and as alternative 'redeemer' represents a possibility which, because of its destabilizing consequences, needs to be contained. This is achieved neither through a punishment sanctioned by laws of human justice (Irene is not given a jail sentence), nor by Catholic acceptance (she is not recognized by the Church as a saint), but instead, through a weakening achieved via the endless interrogations as psychiatric 'cure' of a reality which cannot be read aloud and is thus put beyond the bounds of normal psychic activity.

It is also important to recall that 1951 saw the official closure of the Marshall Plan. The effects of American support throughout western Europe were so significant that between 1947 when the plan was implemented and 1952 most European countries enjoyed a period of unprecedented economic growth. Italy was certainly one of the benefiting countries but the aid had come with a price, that of political compromise. If in *Ladri di Biciclette* the contribution was considered a clear threat to the respectability of a masculinity understood as the ability to produce capital, in *Europa '51* the emphasis is on a gradual loss of a possible focusing of national ego. The suicidal death of a child/redeemer who is asked to 'go to bed and not disturb' the unfolding of a party where adults play with the child's toys is a metaphorical synthesis of a still unfolding history which had seen the desires and energies of new political forces crushed and unlistened to because of the blind excitement and the louder call of consumerism and materialistic wealth.

Rossellini proposes the 'awakening of the captive' (in Neumann's terms, the awakening of the Anima), the temporary rescue of the relating feminine through the spiritual movement of Irene and grants her the 'Latin and Italian' attitude (as he himself had described them)[11] which 'sees both sides' of human nature and is capable of embracing both. So Irene's journey is not only a transformation of the archetypal feminine across the dynamic axis which joins negative mother with positive Anima (Neumann 1963: 64–74), but becomes an attempt at shedding the ambiguous and passing identification with political and religious ideologies in favour of a reunion with a true 'soul', with a spiritual heritage that Rossellini perceives as culturally owned.

Conclusion

The effect of the new organization of government and of new political alliances on cultural attitudes and on the approach to traditional values is systematically explored in these unjustly underrated, intensely moving films. While each of the films remains securely attached to its immediate historical context, there is a richness and clarity in the underlying unconscious message which makes the films stand out from the rest of the texts analysed so far.

Having covered a seemingly positive trajectory of development the narrative solutions of these three films either halt or reverse, each with different expedients, the process of self-discovery which had motivated the protagonist's movement within the diegesis. The halting rather than a regression to an earlier stage of development is both in *Bellissima* and *Europa '51* a measure of protection of a newly acquired consciousness from the aggressive immaturity of its surroundings. In *Miracolo a Milano*, however, the final flight towards the east represents an admission of an unprepared ego to its inability to relinquish a childhood's dream of innocence which the mother's protection promises to 'magically' preserve.

The same unwillingness to step out of the maternal bond and move into adolescence dramatically marks, in *Europa '51*, the beginning of Irene's journey towards individuation. Irene stands to represent, from the very beginning of the film, a national identity temporarily acquired in the fragile form of a persona whose traits

---

11 See page 196.

are borrowed from a repertoire of images of alien cultural origin. Irene's unease with the working classes' communication of a discomfort manifested as a strike, her revealing dress, her independence confirmed by her driving a smart car and her 'ornamental' lapdog are signs which circumscribe, at the same time, the borders of a class and its colonization by new styles of being originating from overseas. Her American husband strengthens the association of such traits with an Anglophone culture and later tries to contain, through all means available, her attempts at shedding what has become a burdensome mask. Moreover, Bergman's presence itself elicits the reading of a subplot encrypted within her star history: she is the Hollywood actress 'imported' to provide an Italian director with a model of stardom and femininity he can analyse and deconstruct so as to make of Bergman's transformation an example of the possibilities for resistance still available.

The child's tragic suicide represents the epilogue of an Oedipal narrative where the conscious maternal rejection precedes her unconscious desire with irreparable consequences and, as such, it is a comment on the dangerous displacement within traditional family structures of parental love on to objects. Understood as a metaphor for a political statement Michel's choice can also be interpreted as representing the first act of a rebellion against the Christian Democrats' rejection of a dialogue with the growing presence of Communism. The boy's evident disapproval of his mother's engagement with a life of glamour and appearances reflects the Communists' suspicion with the assimilation, through the new media, of American cultural traits. The boy's insistent calls, aimed at redirecting Irene's attention towards her role in the process which would lead to a new relationship between them, echo the last hope for the re-establishment of a co-operation between Communism and other leading parties which, effective during the unified Resistance and promising in the first post-war coalitions, is destined to remain unfulfilled.

From a Jungian perspective Michel's suicide has the symbolic value of a fall back into the maternal, and the spiral staircase which 'welcomes' the fall leaves no doubt as to its visual significance as a passage back into a womb fostering both life and death (Neumann 1963: 107). Indeed, Michel's death coincides with Irene's rebirth: his fall coincides with hers in the sense that with his death her 'meanings' lose an assumed point of reference and the pointers holding up her social mask deteriorate, leaving her exposed to that same unconscious he has surrendered to. Irene successfully integrates what Michel represents archetypally as Child (the bringer of light, the future, the ability to deliver what is new) and as a consequence she is propelled into a journey which, with the aid of mediating figures such as the 'animus' embodied by the communist journalist and the prostitute as an aspect of a feminine she is painfully reconstructing, leads her to a new level of awareness.

Like Totò who in *Miracolo a Milano* mimics his fellow citizens' discriminating traits, Irene's search for a new identity takes her to test new possibilities of being which seem to materialize in the space between the two contrasting ideologies (Communism and Catholicism) whose pulls she surprisingly resists.

Maddalena in *Bellissima* also manages to resist the seductive pull of the empty image that her little daughter, as an aspect of the Feminine they together represent, is asked to fill. Maddalena's admission of the ease with which she can 'pretend to be someone else' offers her a choice as it presupposes an identity to which the temporarily selected persona stands as 'else'.

Both Maddalena and Irene are proud embodiments of a utopian idea of nation, undoubtedly reflecting the two directors' radical political perspectives. Both are offered the possibility of 'definition', one through capital, the other by submission to an ideological construct. They both refuse and their refusal seems to condemn them to a life of imprisonment, in a damp basement and in a mental asylum respectively. Paradoxically, however, their freedom is unlimited: liberated from the compromise of partial definitions and from the conditioning and limitations of capital exchange they find a place of untouchable purity. Irene's pursuit of her own personal development has certainly led to an individual salvation and to a new awareness of her place in society, yet her journey appears to remain within the confines of the archetypal, kept in the collective 'unconscious' by her seclusion. The consciousness she represents, however, is held sacred by the working class friends she has found on her way. With this, Rossellini's film is opening a possibility within the negative closure, as he does in *Germania Anno Zero*.

Maddalena and Irene represent that possibility. They are what Italy, in the eyes of Visconti and Rossellini, could and should have become: a place defined by its people's humanity, dignity and tolerance rather than by the corruption of its politics and the products of its rebuilt economy. If political development becomes a weak utopia, and sanctity cannot bring profound changes in spiritual consciousness, all that remains to do is to preserve the values of human love and solidarity even at the cost of isolation. The restricting endings of Rossellini and Visconti are clearly anything but surrenders. Still valid as the directors' conscious elaboration of a disappointment with a political establishment hostile to dialogue, the films also reflect the wisdom of a collective unconscious which, rather than lose an existing but vulnerable beauty, will put her to sleep, with the working classes as witness and guardian, and wait for the ripening of a time when a hero will awaken her to new life.

De Sica's magic, in the context of a narrative with a trajectory opposite to that followed by Rossellini's and Visconti's heroines, produces much wealth but nothing worth fighting or waiting for. The offer by Totò's mother of the magic dove has the never repayable value of the sacrifice made by Annovazzi's mother. Rather than offering the means to personal empowerment both mothers have gifted their children with the unlimited power which comes from the yielding to their generous, nullifying embrace. With Totò the entrapment and the disempowerment have a visual correspondent: with nothing left to do but 'wish' Totò and his people become inundated with objects which are signifiers of a status nobody has thought of asking for. Indeed the status of victims of capitalist exploitation is not modified by the acquisition of objects of capital value, an acquisition which actually only works as fatal distraction from the essential struggle for ego identity.

A desire without an anchoring in reality equates to a circular chasing of a satisfaction which only the quest for consciousness can reopen.

Locked into an infantile stage of development Totò chooses not to engage with the struggle necessary to free his dependent ego. Totò, whose fathering remains mysterious, is an image of that which Neumann describes as 'the "eternal son", the permanent revolutionary. Although not accepting a fate of subordination to father figures the absence of father identification prevents him from ever obtaining his kingdom' (Neumann 1954: 190); a fate which befalls Totò notwithstanding the opportunities he is presented with. His encounter with the shadow figure of Mobbi remains unproductive. Unable to understand Mobbi's intentions because of linguistic limitations, Totò stands in the dangerous position of potential possession by the shadow, effectively amounting to having his people evacuated and his land bulldozed by a dark and powerful 'other' he can only face with the aid of the now lost dove. The fear of becoming enslaved by a softly spoken representative of a corrupt capitalism leaves only the option of escape back into the mother whose magic can do everything but does not seem to do the essential. The evacuation in the trucks is reminiscent of the Germans' deportation of the Jews and it symbolizes a spiritual deportation: the distraction of immediately achievable wealth leads to a seclusion Totò does not have the charisma to rebel against. The American aid distracted Italian politics from its function of representation and of spiritual leadership, leading to an entrapment which, De Sica suggests, can only be resisted by escaping towards the east.

Totò's implementation of Communist ideals did not safeguard his city from the invasion of desire. The failure to materialize the dream of freedom and unity is, in Totò's fable and in the history of post-war Italy, a consequence of immaturity and passivity but it is, most importantly, the consequence of an unwillingness to accept the limitation of the real and to take responsibility for change. The flight reconfirms De Sica's ideological affiliation, clearly pointing towards a socialist east, but it also seals his admission to the value of ideology as a direction, rather than as a goal, as a valid process rather than as solution. De Sica's narrative closes with a return through the maternal to the maternal. Unlike the narrative closure of his fellow neo-realist directors, De Sica's does not contemplate the jealous protection of a precious awareness but simply the safe acceptance of the means of escape.

Witnesses of yet another defeat, this time consumed as the limitation of cultural autonomy and the assimilation of extraneous values into the landscape of their new country, the directors propose different solutions of resistance. Their validity would either be questioned or validated by history.

Conclusion

An approximation of meaning: looking, looking and looking again

This work set out to explore the original hypothesis of the existence of a thread, descriptive of a recognizable psychological process, connecting the cinematic images produced across a specific period of time within a common cultural context.

In the first part of book (Primo Tempo) I discussed the suitability of the Jungian approach to my analysis and isolated the specific potential inherent in the Jungian contribution to film study. I did this by relating its history to that of the Freudian and Lacanian psychoanalytic approaches to the moving image; by exploring the relevance of the Jungian construct, both in its classical and post-Jungian revisiting of the relationship between art and the cultural unconscious; and finally by presenting the analysis of film in relation to national identity as an area where the relatively underdeveloped potential of a Jungian perspective opens new avenues for research.

Supported by the Jungian methodological approach to dreams and anchored to an updated post-Jungian model of the psyche, the theoretical evaluation of film as manifestations of a culture's unconscious has revealed, when considered in relation to the historical context of the films' production, the working of a process characteristic of individual as well as of collective development. The analysis has indeed provided original insight into the social, cultural, economic and political transformations which punctuate the history of a culture contributing to overcome the limitation of ahistoricity often attributed to the Freudian interventions. But the book also wanted to point to the possibility for a constructive dialogue between psychoanalytical and Jungian perspectives on film, a dialogue which ensues from an understanding of the symbol as a moment of intersection between a culture's past and future. To this end I introduced the Jungian discussion of the origin of artistic production in the autonomous creative complex and engaged in a parallel analysis of the Freudian study of fantasy and daydreaming. This analysis has demonstrated how the Jungian suggestion, anchoring the personal creative complex to an archetypal core in the collective unconscious, implies an approach to the artistic image as expression of the interaction between an individual's personal past, the present situation of the culture fostering the image's emergence and, thanks to its archetypal core, the future in which it hopes to re-establish balance.

The threefold temporal frame of reference characteristic of the appearance of the work of art in the Jungian construct finds echo in the development of the Freudian wish through artistic material but the parallel analysis has brought to the foreground, more firmly, analytical psychology's specific appreciation and meaningful analysis of the artistic image as the place of intersection between the historical, psychological, political and religious forces affecting a culture's unconscious. The mutually influencing relationship between these forces and the images invested with archetypal value becomes evident when the process of the appearance of a symbol in consciousness is understood as that of a specific means of communication which, emerging from the collective unconscious, acquires – crossing increasingly individualized unconscious layers – the characteristics which will make it more accessible to the individual or the group consciousness it addresses. The ability to recognize and resonate with the archetypal message delivered through the image both presupposes and conditions the belonging to a community. And indeed, comparative studies of mythology, fairy tales, tribal lore and religious iconography point to consistent, archetypally specific, therefore collectively shared core meanings.

Erich Neumann's extensive analysis of world mythology has provided both the inspiration and a strong point of reference to this study as he convincingly points to a process of transformation within a culture which, traceable across the changes in mythological images, can be considered parallel to the individual process of individuation. If myths once responded to a group's need to represent its cultural process of development, this function now rests with the pictorial narratives which have come to take their place and cinema, because of its wide-reaching scope and accessibility, is certainly to be considered one of them. This work has demonstrated how a comparative study of the cinematic images produced across a specific period of time within a defined cultural environment reveals a pattern of development similar to that isolated by Neumann in ancient mythology. The definition of such cultural environment as national and of the process within it as one which, parallel to that leading to the birth of ego-consciousness, sees the emergence of a national identity has however, required some important revisions.

As well as clarifying the position of distance this work adopts in relation to a Jungian 'psychology of nations', it has also been necessary to reconsider definitions and different approaches to the idea of nation. The revisions of Anderson's original concept of 'imagined communities' within the discussion on national cinema propose an understanding of the idea of nation resulting from a constant negotiation between the imagined unity and the borders which define it. I suggest that the existence and effectiveness of such borders containing political and economic diversity, cultural practices and regional identities cannot be taken for granted and as a consequence the definition of nation becomes fluid and its 'imagining' the result of a continuous dynamic filtering. Moreover, if national identity is understood as a temporarily stable identification of a group with an ideal of unity it is possible to propose the analogy with the relationship of the ego to the Self, a relationship which is at the heart of the process of individuation.

The complexity of the process of formation of a national identity, as it is conditioned by a group historical past and by economic, political and social dynamics within the group and in relation to others, demands, in order to more fully understand the significance of the cinematic images relating to it, the mediation of an interpretative method capable of negotiating across such dynamics.

The Jungian methodological approach to dreams has provided the template for film interpretation, and the process of association Jung used to link the dream image to the psychological background in which it is embedded, together with the definition of a historical setting as the films' past and contemporary context, has been used to link the significant, recurring material across the films of different directors produced within the same short period of time. The comparative method, central to the progress of classical and post-Jungian thought, can only reveal the developmental thread spanning a selected temporal frame if the images describing it can be considered to be recurrent images. Association has indeed revealed a recurrence of images across the films of the chosen directors both at a particular time and across a 'timeline' of historical development. This process led to isolating the images worthy of closer critical attention which took the form of amplification. Involving the use of historical, mythological and cultural parallel, amplification works by 'expanding' possible meanings of the image. In complete contrast to the Freudian tendency to move away from the image and into word association, Jung insists on looking, looking and looking again and in deriving images from images in order to achieve that approximation of meaning which he believes to be the most satisfying result of dream analysis.

With a complex history of unification and often uneven national definition, Italy has provided the ideal cultural background to a search for an archetypal pattern descriptive of the emergence of ego-consciousness related to an historical development of a national identity. Moreover, Italy's history as a nation ran almost parallel to that of its cinema. The troubled process that from the first partial unification in 1861 led to the establishment of the Italian Republic in the late 1940s is, to some extent, traceable in cinematic representations from the beginning of the twentieth century. If the cinema of the interwar period, conditioned by the political and ideological ambiguity of the fascist regime, somewhat reflected its contradictions, the end of the dictatorship coincided with a change in both the style and thematic of the cinematic representations. The tragic decision to enter World War II which fostered the collapse of the illusionary façade on which Mussolini's Fascism had constructed a rather fragile national identity, marks, in fact, the appearance of the first examples of neo-realist films.

This book offers, through a traditional Jungian method of dream analysis, an original reading of the specific symbolism which is so powerfully embedded into the loosely structured narratives of the first decade of neo-realism. This symbolism is brought to the foreground as a positive act of compensation and of necessary psychological processing of both the trauma of the loss of the identity, however false, constructed by Fascism, and that of a complex and in many ways unexpectedly disappointing rebirth into a political settlement which did not honour the unity envisaged during the Resistance.

Neo-realism, rebirth and the alternative outcomes of a Jungian reading

The reading of recurrent images from the selected films by Luchino Visconti, Roberto Rossellini and Vittorio De Sica (Secondo Tempo), and the successful 'amplification' of their meaning, brought together through association, has helped outline a picture of specific moments in the history of the rebuilding of Italian national identity enriched by an understanding of the state of the cultural unconscious as described through the images' archetypal content. A chronological organization of the chapters structured around particularly significant events has been functional to a vertical comparative reading and to associations drawn within the films' present and past. This in itself provided precious insights into the way a cultural unconscious responds to significant and/or traumatic events. Yet, in order to discursively present such a response as consistent with a process of development of a collective ego-consciousness, I shall endeavour to revisit the individual findings within a narrative of archetypal continuity.

The emergence of ego-consciousness is considered, by Neumann, as an early stage in the development of personality. The characteristic presence of children in the films of this first decade of neo-realism, coinciding with the struggle to rebuild the nation, confirms the association between the films, the historical context and this particular stage of psychological development. Indeed it is the image of a child which frames, on both ends, the textual region of analysis of this work, with Prico (*I Bambini ci Guardano*) at the beginning and Maria (*Bellissima*) at the end. Compensating for the negative outcome of the struggle for independence the children appear in De Sica's, Visconti's and some of Rossellini's films as a personification of the potential for renewal and rebirth. In all the films the children embody the energy and the pull towards change and represent the point of reference for the questioning of old systems. The historical situation demands this questioning which finds a response in the unconscious, setting the developmental process in movement. Neumann describes this stage as that of the 'slaying of the father'. I propose that this is the point where, during the early years of the war, the process of the emergence of ego/national identity begins.

The slaying of the father: the end of Mussolini (Chapter 5)

Neumann suggests that 'without the murder of the "father" no development of consciousness and personality is possible' (Neumann 1954: 184). What he is describing is obviously the result of an encounter with a transpersonal factor, namely the authoritarian side of the father archetype, as it becomes projected upon different objects (Neumann 1954: 184). In the case of Italy, Mussolini embodied rather accurately the characteristics of this 'father'. In fact this 'Terrible Male . . . functions not only as a principle that disintegrates consciousness, but even more as one that fixes it in a wrong direction. It is he who prevents the continued development of the ego and upholds the old system of consciousness' (Neumann 1954: 186).

The disposal of this Father, the rebellion against a blindly imposing authority, is an important step towards a more solid acquisition of consciousness; and indeed external circumstances at the beginning of the war suggested that this possibility was now an accessible reality. The war, as it weakened from its onset Mussolini's rhetorical hold on people's loyalty, represented an opportunity for the questioning of his 'paternal' authority. In fact, Mussolini's wild and impulsive belligerency and his insane prioritizing of personal ambition over the protection of his fellow nationals had revealed more explicitly the archetypal traits of a Terrible Father who had to be eliminated before a reconstruction of a damaged national ego could begin. That such an identity was damaged as a result of Mussolini's demand for the nation to be identified with his flamboyant and incoherent persona is evident in the films' narrative resolutions. The murder and/or elimination of the father are accomplished but without the hero's agency and not within a fight which would allow for the strengthening of the victorious ego. Mussolini's removal did not come as the result of a popular revolution which would have been the equivalent of a successfully strengthening fight with a negative paternal authority. The aggression and the energy which would destroy him came from external forces (Allied invasion) and from life-saving treachery (his deposition by vote from the Gran Consiglio, 1943) and that energy was certainly not returned to the unconscious of the Italian nation. In the films the murder (*Ossessione*), elimination (*I Bambini ci Guardano*) or absence (*Un Pilota Ritorna*) of the fathers is also not functional to a positive outcome: the heroes' unwillingness to take the vacant father's place describes the weakness of the national ego at this point in history.

During the years of the dictatorship, resistance was met with either murder (Matteotti, 1924) or imprisonment and exile (Gramsci and Togliatti, 1926). Keeping the 'sons' from overcoming the tyranny by capturing and destroying their consciousness (Neumann 1954: 187), Mussolini enforced what Neumann described as a 'patriarchal castration': a psychological conditioning which deflates the revolutionary spirits and keeps the ego 'captive', imprisoned by its inability either to identify with the old or to renovate the 'kingdom'. The analyses of the films of this period (*I Bambini ci Guardano, Ossessione* and *Un Pilota Ritorna*) have demonstrated how this condition is actually described by the images and, through association, I have also shown how, corresponding to the historical condition, events and actions these images are consistent with a description of the state of Italy's cultural unconscious.

With Mussolini's death the external situation forced Italian consciousness to face the next stage of its development which should consist in the acquisition of authority and in the ability to face the pull from the unconscious. Yet the images which accompany this particular moment in the history of the building of a new national identity are suggestive of an inadequacy represented as either an illness of immobilizing nature (*La Porta del Cielo*) or of dispersion of leadership (*Roma Città Aperta*). I suggest that this points to a tendency to return to a safety preceding consciousness and as such it is described, mythologically, as 'uroboric incest'; a movement described by the films of the post-armistice.

The 'uroboric incest': the Church as safe return (Chapter 5, part two)

The elimination of the tyrant (Terrible Father/Mussolini) and the invasion of the land (Good Mother) by alien forces (both American and German) was to leave the young ego/nation exposed to the pull exerted by the other poles of the respective archetypes: facing the abyss of a frightening unconscious (Terrible Mother) and longing for the acquisition of a higher consciousness (Heavenly Father). The narrative journeys explored through the narratives of the films of the post-armistice period (*La Porta del Cielo* and *Roma Città Aperta*) point to the search for a dissolution of these tensions. The necessity to take a position in relation to other nations and the questions of loyalties and of leadership were the pressing issues which characterized the uncertain years before the end of the war. The loss of identity implied by the armistice was also demanding the emergence of a new one. This newly constructed nation was to take a position of consciousness solid enough to withhold the invasion (Allied) which, felt as 'liberation', threatened to swallow its independence.

De Sica's train (*La Porta del Cielo*) provides a good description of the situation in the unconscious. In the film a good proportion of the infirmities is of a paralyzing nature and the train's movement is towards a miraculous healing as an outcome of fatherly intervention. When left to face the abyss of the maternal unconscious, the ego needs to take a position against the tendency of the unconscious to swallow it back. The opportunity for Italy's rebirth was becoming real as the now orphan nation (that of orphan being a necessary condition for ego independence) faced the difficulty and the complex responsibility of organizing difference; a function of the ego modelled by the archetype of the Self (clearly represented in *Roma Città Aperta*). The overwhelming fear of inadequacy can indeed take over if the ego is unprepared and too weak to withstand the confrontation implied by birth. The infirmities are reminders of the petrifying effect of that confrontation. The beheading of the Medusa requires a reflection suggestive of awareness in the ownership of one's own gaze. In the film this passage is overlooked and a step in the solidification of consciousness missed: the journey of healing is towards a miracle enacted by the Father in the Mother's house.

The awareness of an inadequacy of the new ego-consciousness to fulfil its role of leadership in the landscape of the national psyche is compensated for by its returning to what Neumann calls a 'uroboric' unity with the Parents (Neumann

1954: 16–18): a place of unconsciousness the infantile ego longs for and to which he has to surrender if too weak to withstand the wearisome journey towards consciousness. This return can be a necessary moment of 'recharging', an immersion in energy which will become functional to a rebirth. Yet, both in the films and in reality the responsibility for the rebirth is given to a spiritual principle/ideology. This goal is in itself too ambitious if considered in relation to the spiritual/ideological consciousness which in Italy was in its embryonic, disjointed form. *La Porta del Cielo* points to this unpreparedness and suggests a returning of Italy to an identity predating that of political nation back to that of a Catholic country.

Rather than a move forward towards autonomy there is in the films and in the political attitude of these years a tendency to ask for a rescuing from the orphaned condition. The possibility of forming something new is certainly described in the films, especially in *Roma Città Aperta*. The film's symbolic representation of the archetype of the Self describes the ambitious project of integration of differences which the new government will face after the war. However, the film also warns of the dangers inherent in a lack of pragmatism which in the longing for a higher, spiritual consciousness (Heavenly Father again) forfeits the importance of a mediation with an Earth represented by Pina. What is left is the option of returning to an institution – the Church – which considered as such (an institution) becomes a point of union between Heaven and Earth, between Mother and Father which provides temporary refuge until the ego's readiness for a new birth. Again, the films describe the effect on the Italian unconscious of a negative leadership which left a legacy of distrust in leadership itself and weariness at taking 'alone' the father's place. Notwithstanding the weakness of the ego/national identity, a 'birth' was necessary and in 1948 the new Republic was indeed born. The films of this period describe how Italy managed to overcome instability by shifting the core of its being from ideology to economy and in so doing began to construct a persona consistent with that core. I argue that the period of the election marked the moment of a rebuilding/rebirth which in compensating weakness with affluence fostered the development of an internal split between pragmatism and ideology. The possibility of integration glimpsed during the Resistance was replaced by a drift between Communists and Christian Democrats which the efforts of the intellectuals would, for a long time, be unable to bridge. The new national identity was now required to find the means to manage its interaction with the world. The search for the definition of this interface is described as the acquisition of a mask forged on an economic identity.

An adolescent ego: the mask of an economic identity (Chapter 6)

Neumann points to the fact that the 'adolescent ego' is bound to remain insecure 'until it has finally consolidated itself and is able to stand on its own feet', something which is only possible after the victorious fight with the dragon (Neumann

1954: 121). This insecurity derives from the identification of the ego with a still undeveloped consciousness which nevertheless directs it towards a distancing from the unconscious. At one time the pubertal ego is facing away from the unconscious with an attitude of 'depreciation of the place from which one came' (Neumann 1954: 123) and directing its energy towards the world as the place of its conquest and creation. I propose that at this stage in the process of asserting itself as a nation worthy of international appreciation Italy's condition is described quite accurately as that of a 'pubertal ego'.

The film narratives of this period present heroes whose relationship to the Mother (unconscious) now involves a willingness to move away from her in search of the means necessary to consolidate their presence in the world. Her offers of nourishment (sheets in *Ladri di Biciclette*, mortgage money in *La Terra Trema* and food found in the street in *Germania Anno Zero*) are accepted as borrowings which are not to be repaid. It is the energy derived from this nourishment that allows for the acquisition of the means (bicycle and boat) which make that ego 'visible' to society. The subsequent loss of these means has two consequences: it forfeits the debt to the mother and triggers the movement to a new stage in development.

The autarchic policies of Mussolini's regime had led to Italy's misrecognition and disappearance from the world scene. After the war the country was finally eager to accept any support which would guarantee its meaningful and positive participation. The objects which represent, in the films, the means to such participation are, paradoxically, both a means to independence and a reminder of how that independence is itself dependent on the Mother. Italy's economic resurgence allowed for the rebuilding of infrastructure and for the recovery of industry, marking the beginning of a miracle growth which seemed, for a while, to compensate for other weaknesses. Nevertheless such resurgence depended on American aid, a dependency which while affecting politics was also to affect Italy's sense of worth and the core of identity.

The films appear to be centred on the recovery of the object which supported the recognition of the ego as differentiated from the unconscious and unquestioning (in *La Terra Trema* and in *Germania Anno Zero*) masses. I have argued that the final surrendering to the loss of the object, rather than a defeat, stands as compensation and protection on the part of the unconscious of an ego which, having dissolved false identities, is about to move on to a journey of individuation. To the external conditions which disappointed hopes and led to the consolidation of old political dynamics, the films juxtapose the possibility of a resistance based on an understanding of the process of growth. Both 'Ntoni and Antonio (*La Terra Trema* and *Ladri di Biciclette*) move back into the undifferentiated community but have finally glimpsed the importance of relatedness as the means to independence and as the differentiating element. The inner insecurity characteristic of this stage is then overcome, historically through economic dependency, psychologically through a form of withdrawal which accepts the dependency as necessary but struggles to preserve ideological purity.

The unconscious message seems to insist on the danger inherent in opting for pure ideology and in rejecting compromise: consistent with Neumann's description of the characteristics of puberty, the 'overvaluation of the ego', symptom of an immature consciousness, is compensated for by 'a depressive self-destruction which . . . often culminates in suicide' (Neumann 1954: 123). In Rossellini's film (*Germania Anno Zero*) the detachment from the parents, through a murder which is archetypally explained, brings at once the birth of a new fragile identity and the overwhelming guilt for the undeserved individuality which came from a victory without a fight. The archetypal message is then consistent with one which points to the possibility of another beginning, parallel to the one which, politically, appears to be negatively tinged. This beginning is presented as that of another kind of resistance. The nature of this resistance is presented more clearly in the last films discussed in the book, produced during the years which saw the end of the Marshall Plan.

Consolidating the ego: the American paradise and the salvation of the soul (Chapter 7)

The years immediately after the elections (1949 to 1952) saw the settling into a new organization of government, the establishing of new political alliances and the adjustment to the new cultural attitude imported, together with the financial aid, from America. The insecurity of the newly formed ego/national identity had conditioned the structuring of government around the safe exclusion of the 'unsettling' Communist presence. Jung would describe this presence, condemned by the ego as having negative value, as representing the Shadow part of the personality. Neumann's consideration of the function of the shadow is particularly relevant to the understanding of this particular stage in the development of an Italian national identity. He suggests:

> It is as though centroversion had attached to the aspiring flights of ego consciousness, with its animosity to the body, the leaden weight of the shadow which takes good care that there shall be no 'reaching for the moon' . . . the shadow . . . prevents a dissociation of the personality such as always result from hypertrophy of consciousness and overaccentuation of the ego.
> (Neumann 1954: 352)

If the acknowledgment of the shadow is such an important aspect for the balanced development of consciousness, the exclusion of a dialogue with opposite factions as suggested by the new organization of government was bound to bring imbalance. The films produced in this period describe the potentially fatal consequences of such one-sidedness as well as compensating for it in their archetypal content.

The necessity for the ego to adapt to its social environment corresponds to Italy's striving towards acceptance and participation in the life of the community of nations. In a direct developmental line with the insecurity discussed as characteristic of the previous period, the insistence on creating an acceptable 'persona' is to be partially attributed to a normal unfolding of a process of adaptation. This new necessity marks the end of childhood; it is the end of a 'world of dream and fairy tale' and the time when the energy previously used to prevent a fall back into unconsciousness can now be used to build and consolidate the conscious system. Throughout the narratives in the films of these years the children, in fact, are withdrawn from the screen, in one case literally (*Bellissima*). Letting go of what their presence represents – potential for growth, innocence, beauty – is a complex process honoured in the films. The process which leads to the integration of that potential into an ego, now on its way to the realization of the self through individuation, is in fact beautifully described in the journey of the women in *Europa '51* and *Bellissima*. In De Sica's *Miracolo a Milano* this journey is reversed and the distracting power of consumerism leads to a loss of ground, literal but also undoubtedly symbolic, and consequently to a return to the Mother. While De Sica's film referred to the dangerous effect of consumerism on a still emotionally fragile community, the other films present journeys which suggest the possibility of compensating for the effect of the economic frenzy which is transforming Italy into one of America's ideological colonies.

The women in Rossellini's and Visconti's films, Irene and Maddalena, stand for an ideal of nation that not only corresponds to the directors' radical political perspective but also proposes a model of psychological self-realization which, as it should be according to a healthy process of individuation, rejects homologation and refutes definitions associated with either capital or with standardized and stifled ideological constructs. These last images of a wholeness achieved and imprisoned, conquered but surrendering, are images of hope. They imply that an 'inner voice' is still functioning. Neumann maintains that the 'voice, that inward orientation which makes known the utterance of the self, will never speak in a disintegrated personality, in a bankrupt consciousness, and in a fragmented psychic system' (Neumann 1954: 444). Through these last films this voice is certainly speaking and eventually Italy will listen.

This narrative discussion of the historical events, described through film images and understood through a Jungian analytical perspective, has highlighted the salient moments of a process of development otherwise unconscious. The adopted methodology has successfully aided an understanding of the images as both descriptive of the state of a cultural unconscious and compensating for events and external influences conditioning the process of growth.

A difficult travelling companion: with Jung and beyond Jung

I discussed the possible reasons for the diffident reception Jung has often received in academic circles at the beginning of Chapter 1. Coming closer to his work through this research I have certainly found reasons for understanding that diffidence: his substituting one dogmatic position with another (as I mentioned in Chapter 2) and his rigid classification of differences which places his ideas on nation on rather dangerous ideological ground (Chapter 3).

In the course of the development of this book I have also become increasingly aware of how Jung's own theory was certainly conditioned by his gender and by a particular, personal attitude towards women. In his discussion of the Mother Archetype Jung seems to reflect on his own attitude when he states:

> The mother has from the outset a decidedly symbolic significance for a man, which probably accounts for his strong tendency to idealize her. Idealization is a hidden apotropaism; one idealizes whenever there is a secret fear to be exorcized.
>
> (*C.W.*, Vol. 9i: para. 192)

Although he describes the feared object as 'the unconscious', its relationship to the image of mother becomes revealing when after describing the anima as the 'perilous image of Woman' who is at the same time 'the great illusionist, (and) the seductress' he suggests that rather than a substitute for the mother, the anima is actually the origin of the 'numinous qualities which make the mother-imago so dangerously powerful' (*C.W.*, Vol. 9ii: para. 24–27).

Demaris Wehr criticizes Jung's decontextualized description of such fear-inducing images as they seem to 'elevate men's fear of women to the level of symbol and mythologize it' (Wehr 1987: 110). What she proposed instead is to locate men's fear of women and its correspondence to the anima, and indirectly to the Mother Archetype, within the context of patriarchy in order to heal and maybe understand misogyny. Jung's own position must then be considered within this context yet it remains important to maintain, working within his theoretical construct, a degree of cautiousness when dealing with issues of gender. When writing her introduction to 'Visual Pleasure and Narrative Cinema' Laura Mulvey suggested that the first step out of patriarchal oppression is in the examination of patriarchy with the tools it provides 'of which psychoanalysis is not the only but an important one' (Mulvey 1975: 15). Similarly, an analysis of the way symbols emerge and operate both at a personal and collective level does not preclude an understanding of the Jungian perspective as a symbol system which endorses patriarchy by tending to work towards the legitimizing of a certain social order (Wehr 1987: 25).

This awareness has helped maintain a perspective on neo-realism which, while discussing the film's archetypal contents, has remained sensitive to the underlying social discourses. Moreover, the particular attention paid in the book to the analysis of the women in the films is partially derived from a desire to juxtapose a Jungian insistence on the journey of the male hero with a dedication to an analysis of a woman's process of transformation. This dedication also reflects a desire to partially readdress a balance which, in the case of the academic debate on neo-realism, seems to be favourable to a traditional insistence on the analysis of the narrative led by male protagonists.

A final word

The intention of travelling the 'royal road' from cinema towards a culture's unconscious has actually led to one journey within another: a complex process of negotiation between the stories told in images, those revealed through the analytic methods and the revisiting through both of a country's history. In the way this book has managed this process of negotiation lies its central contribution to film analysis: a methodology which, centred on the image as the bridge connecting history and a culture's unconscious, can finally do that image justice.

Bibliography

Allen, B. and Russo, M. (eds) (1997) *Revisioning Italy: National Identity and Global Culture*, Minnesota, MN: University of Minnesota Press.
Allum, P. (1990) 'Uniformity undone: aspects of Catholic culture in postwar Italy', in Z. Baranski and R. Lumley (eds) *Culture and Conflict in Postwar Italy*, London: Macmillan.
Anderson, B. (1991) *Imagined Communities: Reflections on the Origin and Spread of Nationalism*, London and New York: Verso.
Armes, R. (1971) *Patterns of Realism*, London: Tantivy Press.
Bacon, H. (1998) *Visconti: Explorations of Beauty and Decay*, Cambridge: Cambridge University Press.
Baranski, Z. G. and Lumley R. (eds) (1990) *Culture and Conflict in Postwar Italy: Essays on Mass and Popular Culture*, London: Macmillan.
Barlach, E. (1912) *Der tote Tag* [The Dead Day]. Berlin.
Baudry, J. L. (1970) 'Cinéma: effets idéologiques produits par l'appareil de base', *Cinétique*, 8. Translated as (1974–1975) 'The ideological effects of the basic cinematographic apparatus', *Film Quarterly*, 28, 2: 39–47.
—— (1975) 'Le dispositif', *Communications*, 23: 56–72. Trans. J. Andrews and B. Augst (1976) as 'The apparatus: metapsychological approaches to the impression of reality in cinema', *Camera Obscura*, 1 (Fall). Reprinted in L. Braudy, and M. Cohen (eds) (1999) *Film Theory and Criticism: Introductory Readings*, 5th edn, New York and Oxford: Oxford University Press: 760–777.
Bazin, A. (1971) 'In defence of Rossellini, a letter to Guido Aristarco', in H. Gray (ed.) *What Is Cinema?*, Vol. 2, Berkeley, CA: University of California Press.
Bazin, A. (2000) 'Defence of Rossellini', in D. Forgacs, S. Lutton and G. Nowell-Smith (eds) *Roberto Rossellini: Magician of the Real*, London: British Film Institute.
Bedani, G. and Haddock, B. (eds) (2000) *The Politics of Italian National Identity: A Multidisciplinary Perspective*, Cardiff: University of Wales Press.
Beebe, J. (2000) '*The Wizard of Oz*: a vision of development in the American political psyche', in T. Singer *The Vision Thing: Myth, Politics and Psyche in the World*, London and New York: Routledge.
Bergstrom, J. (1999) *Endless Night: Cinema and Psychoanalysis, Parallel Histories*, Berkeley, CA: University of California Press.
Berry, P. (2001) 'Image in motion', in C. Hauke and I. Alister (eds) *Jung and Film: Post-Jungian Takes on the Moving Image*, Hove, UK: Brunner-Routledge.
Bondanella, P. E. (2001) *Italian Cinema: From Neorealism to the Present*, 3rd edn, New York and London: Continuum.

Breuilly, J. (1993) *Nationalism and the State*, Chicago, IL: University of Chicago Press.
Brunetta, G.P. (1994) 'The long march of American Cinema in Italy from fascism to the Cold War', in D. W. Ellwood and R. Krows (eds) *Hollywood in Europe: Experiences of a Cultural Hegemony*, Amsterdam: VU University Press.
—— (2001) *Storia del Cinema Italiano*, Vols. 1, 2, 3, 2nd edn, Roma: Editori Riuniti.
Buss, R. (1989) *Italian Films*, New York: Holms and Meier.
Caldwell, L. (2000) 'What about women? Italian films and their concerns', in U. Siegluhr (ed.) *Heroines without Heroes: Reconstructing Female and National Identities in European Cinema 1945–51*, London: Cassell.
Chiarini, L. (1978) 'A discourse on neo-realism', in D. Overbey (ed.) *Springtime in Italy: A Reader on Neo-realism*, Stockport: Talisman Books.
Clough, W. R. (2002) *Moving Forward: Clash of Civilizations*, available at www.cgjungpage.org/articles/clough1.html (accessed 20 November 2005).
Conforti, M. (1999) *Field, Form, and Fate: Patterns in Mind, Nature and Psyche*, Woodstock, CT: Spring Publications.
Copjec, J. (1989) 'The orthopsychic subject: film theory and the reception of Lacan', *October*, 49. Reprinted in R. Stam and T. Miller (eds) (2000) *Film Theory: An Anthology*, Oxford: Blackwell.
—— (1994) *Read My Desire: Lacan Against the Historicists*, Cambridge, MA: MIT Press.
Creed, B. (2000) 'Film and psychoanalysis', in J. Hill and P. Church Gibson (eds) *Film Studies: Critical Approaches*, Oxford: Oxford University Press.
Curle, H. and Snyder, S. (eds) (2000) *Vittorio De Sica: Contemporary Perspectives*, Toronto. University of Toronto Press.
De Blasio Wilhelm, M. (1988) *The Other Italy: The Italian Resistance in World War II*, New York and London: Norton.
De Grand, A. J. (1971) 'The Italian Nationalist Association in the period of Italian neutrality, August 1914–May 1915', *Journal of Modern History*, 43, 3: 394–412.
De Grazia, V. (1992) *How Fascism Ruled Women: Italy, 1922–1945*, Los Angeles and London: University of California Press.
De Lauretis, T. (1995) 'On the subject of fantasy', in L. Pietropaolo and A. Testaferri (eds) *Feminisms in the Cinema*, Bloomington, IN: Indiana University Press.
Deleuze, G. (1989) *Cinema 2: The Time Image*, trans. H. Tomlinson and R. Galeta, London: Athlone Press.
Delle Vacche, A. (1992) *The Body in the Mirror: Shapes of History in Italian Cinema*, Princeton, NJ: Princeton University Press.
Doane, M A. (1990) 'Remembering women: psychical and historical constructions in film theory', in E.A. Kaplan (ed.) *Psychoanalysis and Cinema*, London and New York: Routledge. First published 1987, *Continuum, the Australian Journal of Media and Culture*, 1, 2: 3–14.
Dougherty, M. (2001) 'Love-life: using films in the interpretation of gender within analysis', in C. Hauke and I. Alister (eds) *Jung and Film: Post-Jungian Takes on the Moving Image*, Hove, UK: Brunner-Routledge.
Duggan C. (1994) *A Concise History of Italy*, Cambridge: Cambridge University Press.
Ellwood, D. W. (1985) *Italy 1943–1945*, Leicester: Leicester University Press.
Feldman, B. (2003) 'Encountering otherness: anthropological, developmental and clinical dimensions', *Journal of Jungian Theory and Practice*, 5, 2: 23–40.
Feldman, B. (2004) 'Towards a theory of organisational culture: integrating the "other" from a post-Jungian perspective', in T. Singer and S. L. Kimbles (eds) *The Cultural*

Complex: Contemporary Jungian Perspectives on Psyche and Society, Hove, UK: Brunner-Routledge.

Forgacs, D. (2000) 'Mass media and the national community', in G. Bedani and B. Haddock (eds), *The Politics of Italian National Identity: A Multidisciplinary Perspective*, Cardiff: University of Wales Press.

Forgacs, D., Lutton, S. and Nowell-Smith, G. (eds) (2000) *Roberto Rossellini: Magician of the Real*, London: British Film Institute.

Fredericksen, D. (1979) 'Jung/sign/symbol/film', *Quarterly Review of Film Studies*, Spring: 167–192.

—— (2001) 'Jung/sign/symbol/film', in C. Hauke and I. Alister (eds) *Jung and Film: Post-Jungian Takes on the Moving Image*, Hove, UK: Brunner-Routledge.

Freud, S. (1900) *The Interpretation of Dreams*, trans. A.A. Brill (1997), Ware: Wordsworth Editions.

Freud, S. (1907) 'Creative writers and day-dreaming', in S. Freud (1959) *The Standard Edition of the Complete Psychological Works of Sigmund Freud*, Vol. 9, London: Hogarth Press and Institute of Psychoanalysis.

—— (1914) 'Remembering, repeating and working through', *Standard Edition*, London: Hogarth Press.

—— (1915) 'Beyond the pleasure principle', *Standard Edition*, London: Hogarth Press.

—— (1919) 'The "uncanny"', in J. Strachey (1990) *The Penguin Freud Library, Volume 14: Art and Literature*, London: Penguin.

Galli della Loggia, E. (1996) *La Morte della Patria*, Roma and Bari: La Terza e Figli.

Ganser, D. (2005) 'The puzzling story of NATO's secret armies during the Cold War: just what were they up to?', *History News Network*, available at http://hnn.us/articles/12253html (accessed 5 June 2007).

Gellner, E. (1964) *Thought and Change*, London: Weidenfeld and Nicolson.

Gellner, E. (1983) *Nations and Nationalism*, Oxford: Blackwell.

Gellner, E. (1987) *Culture, Identity and Politics*, Cambridge: Cambridge University Press.

Goodwin, B. C. (1989) 'Evolution and the generative order', in B. Goodwin and P. Saunders (eds) *Theoretical Biology: Epigenetic and Evolutionary Order from Complex Systems*, Baltimore, MA: Johns Hopkins University Press.

Gramsci, A. (1971) *Selections from the Prison Notebooks of Antonio Gramsci*, eds and trans. Q. Hoare and G. Nowell Smith, London: Lawrence and Wishart.

Gray, R. M. (1996) *Archetypal Explorations: An Integrative Approach to Human Behaviour*, London and New York: Routledge.

Gundle, S. (1990) 'From neo-realism to *Luci rosse*: cinema, politics, society, 1945–85', in Z. G. Baranski and R. Lumley (eds) *Culture and Conflict in Postwar Italy: Essays on Mass and Popular Culture*, London: Macmillan.

—— (2000) *Between Hollywood and Moscow: The Italian Communists and the Challenge of Mass Culture: 1943–1991*, Durham and London: Duke University Press.

Haddock B. (2000) 'State, nation and risorgimento', in G. Bedani and B. Haddock (eds) *The Politics of Italian National Identity: A Multidisciplinary Perspective*, University of Wales Press.

Hastings, A. (1997) *The Construction of Nationhood: Ethnicity, Religion and Nationalism*, Cambridge: Cambridge University Press.

Hauke, C. (2001) '"Let's go back to finding out who we are": men, *Umheimlich* and returning home in the films of Steven Spielberg', in C. Hauke and I. Alister (eds) *Jung and Film: Post-Jungian Takes on the Moving Image*, Hove, UK: Brunner-Routledge.

Hauke, C. and Alister, I. (eds) (2001) *Jung and Film: Post-Jungian Takes on the Moving Image*, Hove, UK: Brunner-Routledge.

Hayward. S. (2000) 'Framing the nation', in M. Hjort and S. Mackenzie (eds) *Cinema and Nation*, London and New York: Routledge.

Heath, S. (1976) 'Narrative space', *Screen*, 17, 3: 68–112.

—— (1999) 'Cinema and psychoanalysis: parallel histories', in J. Bergstrom *Endless Night: Cinema and Psychoanalysis, Parallel Histories*, Berkeley, CA: University of California Press.

Higson, A. (2000) 'Limiting imagination of national cinema', in M. Hjort and S. Mackenzie *Cinema and Nation*, London and New York: Routledge.

Hjort, M. and Mackenzie, S. (eds) (2000) *Cinema and Nation*, London and New York: Routledge.

Hockley, L. (2001) *Cinematic Projections: The Analytical Psychology of C.G. Jung and Film Theory*, Luton: University of Luton Press.

Hollwitz, J. (2001) 'The Grail quest and *Field of Dreams*', in C. Hauke and I. Alister (eds) *Jung and Film: Post-Jungian Takes on the Moving Image*, Hove, UK: Brunner-Routledge.

Izod, J. (1992) *The Films of Nicolas Roeg: Myth and Mind*, London: Macmillan.

—— (2001a) *Myth, Mind and the Screen: Understanding the Heroes of Our Time*, Cambridge: Cambridge University Press.

Izod, J. (2001b) '*2001: A Space Odyssey*: a classical reading', in C. Hauke and I. Alister (eds) *Jung and Film: Post-Jungian Takes on the Moving Image*, Hove, UK: Brunner-Routledge.

—— (2006) *Screen, Culture, Psyche: A Post-Jungian Approach to Working with the Audience*, London and New York: Routledge.

Jacobi, J. (1959) *Complex/Archetype/Symbol in the Psychology of C. G. Jung*, London: Routledge and Kegan Paul.

Jung, C. G. (1956) *Symbols of Transformation: An Analysis of the Prelude to a Case of Schizofrenia. The Collected Works*, Vol. 5. London: Routledge and Kegan Paul.

—— (1971) *Psychological Types. The Collected Works*, Vol. 6. London: Routledge and Kegan Paul.

—— (1966) *Two Essays on Analytical Psychology. The Collected Works*, Vol. 7, 2nd edn, London: Routledge and Kegan Paul.

—— (1969) *The Structure and Dynamic of the Psyche. The Collected Works*, Vol. 8, 2nd edn, London: Routledge and Kegan Paul.

—— (1968) *The Archetypes and The Collective Unconscious. The Collected Works*, Vol. 9, Part I, 2nd edn, London: Routledge and Kegan Paul.

—— (1968) *Aion: Researches into the Phenomenology of the Self. The Collected Works*, Vol. 9, Part II, 2nd edn, London: Routledge and Kegan Paul.

—— (1970) *Civilization in Transition. The Collected Works*, Vol. 10, 2nd edn, London: Routledge and Kegan Paul.

—— (1969) *Psychology and Religion: West and East. The Collected Works*, Vol. 11, 2nd edn, London: Routledge and Kegan Paul.

—— (1970) *Mysterium Coniunctionis. The Collected Works*, Vol. 14, 2nd edn, London: Routledge and Kegan Paul.

—— (1966) *The Spirit in Man, Art, and Literature. The Collected Works*, Vol. 15, London: Routledge and Kegan Paul.

—— (1966) *The Practice of Psychotherapy. The Collected Works*, Vol. 16, 2nd edn, London: Routledge and Kegan Paul.
—— (1954) *The Development of Personality. The Collected Works*, Vol. 17, London: Routledge and Kegan Paul.
—— (1977) *The Symbolic Life. The Collected Works*, Vol. 18, London: Routledge and Kegan Paul.
Jung, E. (1985) *Animus and Anima*, Dallas, TX: Spring Publications.
Kaplan, A. E. (ed.) (1990) *Psychoanalysis and Cinema*, London: Routledge.
Katz, R. (2003) *Fatal Silence: The Pope, the Resistance and the German Occupation of Rome*, London: Weidenfeld and Nicolson.
Kauffman, S. (1995) *At Home in the Universe: The Search for the Laws of Self-Organisation and Complexity*, New York: Oxford University Press.
Knox, J. M. (2001) 'Memories, fantasies, archetypes: an exploration of some connections between cognitive science and analytical psychology', *Journal of Analytical Psychology*, 46: 613–635.
Kristeva, J. (1985) 'Stabat mater', *Poetics Today*, 6, 1–2: 133–152.
La Costituzione della Repubblica Italiana. (The Constitution of the Italian Republic), available at www.quirinale.it/costituzione/costituzione.htm (accessed 20 January 2007).
Lacan, J. (1975) *The Seminar of Jacques Lacan. Book I Freud's Papers on Technique 1953–1954*, J.A. Miller (ed.), trans. with notes John Forrester 1988, Cambridge: Cambridge University Press.
—— (1977) *The Four Fundamental Concepts of Psychoanalysis*, London: Hogarth Press.
—— (1988) *The Seminars of Jacques Lacan: Book II. The Ego in Freud's Theory and in the Technique of Psychoanalysis. 1954–1955*, J.A. Miller (ed.), trans. Sylvana Tomaselli with notes by John Forrester, Cambridge: Cambridge University Press.
—— (1993) *The Seminars of Jacques Lacan: The Psychoses. Book III 1955–1956*, J.A. Miller (ed.), trans. with notes Russell Grigg, London: Routledge.
Landy, M. (2000) *Italian Film*, Cambridge: Cambridge University Press.
Lebeau, V. (2001) *Psychoanalysis and Cinema: The Play of Shadows*, London: Wallflower Press.
Lennihan, L. (2001) 'The alchemy of *Pulp Fiction*', in C. Hauke and I. Alister (eds) *Jung and Film: Post-Jungian Takes on the Moving Image*, Hove, UK: Brunner-Routledge.
Liehm, M. (1984) *Passion and Defiance: Film in Italy from 1942 to the Present*, Berkeley and Los Angeles: University of California Press.
McDowell, M. J. (1999) 'Relating to the mystery: a biological view of analytical psychology', *Quadrant: Journal of the C. G. Jung Foundation for Analytical Psychology*, 29, 1: 12–32, available as 'Jungian analysis and biology' at http://cogprints.ecs.soton.ac.uk (accessed 4 February 2003).
—— (2000) 'The landscape of possibility: a dynamic systems perspective on archetype and Change', *Journal of Analytical Psychology: An International Quarterly of Jungian Practice and Theory*, available at http://cogprints.org/1084/00/Jap% 5F9.html (accessed 11 April 2003).
—— (2001) 'The three gorillas: an archetype orders a dynamic system', *Journal of Analytical Psychology*, 46: 4.
Mack Smith, D. (1983) *Mussolini*, London: Paladin Grafton.

—— (1997) *Modern Italy: A Political History*, New Haven and London: Yale University Press.
Marcus, M. (1986) *Italian Film in the Light of Neorealism*, Princeton, NJ: Princeton University Press.
Marlan, S. (2002) 'The mixed texture of symbolic thought: a response to and elaboration of some points in Alan Jones's paper "Teleology and the hermeneutic of hope: Jungian interpretation in the light of the work of Paul Ricoeur"', *Journal of Jungian Theory and Practice*, 4, 2: 56–65.
Metz, C. (1974) *Film Language: A Semiotics of the Cinema*, New York: Oxford University Press.
—— (1975/1982) *Psychoanalysis and Cinema: The Imaginary Signifier*, London: Macmillan.
—— (1977) *Le signifiant imaginaire: Psychanalyse et cinema*, Paris: Union Générale d'Éditions. Published in English in 1982 as *The Imaginary Signifier. Psychoanalysis and the Cinema*, trans. C. Britton, A. Williams, B. Brewster and A. Guzzetti, Bloomington, IN: Indiana University Press.
Morgan, H. (2004) 'Exploring racism: a clinical example of a cultural complex', in T. Singer and S. L. Kimbles (eds) *The Cultural Complex: Contemporary Jungian Perspectives on Psyche and Society*, Hove, UK: Brunner-Routledge.
Morley, D. and Robins, K. (1990) 'No place like *Heimat*: images of home(land) in European culture', *New Formations*, 12: 1–23.
Muller, H. J. (1957) *Uses of the Past: Profiles of Former Societies*, New York: Oxford University Press.
Mulvey, L. (1975) 'Visual pleasure and narrative cinema', *Screen*, 16, 3: 6–18.
—— (1989) *Visual and Other Pleasures*, London: Macmillan.
Mussolini, B. (1935) *The Doctrine of Fascism*, Firenze: Vallecchi Editore.
Neumann, E. (1954) *The Origins and History of Consciousness*, London: Routledge and Kegan Paul.
—— (1956) *Amor and Psyche: the Psychic Development of the Feminine*, London: Routledge and Kegan Paul.
—— (1959) *Art and the Creative Unconscious: Four Essays*, London: Routledge and Kegan Paul.
—— (1963) *The Great Mother: An Analysis of the Archetype*, 2nd edn, Princeton, NJ: Princeton University Press.
Neville, B. (1992) 'The charm of Hermes: Hillman, Lyotard and the post-modern condition', *Journal of Analytical Psychology*, 37: 337–353.
Noll, R. (1994) *The Jung Cult: Origins of a Charismatic Movement*, Princeton, MA: Princeton University Press.
Noll, R. (1997) *The Aryan Christ: The Secret Life of Carl Jung*. New York: Random House.
Nowell-Smith, G. (1967) *Visconti*, London: Secker and Warburg and British Film Institute.
—— (2003) *Visconti*, 3rd edn, London: BFI Publishing,
Overbey, D. (ed.) (1978) *Springtime in Italy: A Reader on Neo-realism*, Stockport: Talisman Books.
Penley, C. (2000) 'Feminism, film theory, and the bachelor machines', in R. Stam and T. Miller (eds) *Film and Theory: An Anthology*, Oxford: Blackwell.
Polese, R. (2002) 'Il cinema a Salò', *Corriere della Sera*, 18 January, available at www.romacivica.net/ANPIROMA/FASCISMO/fascismo17c.htm (accessed 3 December 2006).

Rank, O. (1914) *The Myth of the Birth of the Hero*, trans. F. Robbins and S. Ely Jelliffe, Nervous and Mental Disease Monograph Series, New York: Journal of Nervous and Mental Disease Publishing Company.
Restivo, A. (2002) *The Cinema of Economic Miracles: Visuality and Modernization in the Italian Art Film. (Post Contemporary Interventions)*, Durham and London: Duke University Press.
Ricoeur, P. (1970) *Freud and Philosophy: An Essay on Interpretation*, New Haven, CT: Yale University Press.
Rocchio, F. V. (1999) *Cinema of Anxiety: A Psychoanalysis of Italian Neorealism*, Austin, TX: University of Texas Press.
Rodowick, D. N. (1997) *Gille Deleuze's Time Machine*, Durham and London: Duke University Press.
Rohmer, E. and Truffaut, F. (1954) 'Entretien avec Roberto Rossellini', *Cahiers du Cinema*, 37, in J. Hillier (ed.) (1985) *Cahiers du Cinema Vol. 1. The 1950s: Neo-Realism, Hollywood, New Wave*, London: Routledge and Kegan Paul.
Romanyshyn, R. (1989) *Technology as Symptom and Dream*. New York: Routledge.
Samuels, A. (1985) *Jung and the Post-Jungians*, London: Routledge and Kegan Paul.
—— (1992) 'National psychology, national socialism, and analytical psychology: reflections on Jung and anti-semitism', *Journal of Analytical Psychology*, 37, 1: 3–28, 37, 2: 127–147, available at www.history.ac.uk/eseminars/sem9.html (accessed 11 December 2006).
—— (1993) *The Political Psyche*, London: Routledge.
—— (2000) 'The politics of transformation: the transformation of politics', in T. Singer (ed.) *The Vision Thing: Myth, Politics and Psyche in the World*, London and New York: Routledge.
Samuels, A., Shorter, B. and Plaut, F. (1986) *A Critical Dictionary of Jungian Analysis*, London and New York: Routledge and Kegan Paul.
Sheldrake, R. (1988) *The Presence of the Past*, London: Collins.
Shiel, M. (2006) *Italian Neorealism: Rebuilding the Cinematic City*, London: Wallflower Press.
Silverman, K. (1988) *The Acoustic Mirror: The Female Voice in Psychoanalysis and Cinema*, Bloomington, IN: Indiana University Press.
Silvestri, S. 'Dai telefoni ai telefonini bianchi', *il manifesto* 7, available at www.ilmanifesto.it/25aprile/07_25Aprile/9507rs30.01.htm (accessed 2 June 2007).
Singer, T. (ed.) (2000) *The Vision Thing: Myth, Politics and Psyche in the World*, London and New York: Routledge.
Singer, T. and Kimbles, S. L. (eds) (2004) *The Cultural Complex: Contemporary Jungian Perspectives on Psyche and Society*, Hove, UK: Brunner-Routledge.
Smith, A. (2000) 'Images of the nation: cinema, art and national identity', in M. Hjort and S. Mackenzie (eds) *Cinema and Nation*, London and New York: Routledge.
Spackman, B. (1996) *Fascist Virilities: Rhetoric, Ideology and Social Fantasy in Italy*, Minneapolis, MN: University of Minnesota Press.
Spielrein, S. (1912) 'Uber den psychologischen Inhalt eines Falls von Schizophrenie', in *Jahrbuch fur Psychoanalytische und Psychopathologische Forschungen*, Vol. 3, Leipzig and Vienna cited by Jung in vol. 15: 201.
Stam, R. (2000) *Film Theory: An Introduction*, Oxford: Blackwell.
Stevens, A. (2002) *Archetype Revisited: An Updated Natural History of the Self*, 2nd edn, Hove, UK: Brunner-Routledge.

Strickland, B. R. (ed.) (2001) *The Gale Encyclopedia of Psychology*, 2nd edn, Farmington Hills, MI: Gale.

Tomasulo, F. (1982) '"Bicycle Thieves": a re-reading'. *Cinema Journal*, 21, 2: 2–13.

Torriglia, A. M. (2002) *Broken Time, Fragmented Space: A Cultural Map for Postwar Italy*, Toronto: University of Toronto Press.

Ulanov, A. (1992) 'Disguises of the anima' in N. Schwartz-Salant and S. Murray (eds) *Gender and Soul in Psychotherapy*, New York: Chiron.

Von Franz, M. (1966) *The Interpretation of Fairy Tales*, New York: Random House.

—— (1974) *Shadow and Evil in Fairy Tales*, revised edition 1995, Boston, MA: Shambhala.

—— (1980) *Alchemy: An Introduction to the Symbolism and the Psychology*, Toronto: Inner City Books.

—— (1997) *Archetypal Patterns in Fairy Tales*. Toronto: Inner City Books.

Waddington, C.H. (1972) *Towards a Theoretical Biology: 4 Essays*, Edinburgh: Edinburgh University Press.

Wagstaff, C. (2000) 'Rossellini and neo-realism', in D. Forgacs, S. Lutton and G. Nowell-Smith (eds) *Roberto Rossellini: Magician of the Real*, London: British Film Institute.

Wegner, H. (2000) 'Pius Aeneas and Toto il Buono: the founding myth of the Divine City', in H. Curle and S. Snyder (eds) *Vittorio De Sica: Contemporary Perspectives*, Toronto: University of Toronto Press.

Wehr, D. (1987) *Jung and Feminism: Liberating Archetypes*, London: Routledge.

Williams, L. (1987) '"Something else besides a mother" Stella Dallas and the maternal melodrama', in C. Gledhill (ed.) *Home is Where the Heart Is: Studies in Melodrama and the Woman's Film*, London: BFI Publishing.

Wiskemann, E. (1969) *Fascism in Italy: Its Development and Influence*, London: Macmillan.

Wood, M. (2000) 'Woman of Rome: Anna Magnani', in U. Siegluhr (ed.) *Heroines without Heroes: Reconstructing Female and National Identities in European Cinema 1945–51*, London: Cassell.

Wood, M. (2005) *Italian Cinema*, Oxford and New York: Berg.

Woodman, M. (1982) *Addiction to Perfection: The Still Unravished Bride*, Toronto: Inner City Books.

—— (1990) *Ravaged Bridegroom: Masculinity in Women*, Toronto: Inner City Books.

Zavattini, C. (2000) 'Some ideas on the cinema', in H. Curle and S. Snyder (eds) *Vittorio de Sica: Contemporary Perspectives*, Toronto: University of Toronto Press.

Zemon Davies, N. (1975) *Society and Culture in Early Modern France*, Stanford, CT: Stanford University Press, cited by L. Mulvey (1989) *Visual and Other Pleasures*, London: Macmillan.

Zizek, S. (1992) *Looking Awry: An Introduction to Jacques Lacan through Popular Culture*, Cambridge, MA: MIT Press.

—— (2001) *The Fright of Real Tears: Krzystof Kieslowski between Theory and Post-theory*, London: British Film Institute.

Index

affect 40–1, 53, 179
alchemy 62, 197; gold 62, silver 62
Allies 92, 97, 99–101, 118–20, 125, 138–9, 143, 162
America 62–3, 65, 100, 112, 144, 161, 169, 199, 212–13; United States 86, 168, 170; US 143–5, 162, 168–9; USA 13
American: allies 78, 143; colonization of culture 8, 167, 169, 201; influence 61, 87, 170
amplification 21–2, 26–8, 30, 72, 114, 138, 141, 186, 206–7
Anderson, Benedict 48, 57–8, 61, 205
Andreotti, Giulio 170–1
anima 111, 123, 127, 131–2, 176, 179, 200, 214; *see also* archetype; *see also* complex
animus 131, 194, 201; *see also* complex
archetype 3–6, 21, 24, 27–8, 31–46, 50–2, 54–6, 70, 106, 108, 111, 131, 137, 147, 155, 158, 168, 174, 184–5, 208–10; archetype-per-se 21, 39; *see also*: anima, animus, child, father, mother, persona, self, shadow
assumption, dogma of the 124, 170–1, 195–9; and Pope Pius XII 195–7; *see also Europa '51*

I Bambini ci Guardano 7, 98, 109–14, 134, 137, 207, 208; and suicide 110–11, 114; *see also* De Sica
baptism 187–8
Baudry, Jean-Louis 1, 12–14; and apparatus 2, 13–14, 16–17
Bazin, Andre 69, 89
Beebe, John 32, 49, 61–3, 65
Bellissima 8, 90, 108, 167, 171–81, 188, 198, 200, 202, 207, 213; and child 178; *see also*: Anna Magnani, Luchino Visconti
Bergman, Ingrid 92, 191, 199, 201; *see also: Europa '51*, Rossellini
Bicycle Thieves *see Ladri di Biciclette*
birth 140, 142, 150, 164, 183–4, 186–7, 197, 205, 209–10, 212; *see also* rebirth
blindness 116, 123–4; *see also La Porta del Cielo*

Camerini, Mario 86–7, 91
castration 14–5, 115, 140, 208
Catholic; church 64, 84, 102, 133, 158, 170, 195–7; educational system 73; iconography 7, 98; religion 64, 81; *see also* Church
Cavour 74
centroversion 54, 212
Christ 19–20, 120, 123, 134–5, 139, 150, 198; Jesus 123, 127, 129, 131, 134–5; redeemer 192, 199–200; saviour 139, 177, 197
Christian Democratic Party, DC 118, 136, 143, 163, 165
Church 7, 75, 77, 104, 109–13, 116–17, 121, 133–4, 136, 139–40, 145, 168–71, 195–7, 209–10; and Mussolini 78, 81; and the Resistance 98, 126–9; and women 83, 102, 170, 199; *see also* Vatican
CIA 171
cinema 1–3, 6–7, 11–15, 17, 24, 27, 73, 91–4, 169–70, 180, 205–6, 215; Italian cinema 63–4, 84–8, 94, 206; national cinema 47–9, 57–8, 60; *see also* neo-realism
collective unconscious 3–4, 6, 21, 24, 27,

31–2, 38–48, 50, 52, 62–3, 70, 142, 202, 204–5
Communist Party 79,118–19,136,144; PCI 80, 165, 169
complex 6, 31–2, 39–44, 46, 48–51, 54, 59, 204; ego-complex 41; mother complex 102, 188; feeling-toned complex 41, 49
Conforti, Michael 37–8, 46
consciousness 3–6, 20–1, 25–7, 33–9, 41–4, 50–2, 54–6, 62–5, 71, 103, 106, 111, 113, 124–5, 131, 136–7, 149–50, 152, 155, 158, 163–4, 177, 183, 185–9, 192, 195, 200, 202–3, 207–13; collective consciousness 27, 72, 83, 164, 180; ego-consciousness 5, 47–8, 56, 59–60, 97, 116, 139, 142, 164, 189, 205–7, 209, 212; national consciousness 94, 116, 139–40, 142, 164
constitution 74, 76, 81, 144, 160, 190
Copjec, Joan 12, 16–19, 29
cross 19, 20, 134–5

daydream 47
DC *see* Christian Democratic Party
De Gasperi 136, 144–5
De Sica, Vittorio 7–8, 88, 90–2, 98, 109–14, 116, 120–1, 139, 156, 165, 170, 182, 189–90, 202–3, 207, 209; *see also*: *I Bambini ci Guardano, Ladri di Biciclette, Miracolo a Milano, La Porta del Cielo, Umberto D.*
death 105–10, 112, 114, 116–17, 123, 127, 129, 131–5, 137–9, 150–2, 161, 163–5, 190, 192–3, 198–201, 208
Delacroix, Eugene 128–9
Deleuze, Gilles 72, 89–90
dictatorship 7, 65, 73, 80, 83, 87, 132, 143, 151, 206, 208; *see also* Mussolini
divismo 85, 94
Doane, Mary Ann 13, 17
dove *see Miracolo a Milano*
dream 1–2, 4, 13, 20–2, 24, 26–7, 32, 34, 38–40, 51–2, 62, 69–72, 145, 149, 174, 181, 185, 204, 206, 213; American dream 161,167, 175, 180, 190
dynamic systems 36, 39–40, 46

ego 5–6, 14, 21, 25, 36, 41, 47, 53–4, 56, 59–60, 111, 115, 131, 140, 142, 149–50, 159, 163–5, 176, 185, 187–8, 194, 202–3, 206–13; *see also*: consciousness, complex

election 8, 77, 144–5, 152, 154, 165, 167–70, 210, 212; general elections 79, 129, 141, 152, 161
Europa '51, 8, 90, 92, 167, 171, 180, 190–200, 213; and child 180, 192–3; and suicide 111, 192–3; *see also*: Ingrid Bergman, Rossellini
extraversion 54

fascism 71, 77–82, 86–7, 90, 92–4, 97–8, 100–1, 106–7, 109, 116, 139, 142, 150, 157, 183, 207; *see also* Mussolini
father 50, 59, 98, 103–4, 106–7, 111–12, 114–16, 124, 134, 139, 148–9, 151, 154–5, 157, 165, 183, 185, 187–9, 198, 203, 207–10; fatherland 59, 151; Terrible Father 115, 208–9; tyrannical father 116, 149, 187
feeling 40–2, 50, 63, 179, 180, 196; feeling function 179–80; feeling tone 40–2; feeling-toned images 42; *see also* complex
female *see* gender
feminine 54, 62–3, 85, 103–4, 106, 109, 111–12, 124, 127, 131–2, 138, 154, 157–9, 163, 179, 180, 187, 197–8, 200–2
feminist 13, 15, 142; film criticism 2, 14; *see also* film theory
fertility 93, 106, 116, 147; egg as symbol of 105
film theory 1, 11–13, 16–19, 26, 29; feminist film theory 2, 13–15; *see also*: Copjec, Doane, Mulvey
food 105, 211; egg 105; milk 179, 182–3; in *Ossessione* 105
Fredericksen, Don 12, 18–22
Freud 1, 5–6, 13–15, 18, 23, 31–2, 42–3; psychoanalysis 1–3, 6, 11–15, 17–18, 214; reductive method 42; repression 14, 26; repressed 2–3, 26, 31
function 197; extraverted 63, 65; introverted 65; feeling function 179–80

gaze 12, 14–16, 105, 107, 140, 164, 173, 176–7, 181, 209
gender 15, 25, 62, 64, 128, 214; female 14–15, 59, 102, 111–14, 138, 147, 157–8, 176, 181, 199; male 14–15, 103, 112–13, 126, 137–8, 142, 153, 157–8, 176–7, 179, 181, 183, 190, 214; *see also* women
genre 71, 92; melodrama 85–6, 181

Germania Anno Zero 8, 90, 92, 137, 141, 145–52, 162, 164–6, 202, 211–12; and murder 151; and suicide 150, 164–5; *see also* Rossellini
Giolitti, Giovanni 77–8
Gramsci, Antonio 61, 75–6, 79, 91, 112–13, 129, 154, 165–7, 194, 208; passive revolution 74–5, 93

Hauke, Christopher 3, 6, 12, 19, 22, 25–6
Helios, 147; *see also* horse
Hermes *see* trickster
hero 15, 24–6, 111, 114–15, 132, 149, 151, 154, 181, 183, 185–9, 202, 208, 214; child-hero 147, 164; hero myth 188
Hillman, James 28
Hitler 71, 82, 100–1, 118, 149, 151; Führer 149, 151
Hockley, Luke 3, 6, 12, 18, 23–5, 71
Hollywood 87, 161, 163, 169–70, 175, 201
homosexuality 83, 87, 91, 98; in *Ossessione* 108, 115; in *I Bambini ci Guardano* 110; in *Roma Città Aperta* 138
horse 122, 147, 149

identification 13–16, 41, 52–3, 64, 89, 110–12, 125, 132, 136, 203, 206, 211
identity 44, 53–6, 58, 61, 64–5, 82–3, 87, 114, 116–17, 124, 135, 151, 156, 161, 163–4, 168–9, 187, 198, 202, 207–12; gender identity 25; national identity 5, 8, 47–9, 52, 56, 58–61, 64, 70–1, 75–6, 93, 97, 139, 143, 151, 200, 204–7, 209–10, 212; social identity 14
image 1–8, 15–16, 19–21, 24–8, 29, 30, 39–45, 61, 64–65, 70, 72–3, 84–7, 89–91, 105–8, 135, 139, 173, 176–7, 179–81, 185, 202, 205–7, 214–15; archetypal image 5, 24, 28, 33–5, 38–40, 44–5, 50, 54, 64, 135, 138, 159, 194; cinematic image 1–2, 4, 7, 22, 27, 38, 46, 48–9, 56–7, 65, 71, 85, 204–5; dream image 1, 22, 26, 32, 40, 206; and Freud 3, 18; God-image 135; and Jung 1, 3, 6, 11, 18, 22, 24, 27, 29, 31–5, 40–1, 45–6, 57, 61, 206, 213; and Lacan 13–14; mythological image 44, 55, 64, 205; primordial image 6, 33, 35
imaginary signifier 12, 14; *see also* Metz
imagined communities 48, 205; *see also* Benedict Anderson

incest 110, 112, 114, 209; in *I Bambini ci Guardano*, 110–12; *see also* uroboric incest
individuation 3–4, 8, 18, 20, 24–5, 29–30, 33–4, 36–9, 45, 54, 56, 71, 132, 135, 139, 168, 174, 200, 205–6, 211, 213
inductive method 4, 24
instinct 21, 36–7, 147; maternal instinct 102, 147
introjection 27
introversion 54
introverted *see* function
Italian Communist Party *see* Communist Party
Italian Socialist Party *see* Socialists
Italy 7, 49, 57, 60–1, 64–5, 69, 71, 73–83, 85–7, 90, 93–4, 97–8, 108–9, 116, 120, 125, 130–3, 135, 140–2, 150–2, 160–1, 170–1, 175, 181, 189–90, 199, 202–3, 206, 208–13; history of Italy 7, 8, 73–83, 99–100, 116–17, 120, 141–2, 206
Izod, John 2, 3, 6, 12, 18, 22, 25–8, 29, 174

Jacobi, Jolande 41, 50
Jung and anti-semitism 23, 59; and archetype 21, 33–9, 41, 44, 52, 110, 184; and art 6, 32, 40, 42–6, 49, 51–2, 54, 70; and dreams 4, 34, 38, 70–2, 206; and feminism 214; and film 11–12, 18–19, 22, 26, 31; and Freud 23–4, 32, 42–3, 46–47, 206; and individuation 3, 33, 36, 38–9, 56, 71, 135, 139; and nation 23, 57, 59–60, 205; and politics 63; and symbol 19–20, 22, 25, 48–9, 147, 192; teleological approach 3, 19, 30; and unconscious 6, 19, 31, 33, 70
Jung, Emma 127, 132

Kristeva, Julia 179, 198–9; Stabat Mater 179, 198

Lacan, Jacques 12–17, 21–3
Ladri di Biciclette 8, 90, 110, 141, 155–62, 164–5, 172, 200, 211
Liberty Leading the People see Delacroix
Litany of Loreto 123

Magnani, Anna 92, 126, 129, 172, 176, 181; *see also*: *Bellissima*, *Roma Città Aperta*
Marshall Plan 154, 162, 170

Marx 18; Marxism 132; Marxist 12, 91, 154
Mary 83, 123–4, 129, 171, 180, 189, 195–8; *see also* Virgin Mary
masculine 62, 104, 106, 122–7, 132, 142, 176, 179, 183, 185, 194, 198
mask 44, 61, 164, 201, 210; *see also* persona
Matteotti, Giacomo 80, 208
Mercury *see* Hermes
Metz, Christian 1, 12–14, 16, 19–20; *see also* imaginary signifier
Michelangelo 129–30; Pietà 129–30, 178
miracle 120–1, 124–5, 138, 140, 173, 177, 182, 189–90, 209; economic miracle 190, 211; *see also* Miracolo a Milano
Miracolo a Milano 8, 137, 167, 171, 182–90, 200–1, 213; and consumerism 167, 171, 213; *see also* De Sica
mirror 127, 140, 176–7; Lacan's mirror 13–17
moon 188, 212; in *Miracolo a Milano* 188
mother 14, 59, 102, 104–5, 108–12, 114, 116–17, 122–3, 126, 131–2, 137, 140, 142, 147, 152, 154–6, 158–9, 163–5, 173, 176, 177–81, 183, 187–94, 199–203, 211, 214; Great Mother 55, 103, 106, 108, 112, 123, 137, 158, 189; Terrible Mother 108, 111, 132, 137, 140, 155, 159, 176, 183, 209; *see also* complex
motherhood 7, 83, 98, 102, 105, 109, 117, 123, 176, 193, 198
motherland 59, 93, 151
Mulvey, Laura 2, 14–15, 18, 29, 214; scopophilia 15
murder 80, 109, 137, 207–8, 212; and *Germania Anno Zero* 146, 149–51, 163–4, 212; and *Ossessione* 105–8, 114–16, 137, 208
Mussolini 73, 76, 78–84, 86, 93, 97–102, 104, 112, 115–22, 124–5, 133, 135, 138–9, 143, 151, 168, 189, 206–9, 211
myth 27, 32–34, 47, 49, 52, 55, 60–1, 71–2, 115, 155, 177–9, 188, 205; creation myth 55; Cronos 104; Demeter 179; Helios 147; Icarus 115; Medea 158; Oedipus 44; Osiris and Isis 155
mythology 4, 6, 35, 43–5, 47, 54–5, 65, 71, 104, 111, 122, 147, 192, 205

nation 5, 7, 23, 45, 48, 53, 56–65, 70, 74, 76–8, 80–4, 93, 117–18, 124–5, 129, 132, 136–8, 142–3, 151, 154–5, 162, 165–6, 202, 205–11, 213–14
nationalism 57–59
NATO 171
La Nave Bianca 101–2; *see also* Rossellini
neo-realism 4, 7, 70–2, 87–94, 98, 105, 152, 159, 165, 167, 172, 196, 206–7, 214; pink neo-realism 175; *see also*: De Sica, Rossellini, Visconti, Zavattini
Neumann, Erich 4, 25, 37, 49, 54–5, 60, 64–5, 71, 103–6, 108, 111, 115–16, 122, 132, 136–7, 147, 155, 158–9, 163–4, 183, 185, 187–9, 194, 200–3, 205, 207–13
neuroscience 33, 36, 38–9
numinous 19, 35, 40, 55, 198–9, 214

Ossessione 7, 87, 90, 98, 104–9, 111, 114–15, 127, 137, 139, 154, 172, 208; and child 108–9; and Terrible Mother 108; *see also* Visconti

Partito Comunista Italiano *see* Communist Party
Partito Socialista Italiano *see* Socialists
pattern 30–1, 36, 205–6
PCI *see* Communist Party
persona 44, 61, 110, 192–4, 200, 202, 208, 210, 213; *see also* mask
Pietà *see* Michelangelo
Un Pilota Ritorna 98, 100–2, 114, 208; *see also* Rossellini
politics 8, 49, 61–5, 105, 126, 137, 140, 144, 158, 168–9, 175, 202–3, 211
La Porta del Cielo 7, 98, 119–25, 137–8, 140, 209–10; *see also* De Sica
projection 27, 41, 65, 176, 179, 187, 199
PSI *see* Socialists
psyche 3–4, 20–1, 23–4, 27, 30, 32, 41–2, 49–51, 54, 61–2, 204, 209; Eros and Psyche 106
psychoanalysis 1–3, 6, 11–14, 17–18, 214

rebirth 74, 112, 135–6, 139, 155, 180, 187, 198, 201, 207, 209–10
relatedness 38–9, 109, 132, 149, 211
religion 5, 54–5, 64, 81, 115–16, 199; *see also* Catholic
Resistance 7, 75, 98, 118–21, 125–6, 129, 131–6, 138–9, 141–3, 145, 151–2, 154, 162, 165–6, 171, 190, 193, 201, 207, 210; and the Church 126–7, 129, 131–4, 136; partisans 118, 120, 125, 142–3

revolution 74, 76, 128, 165, 187, 194, 208; French revolution 74, 128–9; passive revolution 74–5, 93
Roma Città Aperta 7, 92, 98, 119, 125–38, 141, 145, 149, 191, 209, 210; see also Rossellini
Rome Open City *see Roma Città Aperta*
Rossellini, Roberto 4, 7–8, 88–93, 98, 100–4, 113–15, 127–9, 133, 135–6, 139, 141, 145, 149–50, 152, 165–7, 191, 195–6, 199–200, 202, 207, 212–13; and Ingrid Bergman 92, 191, 199; see also: *Europa '51*, *Germania Anno Zero*, *La Nave Bianca*, *Roma Città Aperta*, *Un Pilota Ritorna*
sacrifice 116, 119, 135, 139, 141, 156–7, 163, 176–8, 181, 193, 202
Screen 2
self 5, 13, 38, 41, 53–4, 56, 59–60, 74, 82, 84, 93, 124, 131–2, 135, 139, 168, 171, 189, 206, 209–10, 213
semiotic 12, 19, 21, 25, 179; see also sign
Senso 75, 172
shadow 8, 31, 59, 131, 159, 174, 203, 212
sign 19–20, 25, 60
signifier 15–16; see also: imaginary signifier, Metz
skin 52–3, 56, 65
Socialists 80, 94, 118, 144, 154, 160–1, 165, 171
Spielrein, Sabina 49–50
suicide 8, 111, 114, 134, 164, 186, 212; in *Europa '51* 191–2, 198, 201; in *Germania Anno Zero* 146, 150–1, 164; in *I Bambini ci Guardano* 109–11, 134
symbol 6, 19–22, 25, 27–8, 30, 37, 48, 52, 58, 135, 139, 147, 192, 204–5, 214
symptom 2, 42, 50

tears 173, 176, 179–80
teleological 3, 17, 19, 23, 30
La Terra Trema 8, 90, 108–9, 141, 144, 152–6, 159, 161, 164–5, 172, 181, 211
trasformismo 76
trickster 174
trilogy 144; war trilogy 100–1, 145
Trinity 124

Umberto D. 156, 170; see also De Sica
Un Pilota Ritorna 7, 98, 100–4, 114, 208; see also Rossellini
unconscious as collective unconscious 3–4, 6, 21, 24, 27, 31–2, 35, 38–42, 44–8, 50, 52, 62–3, 202, 204–5; as cultural unconscious 1–6, 25–6, 28, 30, 47–8, 70–1, 204, 207–8, 213; as group unconscious 52, 58, 70; as personal unconscious 31, 33, 48, 50, 70
unification 7, 65, 71, 74–6, 83–4, 93, 143, 154, 206
United States 86, 168, 170; US 143–5, 162, 168–9; see also America
uroboric incest 164, 209

Vatican 81, 118–19, 144–5, 170; see also Church
Verga, Giovanni 87, 152, 154; *I Malavoglia* 152; see also *La Terra Trema*
virgin 111, 115, 122–3, 183, 194; Virgin Mary 121, 131, 133, 170, 195–6, 198
Visconti, Luchino 4, 7–8, 75, 87–8, 90–2, 98, 105, 107–9, 111, 113–14, 141, 144, 152, 154, 167, 171–2, 174–5, 177, 180–1, 202, 207, 213; see also: *Bellissima*, *Ossessione*, *La Terra Trema*, *Senso*
Vittorio Emanuele II 74
Vittorio Emanuele III 119, 121, 143
Von Franz, Marie Louise 66, 69

war trilogy *see* trilogy
water 112, 187–8
women 2, 7, 12, 15, 71, 73, 83–5, 93, 102–6, 109, 112–14, 116, 129, 131–2, 137–8, 142, 154, 156, 159, 164, 170, 181, 196–9, 213–14
World War I 64, 77–8, 84–6, 94, 97, 99, 206
World War II 7, 62, 65, 69–71, 75, 94, 97, 99, 206

Zavattini, Cesare 72, 88, 90–1, 165, 172, 182